The
Invention *of*
Charlotte
Brontë

The Invention *of* Charlotte Brontë

HER LAST YEARS
AND THE SCANDAL
THAT MADE HER

GRAHAM WATSON

First published 2024

The History Press
97 St George's Place, Cheltenham,
Gloucestershire, GL50 3QB
www.thehistorypress.co.uk

British Library Cataloguing in Publication Data.
A catalogue record for this book is available from the British Library.

ISBN 978 1 80399 537 3

Typesetting and origination by The History Press
Printed and bound in Great Britain by TJ Books Limited, Padstow, Cornwall.

Trees for LYfe

For my mother
Elizabeth McDermott Watson
(1946–2023)

'The daily life into which people are born, and into which they are absorbed before they are well aware, forms chains which only one in a hundred has moral strength enough to despise, and to break when the right time comes …'

Elizabeth Gaskell, *Ruth*

'Every book, as we know, has its secret history, hidden from the world.'

T.W. Reid, *Charlotte Brontë: A Monograph*

Contents

Acknowledgements   9

Part One: Visiting (1850–1854)
Chapter 1: The Great Unknown   13
Chapter 2: Wild, Strange Facts   29
Chapter 3: A Passionate Life   40
Chapter 4: A Tigress Before Calamity   47
Chapter 5: Eclipse   63
Chapter 6: Debatable Land   86
Chapter 7: Treachery   101
Chapter 8: Providence   106

Part Two: Departing (1854–1857)
Chapter 9: A Strange and Perilous Thing   119
Chapter 10: Spring Flowers   132
Chapter 11: A Grave Duty   145
Chapter 12: The Promised Land   171
Chapter 13: Treason   185
Chapter 14: The Life of Charlotte Brontë   196
Chapter 15: That Unlucky Book   207

Part Three: Remaining (1857–1896)
Chapter 16: Fugitive Pieces   235
Chapter 17: Resurgam   242

Epilogue   245
A Chronology of Charlotte Brontë and Elizabeth Gaskell   246
Notes   251
Select Bibliography   271
Index   275

Acknowledgements

First thanks must go to those scholars whose research and writing on the Brontës and Elizabeth Gaskell are of inestimable value: primarily Dr Christine Alexander, Dr Juliet Barker, John Chappelle and Arthur Pollard; Winifred Gerin, Dudley Green, Margaret Smith, Prof Patsy Stoneman, Dr Jenny Uglow, and the incomparable Ann Dinsdale, whose generosity and dedication make her my hero. All who write about the Brontës owe these specialists a considerable debt. Sincerest thanks also to those institutions who kindly granted permissions for the reproduction of their material.

At The History Press, I'm deeply grateful to Claire Hopkins, whose judgement and vision made this book a reality, to Rebecca Newton for steering it towards publication, and to my editor Gaynor Haliday for her acute insights and meticulous attention to detail.

I'm thankful to those friends and family who listened to me bring the Brontës into otherwise normal conversations: Elaine Cartney, Claire Michie, Dr Amber Pouliot, Claire Woodmore.

Finally, thanks to my beloved friend Jennie Hood, who was first to read this book. It couldn't have had for a fiercer champion.

And to Craig Turner for his inexhaustible enthusiasm, love and support, for being a sounding board for all this and more.

Part One

Visiting

(1850–1854)

CHAPTER 1

1850

The Great Unknown

By August, the summer had squalled to thunderstorms. Lightning struck northern England, hailing sheets of warm rain to drown the great valleys of Lancashire and Yorkshire. Newspapers described torrents of lightning smashing down entire houses. Those who sheltered under trees reported being burned and blinded by showers of 'electric fluid', rain energised by lightning.[1]

Ploughing through the torrential Lake District on a steam train, the novelist Elizabeth Gaskell was denied a late summer sunset, and disembarked in unseasonably early darkness. She had come for the week, on the offer of a friend, to meet the country's most mysterious celebrity, a writer whose true identity was forbidden knowledge. In their holiday home, sheltered by a spinney on a slope above Windermere, she met her hosts Lady Janet Kay-Shuttleworth and her husband Sir James. After hours in the dusk, Elizabeth was momentarily dazzled by the bright oil lamps and firelight. Once it lifted, there was the third figure, the one she had come to see. At last, here was England's great enigma: a lady in black at a table set for tea.

One of Elizabeth's friends encountered her the year before. She repeated what they told her in confidence of how, without even introducing herself, this 'mysterious visitor … a little, very little, bright haired sprite, looking not above fifteen, very unsophisticated' demanded an opinion about the novel scandalising Britain. When told it was first rate, 'the little sprite went red all over with pleasure.'[2] No longer in need of assurances, she stood at once to shake Elizabeth's hand. Finally, Elizabeth could study Currer Bell, the notorious and, until now, invisible author of *Jane Eyre*.

After introductions, Elizabeth went upstairs to take off her bonnet and refresh. When she came back down, Currer Bell was self-consciously absorbed in needlework. 'But I had time for a good look at her,' she reported to a friend:

She is (as she calls herself) *undeveloped*; thin and more than half a head shorter than I, soft brown hair not so dark as mine; eyes (very good and expressive looking straight and open at you) of the same colour, a reddish face; large mouth and many teeth gone; altogether *plain*; the forehead square, broad and rather overhanging. She has a very sweet voice, rather hesitates in choosing her expressions, but when chosen they seem without an effort, admirable and just befitting the occasion.[3]

As suspected, Currer Bell was not the man the press made him out to be. Speculation about his sex and class had been a popular by-line for the past three years, since the publication of *Jane Eyre* in October 1847, when reviewers diluted praise with suspicion. By the standards of the time, the novel's morals were questionable and, suspecting its author's name was bogus, critics sought a sex through which to frame their condemnation. A consensus formed that Bell was a northerner, a man, the dominant voice in a family of hot-tempered brothers who wrote three of the most shocking novels of the day: *Jane Eyre*, *Wuthering Heights* and *The Tenant of Wildfell Hall*. Opinion split into generalisations. Female critics thought Bell had too much insight into women's minds to be male, whereas male critics thought him too coarse, with too much carnal experience, to be female. Set outside the rarefied London squares of popular fiction, without lords or duchesses for heroes, *Jane Eyre* was disdained by one paper as 'anything but a fashionable novel'. Its reviewer wrote: 'on the contrary, the heroine is cast amongst the thorns and brambles of life; an orphan, without money, without beauty, without friends, thrust into a starving charity school, and fighting her way as a governess with few accomplishments.'[4] Unintentionally, they shone a scrutinising light on its hidden author's life.

Some journalists looked beyond sex and wondered if such an accomplished narrative could have been written by an amateur, or if an already-famous writer was testing them. Enquiries with *Jane Eyre*'s publisher found even they had been kept in the dark. They had rushed the novel into print only two months after accepting its handwritten manuscript, knowing nothing of its author beyond his name and location; Currer Bell asked for all correspondence to go through a vicarage near Bradford. Yet when they sent press clippings, delivery was delayed because the postmen could not find anyone with that name. 'It would be better in future not to put the name Currer Bell on the outside,' came the reply, 'if directed simply to Miss Brontë they will be more likely to reach their destination safely. Currer Bell is not known in this district and I have no wish that he should.'[5] This pretence continued for another eight months of near-daily communication until the author was forced to reveal herself in person.

While Elizabeth, with thousands of others, was intrigued by *Jane Eyre*'s passion and unconventionality, she doubted it was a man's work. Her friend, fellow writer Harriet Martineau, was convinced knowledge of feminine activities gave them away. 'Passages about sewing on brass rings could have been written only by a woman – or an upholsterer,' she observed dryly.[6] Strangely, the deprivations of Jane Eyre's girlhood were so like Harriet's that her relatives thought she had written it and teased her to confess. While she could honestly deny it, she began to suspect there might be a spy in her midst, extorting information from confidantes or observing her at close hand to repurpose her life for their fiction. But who?

Harriet was staying with friends in November 1849 when a gift copy of Currer Bell's new novel, *Shirley*, came by post. She scrutinised the handwriting in the accompanying note for clues. It looked 'cramped and nervous' she surmised, the inelegant hand of a compulsive writer. And what of the writer's sex? There was a potential slip. They had written: 'Currer Bell offers a copy of *Shirley* to Miss Martineau's acceptance, in acknowledgement of the pleasure and profit *she* has derived ...' They stopped, inked a line through 'she' and replaced it with 'he', before continuing 'has derived from her works'. That settled it: Currer Bell was a woman in disguise. Harriet decided to test her hunch. She had to prove she had worked them out and was discreet. She addressed a reply to 'Currer Bell Esquire' but started the letter boldly, risking offence for a potential male recipient, hailing him, 'Madam ...'

At the same time, another copy went to Elizabeth Gaskell. She read it straight away. Catching up with a friend afterwards she realised they might help identify its author. 'Do you know Dr Epps?' she asked, remembering he was her father's friend. 'I think you do. Ask him to tell you who wrote *Jane Eyre* and *Shirley*. Do tell me ...'[7]

She must have heard that the homeopath John Epps received a plea for help from William Smith Williams, the editor at Smith Elder & Co. At the beginning of December 1848, Williams told Epps the sister of one of his authors was in an unexplained decline and wondered if he could recommend treatment from a written description of her symptoms.[8] Epps agreed with stipulations: the questioner could not be anonymous, noting that 'if a lady has not sufficient confidence in him to give her name when consulting him, it cannot be expected that he should give his opinion of her case.'[9] Within days, Williams passed him a two-page statement describing a woman not yet 30 with 'a peculiar reserve of character', emaciated and feverish with seizures of coughing. So far, it said, she had refused all medical attention 'insisting that Nature shall be left to take her own course'. It was signed *Miss Brontë of Haworth parsonage, near Bradford.*[10] Although Epps replied immediately with homeopathic remedies and generalised advice, it was already too late – it would have been too late for twenty-first century medicine – to avert or relieve the final agonising stage of tuberculosis that killed the author's sister a few days before that Christmas.

Elizabeth was left guessing. Sensing parts of *Shirley* were written by someone in the early days of a devastating bereavement she sent Currer Bell her sympathies. Her pity cut through the artifice, winning trust where public praise and blame failed. In the grateful note she received back, she read, 'Currer Bell *must* answer Mrs Gaskell's letter. Whether forbidden to do so or not she must acknowledge its kind, generous sympathy with all her heart.'[11]

She. Her. The mask was lifting, the mystery was unravelling. *She* was being revealed.

Despite this, the writer – Charlotte Brontë – still withheld her name. Only in the vulnerable moment of using her own voice did its protection fail. She could not deny her grief for the mother and two elder sisters she lost as a child, or her remaining three siblings who all died within eight months of each other, and referred to herself by the shared initials she used for her real and assumed identities. It let her admit the truth:

> Dark days she has known; the worst perhaps were days of bereavement, but though CB is the survivor of most who were dear to her, she has one near relative still left, and therefore cannot be said to be quite alone.[12]

Elizabeth's intuitive sympathy flared through the darkness enclosing Charlotte Brontë. Desperate to force any resemblance between the two sisters she lost in the last eleven months and famous new admirers like Elizabeth Gaskell and Harriet Martineau, Charlotte turned gratefully to William Smith Williams. 'It mournfully pleases me to fancy a remote affinity,' she wrote, straining for any connection. 'Proud am I that I can touch a chord of sympathy in souls so noble.'[13]

Triumphantly, Elizabeth wrote to her friend Katie, 'What will you give me for a secret? She's a she – that I will tell you.'[14]

This set the tone between Charlotte Brontë and Elizabeth Gaskell. In the years to come, it would express itself in ways neither could imagine but both were, as if by a sense of precognition, preparing. It was the start of Elizabeth winning intimacies, encouraging this deeply private woman to expose herself in confessions she could read aloud to her family then pass around for her friends' amusement.

'This place is exquisitely beautiful,' Charlotte Brontë wrote to her father, the elderly vicar of Haworth, 'though the weather is cloudy, misty and stormy – but the sun bursts out occasionally and shows the hills and the lake. Mrs Gaskell is coming here this evening ...'[15]

She was dejected, having hitherto avoided the Kay-Shuttleworths until their promise of Elizabeth swayed her. Keen to collect celebrities, they courted her from the moment they heard she was Currer Bell and flooded her with letters and invitations, unaware how demanding attention exhausted her, then travelled to Yorkshire on what Charlotte wearily described as 'the wise errand of seeing the scenery described in *Jane Eyre* and *Shirley*'.[16] They were not alone. Charlotte had already noticed sightseers appearing in the village, while others she did not notice were slipping her father's sexton half a crown to point her out in church.[17]

The revelation reached the Kay-Shuttleworths, as it did many in England, as whispers that swept from district to district. Rumours spread through the West Riding for twelve months, filtering into newspapers then back into public conversations as more and more readers recognised the originals of places, institutions, even individuals described in Currer Bell's two bestsellers.

What started as Charlotte and her sisters' project of assumed identities and opposite pronouns was threatening her provincial reality. As children, she and her younger siblings – her brother Branwell and sisters Emily and Anne – played the chroniclers of secret countries colonised by celebrity politicians, jostling with queens and statesmen of their own invention, voicing narratives, poems and works of pseudo-biography and history. This repurposing of reality began with toy soldiers and ended with the sisters publishing a poetry collection and novels under fictitious names: Currer, Ellis and Acton Bell. The inner and outer worlds of their lives never merged until *Shirley* blew the charade apart.

Over the Christmas and New Year period of 1849–50, Charlotte had one of her best friends staying with her. Ellen Nussey was the twelfth child of a local cloth manufacturing family in diminishing fortunes, a meek, vivacious young woman whose eighteen-year friendship with Charlotte began when they were homesick teenagers boarding in a school run by Margaret Wooler, a benevolent spinster still friends with both. 'She makes me indolent and negligent,' Charlotte wrote, rescued with happy relief from depression, 'I am too busy talking to her all day to do anything else.'[18]

Unexpectedly, Ellen received a letter forwarded from home. It was from her local vicar. 'You are on a visit with the renowned Currer Bell,' he announced, 'The great unknown of the present day.'[19] He wanted a favour. He recognised characters in *Shirley* as men and women in his parish and was certain he and his sister were among them with no disguise as a vicar and his sister. They had a right to know who wrote it, the Rev. Heald insisted, after all 'I had no idea I should ever be made a means to amuse the public.' Ellen was culpable, he suggested, having introduced him to Charlotte at a church service. At the time, he left Charlotte feeling he would reckon a dog more able to write a book than she. But for Heald, everything was different now the rumours sounded true. He told Ellen if she confirmed who Currer Bell was he would keep it quiet. If not, he would share his suspicions with everyone. After all, he concluded ominously, one should be wary of those amongst us taking notes, ready to reveal more than they should. 'Best wishes of the season to you and C.B.,' he added, closing with a faintly menacing tone to leave her in no doubt he knew precisely where she was, 'Give my best respects to Mr Brontë ...'[20]

The net was closing. By the first months of 1850, Charlotte felt that only she was still keeping her secret. 'I thought I should escape identification in Yorkshire. I am so little known,' she confided to Williams, trying to nullify similarities between herself and her material. 'It would be difficult to explain to you how little actual experience I have had of life, how few persons I have known and how very few have known me.'[21] The world had not given her enough, she suggested, to be fabricated into fiction.

Shortly after Ellen left, the rumours reached Charlotte personally. One day in January, her father's saturnine Irish curate, 29-year-old Arthur Bell Nicholls, approached her 'cold and disapproving', to ask if what he heard about her in Keighley was true.[22] If it was, he told her, she should know he had read *Jane Eyre* and now wanted 'the other book', *Shirley*, little suspecting he too was a character in it. Charlotte must have admitted it was true, for by the end of the month he was reading it in fits of laughter, 'clapping his hands and stamping on the floor', sharing the clerical set-pieces with Charlotte's bemused father. Arthur was delighted, she told Ellen in relief, and thankfully pleased with her depiction of him as 'decent, decorous, and conscientious'.[23]

Like his fictional counterpart, Arthur taught in the Sunday School at weekends and in the village school during the week. 'Being human, of course he had his faults ... Otherwise he was sane and rational, diligent and charitable.'[24] Taciturn and reserved until now, he could hardly fail to be flattered at being praised so unexpectedly and so publicly. If he ever wondered what Charlotte thought of him, now he knew. As did the rest of the western world.

He lived across the lane from the Brontës, lodging with their nearest neighbours, John Brown and his family. As the sexton and memorial stonemason, Brown was responsible for church maintenance, ringing its bells, digging new graves for the dead then carving and erecting their headstones. This brought all the village families to his workshop in a barn opposite the Brontës' back scullery, a prime location to hear the parson's family business. And although *Jane Eyre* kept him up all night, he never suspected who had written it, until he came home with an 'astounding declaration': Currer Bell was none other than the parson's shy daughter, Charlotte.[25] He heard about it 10 miles away in Halifax, his daughter, 22-year-old Martha, explained to Charlotte. She had been running errands for the family since she was 8, before she moved in as a servant at 13 to help their elderly cook, Tabitha Aykroyd. A few days after the Browns heard Arthur roaring with laughter in his room over *Shirley*, Martha interrupted Charlotte to ask if she really was the author of 'the grandest books that ever was seen', as she described them. Charlotte fell into a cold sweat as Martha explained her father told them he knew three other influential Bradford men who heard the same. With a famous writer somewhere in their midst, the men were donating copies of *Jane Eyre* and *Shirley* to the new lending library a few minutes' walk from the Brontës' front door.[26] Soon her characters would be scrutinized by the locals who inspired them. While Arthur was flattered, she knew his hapless colleagues would be upset or angry enough to hold her to account. 'God help, keep and deliver me!' she wrote to Ellen.[27]

But the press was already on to her. Two weeks later, she was exposed in a national newspaper. On Thursday, 21 February the *London Morning Post* reported:

> It is understood that the only daughter of the Rev. P Brontë, incumbent of Haworth, is the authoress of *Jane Eyre* and *Shirley*, two of the most popular novels of the day, which have appeared under the name of Currer Bell.[28]

The regional papers picked up the story and repeated it over the following weeks into March. By April, the London papers had more. Reports reached them from an American source that all three Bells were not brothers but sisters.[29] The story was broken by *The Boston Weekly Museum*, on 9 February:

> We are assured that a Miss Brontë is the authoress of *Jane Eyre* and *Shirley*. She is the survivor of three sisters, Charlotte, Emily, and Anne, who each have been before the public under the assumed name of Bell. Emily and Anne both died of consumption, but Charlotte remains.

The paper followed it up with a reader's letter confirming everything. It came from a weaver who migrated to Massachusetts four years before.[30] Having recognised locations and persons in both novels Johnathan Berry no longer doubted the author's identity. He had been a mill child, he explained, 'born and bred within a stone's throw' of the house of the vicar who baptised him, Patrick Brontë. 'I know some of the characters in *Shirley* as well as I know my own father … The authoress is young … the public may expect much more from her.'[31]

Charlotte's guise of concealment and assumed names was over. Without her siblings, she faced public scrutiny alone. She sent Ellen a clipping of Berry's letter. It 'amused and touched' her, she said, 'for it alludes to some who are in this world no longer … you will find it a curious mixture of both truth and inaccuracy.'[32]

The London papers lifted these new specifics and let the regionals distribute them through the counties. As Haworth and the Brontës were described to all, the public wanted to experience the landscape of their novels for themselves. Many wanted more: to visit the church, the parsonage, even to see Charlotte herself. Generally, she deterred them, largely from social nervousness but also certain she would disappoint anyone hoping to meet her avatars, Jane Eyre or Currer Bell. Nevertheless, when those around her obliged, she struggled to refuse.

Among the insistent was Lady Kay-Shuttleworth. She made it clear she and her husband wanted to absorb her into their circle. When they offered to drop by one Friday in early March, Charlotte submitted, warning them it would be 'so little worth your while' they need not bother.[33] They ignored that and appeared at her door. To her surprise they were younger than she expected, friendly and seemingly without pretensions. Charlotte's father was enamoured, more so when they restated their offer to Charlotte of a holiday at Gawthorpe Hall, their Elizabethan manor near Burnley. When invitations came by letter, Charlotte could use her father as a justification not to leave home, but if made in person, as perhaps the Kay-Shuttleworths suspected, 'Papa took their side at once' and 'would not hear of my refusing; I must go – leaving me without plea or defence.' She objected when they wanted to take her immediately but promised to come the following week, then went reluctantly, feeling their generosity incurred a debt of obligation. It was 'always a difficult and painful thing to me,' she confided to Williams, 'to meet the advances of people whose kindness I am in no position to repay.'[34]

Before going to see them a second time, in Windermere that August, she told Ellen she was so dreading it she would only stay a few days. 'I consented to go with reluctance – chiefly to please Papa whom a refusal on my part would have much annoyed.' Leaving him behind tortured her with anxiety. He had been ill for about four weeks, complaining of chronic bronchitis and weakness, without growing weaker. They were the last, lost-feeling survivors of a family of six, decimated by tuberculosis, giving both cause to fear the imminent loss of the other. 'Grief is a double-edged sword,' Charlotte explained, 'it cuts both ways – the memory of one loss is the anticipation of another.'[35] The onset of a cold at the start of July brought her fevers and chills that reminded her father of the first symptoms of her sisters' terminal declines. 'I am rather prone to look at the dark side of things and cunningly to search out for it, and find it,' he told Ellen when Charlotte stopped off at hers on her way back from London. Evidently, reading between the lines of a letter Ellen sent him saying Charlotte was unwell, he became uneasy yet tried to be rational. 'Tell Charlotte to keep up her spirits. When once more she breathes the free exhilarating air of Haworth, it will blow the dust and smoke and impure malaria of London out of her head and heart.'[36] Three days later, Charlotte had no sooner reached Haworth when her cab was stopped in the valley by the ingratiating village stationer, John Greenwood. He told her he was sent to fetch her from Ellen's because her father was so worried. Once home, the household was in distress:

Papa had worked himself up to a sad pitch of nervous excitement and alarm – in which Martha and Tabby were but too obviously joining him – I can't deny it but I was annoyed; there really being small cause for it all.[37]

Managing her father's 'great discomposure' was not new. She told Ellen she realised his anxiety had two roots: that he would lose her to either death or marriage. Without bitterness, she assured him there was little prospect of the latter, despite his suspicions she was secretly receiving 'some overtures' and being 'somehow' about to marry. For a peaceful life by her father's rule, she accepted her prospects were binary; to avoid distressing him she must stay alive but stay alone. The message was clear. Death would be welcomed before a suitor.

Ellen urged Charlotte to stay as long as possible in the Lake District.[38] The journey from Haworth was long and arduous, requiring four trains and hansom cabs at either end. Sir James collected her at Windermere and she spent her first evening at Briery Close looking forward to meeting Elizabeth after a year of writing to each other.

The Kay-Shuttleworths had brought their entire household for the autumn. Here, Charlotte found Lady Janet to be 'a little woman 32 years old with a pretty, smooth, lively face', frank, good-humoured and without the airs she detected in James Kay, a doctor who adopted Lady Janet's aristocratic surname when they married. Charlotte thought he had the intellectual gravity his wife lacked, but an irascibility saved by her graciousness.[39] Their four children (a fifth would arrive in 1851) were corralled by a charismatic German-Polish governess, Rosa Poplawska, a woman with possessive designs on Lady Janet, watching her, a family friend noticed, as a cat watches a mouse.[40] When she and Charlotte saw each other 'she was almost as pleased to see me as if we had been related,' Charlotte told Ellen. They first met at Gawthorpe when the Kay-Shuttleworths hoped Charlotte would be impressed by their estate, their standing and conspicuous wealth. Seeing beyond the castellations and shields, Charlotte flinched at the spectacle of a governess surrounded by small children. For here was the woman she had once been, before she won the celebrity that now attracted the class of people who once employed her as an ignorable underling. A governess, without prospects or means, had to separate herself from her family and migrate into the friendless territory of live-in role between servants and masters, respected by neither. Talking with Rosa confirmed a kinship Charlotte could not feel with Sir James or Lady Janet, despite their generosity towards her (and to Rosa, in fact). Meeting again at Briery Close, Charlotte was glad to see she was better treated than she herself had been and that the children, at least, liked her enough to co-operate, making 'great alleviations of the inevitable evils of her position'.[41]

Elizabeth came the next evening, Tuesday, 20 August. 'Of course, we went to bed; and of course we got up again,' she wrote in summary.[42] Janet was unwell, so stayed in her room all week. Practised in running a large household, Elizabeth took over and made breakfast. On Wednesday, the first morning she and Charlotte had together, they were joined by another of the Kay-Shuttleworths' friends, Rev. Henry Moseley, previously a professor of philosophy and astronomy at King's College until James made him one of England's first school inspectors. After breakfast he joined them for a sail on the lake, where they talked about modern architecture, art criticism and Cardinal Newman's opinions on Catholicism. Before he left, he wondered if they had heard that Tennyson was nearby, honeymooning with his new bride at Coniston Water. James knew him slightly so proposed a visit after dinner. Being a fan with connections through mutual friends, Elizabeth was enthusiastic. Charlotte was not. Her lukewarm response might have looked like a lack of regard for his poetry, but the truth was more personal. Unknown to the others, she had introduced herself to him before and met his discouraging silence.

A few years earlier, she had sent him a remaindered copy of the poetry book she self-published with her sisters. Cringing with self-deprecating humour that they had been 'heedless' to go against the advice of 'respectable' publishers, Charlotte, with false-sounding resignation, wrote that as no one wanted or needed it, the stock would be recycled. Out of gratitude for his own work she saved him a copy, she said, unaware how unappealing she made it sound. Phrase for phrase she told at least six other well-known writers the same. Far from writing it off, she was trying to promote it, fishing to be discovered by a great man of letters. The books were never planned to be pulped and just over a year later she used similarly feigned resignation to encourage Smith Elder & Co into taking the stock and reissuing it in a new edition. No one replied to her six near-identical notes, yet Tennyson never threw his away and nearly half a century later it resurfaced in the pages of a memoir by his son. He remembered his father always had 'the highest admiration' for the Brontë sisters.[43] But as Charlotte never heard from him, she read his silence as disdain and recoiled from being revealed as Currer Bell in person. While she withdrew, Elizabeth made plans.

Charlotte changed the subject at dinner when one of the Kay-Shuttleworth children refused to eat. Addressing him in a low voice she said she would have been grateful for a little piece of bread at his age.[44] When someone asked what she meant, she talked about how she and three of her sisters were sent to a brutal boarding school where they were fed scraps hardly fit for animals.[45] Her eldest sisters died as a result, she said, it was all in *Jane Eyre*, and she could not have imagined such a hell had she not experienced it. Regardless of any exaggeration, Elizabeth noted, Charlotte was undeniably still suffering 'in heart and body from the consequences of what happened there'.[46]

Dinner over, James shut Elizabeth and Charlotte into a landau and directed them into the rain. They made little progress until the driver called it off and turned them back. Thwarted and furious, Elizabeth said nothing and 'held my piece and bit my lips', writing that James wasted their time on similar wet expeditions, pointing out vague mountains through the rainy carriage windows.[47] His well-intentioned but misjudged hosting satisfied neither woman. By deciding what was best for both, he only ensured Elizabeth was denied making new connections and Charlotte, who shrank from that, was barred from solitary walks. Both politely complied, but Charlotte especially felt more frustration than enjoyment. A captive guest, she was obliged to suppress her instinct for solitude and tried to discourage the role James was casting for her, as a celebrity he could boast enviable access to. She kept guarded, suspecting writers like herself and Elizabeth made him self-conscious. Eighteen years after publishing his own book, about Manchester mill workers, he felt he had missed his vocation as a social novelist and was critical of theirs. He lectured Charlotte 'on the faults of the artist class' to which she belonged and told them writing fiction demeaned women, leading some into indecency.[48] Only one writer in the room had been charged with that: her. They all knew *The Spectator* said this when it reviewed *Jane Eyre*. Charlotte replied that offending conventionality was an occupational hazard for writers of either sex. It was the natural consequence of an imagination working to the best of its capabilities, she said. Acting quickly to rebalance the exchange, Elizabeth said authors should not be held accountable unless the coarseness was provocative. It sounded like diplomacy yet she said it again years later when she defended Charlotte for being 'utterly unconscious' of impropriety. 'I do not deny for myself the existence of coarseness here and there in her works, otherwise so entirely noble. I only ask those who read them to consider her life ... and to say how it could be otherwise.'[49]

Charlotte would not be stalled. As a writer, she told James, she asserted both her right to express herself as she wished, and to appeal to the higher authority that granted her capabilities. Elizabeth remembered her saying, 'I trust God will take from me whatever power of invention or expression I may have, before He lets me become blind to the sense of what is fitting or unfitting to be said!'[50] If Charlotte's hand was guided by God, those who condemned her must be in moral darkness, James concurred. Elizabeth was impressed. She thought her rebuke perfectly judged, mighty without being petty, judicious without being personal. Despite her shyness and sense of insignificance, Charlotte could rise with controlled ferocity when challenged. 'She is sterling and true,' Elizabeth observed, 'and if she is a little bitter she checks herself ... the wonder to me is how she can have kept heart and power alive in her life of desolation.'[51]

The next day, Thursday, 22 August, James announced the last excursion of the week, an evening with the Arnold family at their house a mile from Harriet Martineau's, on the incline of Lough Rigg Fell. To Charlotte's regret, Harriet was away ('to avoid the constant influx of visitors,' she noted), so escape was impossible.

The Arnolds were not only old friends of the Kay-Shuttleworths but of the Gaskells too, making Charlotte the only stranger in the company. She was 'frightfully shy', Elizabeth observed, 'and almost cries at the thought of going among strangers' but she was particularly apprehensive at the prospect of being shown off that night when even assurances from James that there would be less than half a dozen other people brought her incapacitating headaches.[52] Mary Arnold was the widow of the pioneering educationalist Dr Thomas Arnold, and of their six surviving children, Matthew – third eldest like Charlotte, and seven years her junior – had already achieved an exemplary academic career, a literary apprenticeship with Wordsworth, and an acclaimed volume of verse. He was a comparable opposite to Charlotte, a living demonstration of the trajectory her own life could have taken had she been born into another class and another sex.

They arrived just before dark. Charlotte felt sick with nerves. Flinching at anything less than excessive warmth, she found Mary Arnold unwelcoming, exposing her to strangers keen to scrutinise her. One of Mary's daughters lived to be 90 and still remembered that evening when she was interviewed in 1910. Frances, longest lived of the household, never married and succeeded her mother as matriarch until her own death in 1923. Revealingly, she recalled her family had not invited James or his guests, but that he had sent them an offer to show off his new celebrity friend, Currer Bell. Despite knowing how painful this was for Charlotte, he arranged to trade her anguish for his social cache. Until then, Elizabeth wondered if Charlotte's anxiety was congenital or neurotic. Now she realised James had set them up and her vulnerability to humiliation came from situations just like this where, duped or compromised, she had to act against self-preservation.

Sixty years on, Frances Arnold remembered they waited for Charlotte in the drawing room and watched her arrive looking exhausted and fright-ened. Just as she appeared to sink from the weight of their collective stares, everyone was distracted. In a burst of conviviality, Elizabeth took com-mand. She assumed the role of the vivacious guest of honour, took a chair by the fire and began to regale the whole room with anecdotes. The guests laughed. Charlotte slipped out of sight.[53]

Frances remembered Charlotte invited her to sit beside her and was 'most affectionate'. They thought Elizabeth 'the most beautiful woman of the party ... She possessed the most joyous disposition which could make itself at home anywhere.' Charlotte, at home nowhere, realised her silence had been filled, her deficiencies compensated and the attention she loathed swept away. Deftly, majestically, Elizabeth had saved her and the evening before they could falter. 'I was truly glad of her companionship,' Charlotte admitted. 'She is a woman of the most genuine talent – of cheerful, pleasing and cordial manners and – I believe – of a kind and good heart.'[54]

On their way back to Briery Close, Charlotte mentioned Mrs Arnold's cold reception but was told she ought not to take formality personally. She would change her mind by the time she met her again four months later, once familiar with her on the terms she preferred, having read about her. Away from drawing rooms filled with expectant guests, she could tower over Mrs Arnold in a territory she ruled as a shrewd and imperious reader. In the sealed, completed world of a biography of Dr Arnold, where there were no mixed signals brought by awkward handshakes, Mrs Arnold shone as a dutiful support and an attentive mother. Had Charlotte read it before they met, she accepted, she would have given her the benefit of the doubt and gained more than she had from the evening.[55] As was her habit, Charlotte had reacted, reflected, and then seen things differently.

When not stalled in carriages on sodden hill tracks or shown off in candle-lit parlours, Elizabeth and Charlotte found time to talk alone. 'She and I quarrelled and differed about almost everything,' Elizabeth reflected. 'She calls me a democrat and cannot bear Tennyson – but we like each other heartily, I think, and I hope we shall ripen into friends.'[56] Her warmth and sympathetic intelligence drew Charlotte out from her silence, encouraging candour with good-humoured understanding. Unlike with James, their disagreements required no speeches of self-justification. To Elizabeth, Charlotte was a curiosity; mercurial, paradoxical and barely socialised, yet had somehow produced one of the boldest works of literature in recent times. None of it made sense.

Their rooms looked across Lake Windermere to the blue peaks in the west. Taking it in together, she noticed how Charlotte studied the sky, reading cloud formations for coming weather. Having heard from Janet that Charlotte came from a village 'of a few grey stone houses perched up on the north side of a bleak moor', she commented it must remind her of home.[57] Charlotte said it did, except home felt very different now. She may have explained, as she did to William Smith Williams, that bereavement had ruined it. Her siblings' hard deaths had atomised their identities into the very earth of Haworth:

> I am free to walk on the moors but when I go out there alone everything reminds me of the times when others were with me and then the moors seem a wilderness, featureless, solitary, saddening. My sister Emily had a particular love for them, and there is not a knoll of heather, not a branch of fern, not a young bilberry leaf not a fluttering lark or linnet but reminds me of her. The distant prospects were Anne's delight, and when I look round, she is in the blue tints, the pale mists, the waves and shadows of the horizon. In the hill country silence their poetry comes by lines and stanzas into my mind: once I loved it – now I dare not read it.[58]

In a dream, the orphaned Jane Eyre sees her late mother where the moon would be, parting clouds to whisper consolation. Cut down by grief, it was now Charlotte who searched the sky for solace. Stripped of all who meant anything to her, it was her only friend now, she told Elizabeth – wife, mother, success – who 'could have no idea what a companion the sky became to anyone living in solitude'. To the lonely, the sky was all-encompassing and faithful and meant more 'than any inanimate object on earth, more than the moors themselves'.[59]

Her grief was obliterative, wiping out her family's shared pasts and futures. Emily and Anne perished 'of rapid consumption, unattended by any doctor', she explained ('Why, I don't know,' Elizabeth commented incredulously when she relayed it to a friend). And without a 'friend or relation in the world to nurse her, and her father dreading a sick room of all places', Charlotte expected a lonely, pitiful decline of her own. Her depression and fatalism led Elizabeth to conclude she was barely hanging on to what was left of her life, leaving 'little doubt she herself is already tainted with consumption'.[60] Charlotte had gone through 'suffering enough to have taken out every spark of merriment and [was] shy and silent from the habit of extreme intense solitude', Elizabeth told her friends. 'Such a life as Miss B's I had never heard of until Lady KS described [it].'[61]

Having shut herself away, Lady Janet hardly features in Elizabeth and Charlotte's accounts of their stay, yet Elizabeth must have made time to speak with her at length. In the letters she dashed off when she got home, she recounts details from their lengthy conversations carried out behind a closed door. Unknown to Charlotte, they were all about her.

And not for the first time. The subject of Charlotte had come up between them four months earlier, when Elizabeth and Janet first met. Janet asked her if she told her about when Charlotte stayed. 'No!' Elizabeth exclaimed in response, 'I never heard of Miss Brontë's visit; and I should like to hear a great deal more about her, as I have been so much interested in what she has written.' Not necessarily the narratives in her novels, she explained, more 'the glimpses one gets of *her*, and her modes of thought, and all unconsciously to herself, of the way in which she has suffered. I wonder if she suffers *now*?'[62]

She was surprised she might be of use to Charlotte. 'I am half amused you think I could do her good. I *never* feel as if I could do anyone good.' She often needed strength and faith herself, she added, possibly indicating where Janet felt Charlotte's weaknesses lay, before accepting their personalities might clash. 'I suppose we all *do* strengthen each other by clashing together, and earnestly talking our own thoughts and ideas.'[63] And yet, her curiosity was impossible to ignore.

Having already met Charlotte's father, Janet had anecdotes about the family, their home, and how Charlotte's hard-won successes were almost capsized by their poverty. It was a tale intended to move and it succeeded. It was distressing and, more importantly for a storyteller like Elizabeth, captivating. Here was an extraordinary young woman abandoned by a sequence of bereavements to the grim servitude of a volatile, emotionally absent father. Destitution and grief robbed her of the comforts, safeguards and opportunities most counted on for a start in life. Yet her education, allowance, everything, had to be fought for, with little won in the end. In some ways this sounded like an explanation *for* Charlotte, an individual so curious to others, so unsocialised and sad, so fierce and frightened, that justifications were offered out of her earshot. As with any unpalatable aspects of Charlotte's fiction, Elizabeth decided, the sharp and defensive expressions of her personality could only be rationalised by understanding her life. Only then did she make sense. After all, Elizabeth wrote, 'her faults are the faults of the very peculiar circumstances in which she has been placed.'[64]

As Elizabeth heard it, the life of Charlotte Brontë was tragic to the point of being almost unbelievable. However, as she would discover, what she heard could hardly be called an exaggeration. To this woman of the most exceptional talents and nature, as Elizabeth described her to friends, for whom comfort, love, recognition and reward were always denied, nothing good had seemingly ever happened.

'Poor thing,' Elizabeth reflected, 'she can hardly smile ...'[65]

CHAPTER 2

1850

Wild, Strange Facts

'You said I should stay longer than a week,' Charlotte told Ellen when she got home, 'you ought by this time to know me better.'[1] Abstemious to a fault, she was proud of taking less than her entitlement and left Windermere on Saturday, 24 August for the empty silence of home, the rank graveyard around it, to books and knitting and her father. After the weekend, she wrote to Elizabeth:

> Papa and I have just had tea; he is sitting quietly in his room, and I in mine; storms of rain are sweeping over the garden and churchyard; as to the moors – they are hidden in thick fog. Though alone – I am not unhappy; I have a thousand things to be thankful for, and – amongst the rest – that this morning I received a letter from you, and that this evening – I have the privilege of answering it.[2]

In contrast, Elizabeth's house in Manchester resounded with voices and activity. She got back to find her curate husband gone to Birmingham for a few days' preaching, leaving their daughters with the governess. Bursting to share her impressions of Charlotte and relay everything she heard about her, she went to work. In at least five long letters written over a forty-eight-hour period she repeated Charlotte's life story as Janet told it, combining Janet's gossip and impressions of Haworth with her own assessments. 'Miss Brontë *is* a nice person,' she told one friend, 'Like you ... without your merriment.'[3] To another, 'Her hands are like birds' claws, and she is so short sighted that she cannot see your face unless you are close to her.'[4] And to yet another:

> She is very little and very plain. Her stunted person she ascribes to the scanty supply of food she had as a growing girl, when at that school of the

Daughters of the Clergy … She is truth itself and of a very noble sterling nature, which has never been called out by anything kind or genial.[5]

Weaving the elements into a story for her friends, Elizabeth set the grim scene:

She is the last of six; lives in a wild out of the way village in the Yorkshire Moors with a wayward eccentric wild father – their parsonage facing the North – no flowers or shrub or tree can grow in the spot of ground, on account of the biting winds.

The house had never been painted or refurnished in thirty years, when Charlotte's mother died of cancer when she was 5 years old, crying in her bedridden final weeks, 'Oh God my poor children!'; her father was a 'strange, half mad' Irishman prone to violent outbursts. Elizabeth reported:

For instance, once in one of his wife's confinements something went wrong, so he got a saw, and went and sawed up all the chairs in her bed-room, never answering her remonstrances or minding her tears. Another time he was vexed and took the hearth-rug & tied it in a tight bundle & set it on fire in the grate.[6]

He was frugal and stern, eating separately from his six motherless children and leaving them to be educated by the servants, destroying their colour-ful shoes and depriving them of meat to staunch vanity and indulgence. Charlotte and three of her sisters boarded at the charity school where the eldest, Maria and Elizabeth, contracted the tuberculosis that killed them six weeks apart aged 11 and 10 after they were brought home. 'All this Lady Kay-Shuttleworth told me,' Elizabeth wrote.

How Janet could share such a comprehensive biography when she and Charlotte barely knew each other is a matter of conjecture. One of her sources was an acquaintance, an old Burnley woman who nursed Charlotte's mother in her final months. Martha Wright worked for the family through the summer of 1821 and remembered the uncommonly quiet children shep-herded by Maria, the eldest – their mother weeping in bed – and heard stories about Patrick's rages from before her time with the family. Yet in Elizabeth's retelling of Janet's account another voice is implicit. She says Charlotte described *herself* as 'stunted' by school and quotes her own account of asking her father for an allowance that he refused, deciding instead to try to escape penury by becoming a governess for wealthy families, indicating

Charlotte volunteered the information on her own. As the stories describing her deprivations and defeats finally overcome are more self-justifying than speculative, more self-preserving than the interests of gossips, they indicate origins more intimate than the prurience of Brontë acquaintances, or in any embellishments by Janet. None of the stories has the perspective of Charlotte's siblings, parents or aunt, or are as objective or inaccurate as they should be had they been invented by acquaintances. Throughout the narratives about a household of two parents, an unmarried aunt, three servants and six children only one subjective perspective remains consistent: Charlotte's. This presents the possibility that the narrative relayed from Janet to Elizabeth, and then to Elizabeth's circle of friends was a rhetorical life story originally told by Charlotte herself. A few years later, when she stayed with her at Haworth, Elizabeth noticed how much Charlotte talked about herself and her family:

> There are some people whose stock of facts and anecdotes are soon exhausted; but Miss B is none of these. She has the wild, strange facts of her own and her sisters' lives – and beyond and above these she has the most original and suggestive thoughts of her own; so that like the moors, I felt on the last days as if our talk might be extended in any direction without getting to the end of any subject.[7]

Harriet Martineau heard similar stories from Charlotte the night they met. To her, Charlotte was elemental, 'full of life and power', volunteering 'her name and the history of her life' in an intense two-hour dialogue. Charlotte told Harriet – who told Elizabeth, who relayed it to her friends – that her father had 'never slept out of his house for 26 years; she has lived a most retired life … never been in society, and many other particulars.'[8]

Insatiably curious about Charlotte's life and how far it inspired her fiction, the Kay-Shuttleworths prompted her to tell these stories again at Gawthorpe. Once certain of sympathy, she produced set-piece anecdotes about how the comfortless childhood produced an isolated adulthood. They were a form of explanation for her self-perceived shortcomings in status and looks. Her friends, teachers and the staff of her publisher all heard them. This was Charlotte's courtship with the outer world, her way of drawing people into her influence and keeping them there. These were the stories Janet transmitted to Elizabeth after Charlotte's visit, and when all three were together again at Briery Close. They would become foundational in the century of Brontë biographies that followed, colouring the family reputation and obscuring historical truth with imperishable elements of myth. Even one of Elizabeth's recipients commented in appalled fascination:

> Poor Miss Brontë, I cannot get the look of the grey, square, cold, dead-coloured house out of my head. One feels as if one ought to go to her at once and do something for her … Her life at least *almost* makes one like her books, though one does not want there to be any more Miss Brontës.[9]

At its core, this mythology contains the fugitive pieces of Charlotte's own autobiography never committed to paper. It was a story of self-justification and self-glorification honed over years, which in 1850 met its most responsive listener: Elizabeth Gaskell. But before the end of the year, Charlotte would expand her self-mythologising further than even she had dared take it before.

In the weeks afterwards, Charlotte reflected on what she had told Janet and Elizabeth about the brief lives and hasty deaths of her siblings. Coming home always drew her into a depression so engulfing it undid the relief any holiday brought. 'The deadly silence, solitude, desolation were awful,' she told Ellen, 'the craving for companionship – the hopelessness of relief – were what I should dread to feel again.'[10] Compounding her deflation and loneliness was the approaching anniversary of her brother's death, into the season when her sisters failed and followed him. 'I need say no more,' she told Elizabeth, 'As to running away from here every time I have a battle of this sort to fight – it would not do.'[11]

She turned to all she had left of them: their belongings. Handling their pens, used paint boxes and needlework sets, trinkets and small pieces of cheap jewellery only deepened her sense of isolation and in seeking comfort, Charlotte found the opposite. 'I lost in some days of indisposition the additional flesh and strength I had previously gained,' she told a friend. 'This resulted from the painful task of looking over letters and papers belonging to my sisters. Many little mementoes and memoranda conspired to make an impression inexorably sad which solitude deepened and fostered till I grew ill.'[12] She expanded with another, 'My mind had undergone some painful laceration in the course of looking over my sisters' papers – mementoes and memoranda that would have been nothing to others, conveyed for me so keen a sting.'

Without friends physically nearby and having resolved to protect her father from her grief like a child, she found 'no means of lightening or effacing the sad impression ... Continuous solitude grew more than I could bear.'[13] Reading Emily's and Anne's poetry manuscripts, she wondered if anything new from them could be published. Both had made their own selections in life, releasing with Charlotte what they saw fit for public consumption, and kept their personal and authorial identities separate. All three contributed to *Poems by Currer, Ellis and Acton Bell*, published in the summer of 1846, with Emily's novel *Wuthering Heights* and Anne's *Agnes Grey* issued together in a set in December the following year. Anne published her second and last novel *The Tenant of Wildfell Hall* in June 1848, before *Poems* was reissued the following November. By then, Branwell had died and Emily and Anne had symptoms of the tuberculosis that would kill Emily before the end of the year, then Anne the following spring.

After a lifetime of preparation, their literary careers were over after only three years, amounting to ignored poetry and three disdained novels. Branwell's predicted glories never rose beyond a few published verses, leaving stacks of unpublished poems and stories. Precocious and gregarious as a child, he identified with the esteemed men of letters and wrote newspaper satires from around the age of 11 when he and Charlotte made tiny hand-sewn booklets crammed with his classically inflected odes and long-form political diatribes. From adolescence, Branwell cultivated the rakish air of an effortlessly talented Romantic poet: garrulous, supremely self-assured but personally reckless. He published poems and an article in the regional press under the cover of a false name without telling his family, guarding his solitary achievements while he took on dead-end jobs as a railway clerk and a children's tutor. He had started a novel by the summer of 1845, keeping it as secret from his sisters as they kept theirs from him. Addiction, depression and tuberculosis brought him a pitiful death at 31, leaving his novel unfinished and scores of poems unread. After being collaborators in childhood, a divergence had opened between them in their twenties which appears to have never closed, even in memory. Nothing in the surviving record indicates Charlotte ever considered publishing his writing alongside their sisters'. 'It seems a sort of injustice to expose in print the crude thoughts of the unripe mind, the rude efforts of the unpractised hand,' Charlotte reasoned, 'yet ...'[14] And yet the alternative was oblivion.

While she wanted to put more of their writing into the world, she was full of doubts about acting without their sanction, especially when it came to their early work, intended for no eyes but their own. Emily and Anne could have made further selections from their poetry or written more novels, but without their counsel Charlotte had to balance her conjectures with their likely judgements. Now all their names were known to the world, their masquerade of secrecy, essential for Emily at least, was no longer required, surely a more open approach could be taken? The pen names that protected them in life were obscuring them in death, hastening the tide that had swept away the rest of the family, pulling them further from her reach.

She compromised and decided their rehabilitation should start with what was already published. Copies of *Wuthering Heights* and *Agnes Grey* were scarce after only two years, suggesting their publisher, T.C. Newby, had sold out without reprinting them. While he accepted both two months before Charlotte herself found a publisher, Newby waited until *Jane Eyre* was a sensation then capitalised on its success and recklessly printed Emily and Anne's texts in editions spoiled by printing errors, mixed up their names in adverts, and attributed their books to each other or suggested both were by the author of *Jane Eyre*. Deliberately or accidentally, he fed the growing speculation that Currer, Ellis and Acton Bell were interchangeable or might even be the same person.

Charlotte wondered if her own publisher would be interested and explained that as well as being indifferent to her sisters' work, Newby defaulted on royalties and still owed money. Smith Elder's owner, George Smith would have advised that as Emily and Anne's publisher only Newby held the rights to reissue their work and must be persuaded to either release them to an inheritor, their father, or sell them. If it came to the latter, Newby unquestionably had the upper hand and could ransom them for any price or keep them without reprinting them and consign them to literary oblivion. While George balked at the former, Charlotte feared the latter. Newby, it seemed, had all power over them. But neither Newby nor the men of Smith Elder reckoned on Charlotte's ingenuity.

Searching through her sisters' papers, she found Newby's letters and in them the loophole she needed. She discovered Emily and Anne's publishing agreement had been different from her own; they never sold their rights and only contracted him for printing and distribution, meaning he never had a say in who could issue them next. The power shifted back to her.

Urgently, she wrote to Williams and George, telling them she was going to confront Newby. She wanted to know how many copies they had left of *Wuthering Heights*, *Agnes Grey*, and *The Tenant of Wildfell Hall* as they appeared to be out of circulation. According to what she now knew, if all stock was sold the agreement had ended and Newby had to honour it and pay what was owed. Before she could reach Newby, George cut in, asking her to write a statement of facts and leave the rest to him. She did and as no correspondence survives about this between George and Newby, it could indicate he personally visited their offices in Marylebone, 2 miles from his own in the City of London. It is likely he knew what Charlotte did not, that Newby was notorious for this. Some months before *Wuthering Heights*, Newby had published another debut novelist, the young Anthony Trollope. Not only did they falsely advertise *The Macdermots of Ballycloran* as the work of his mother, established novelist Frances Trollope, they never paid him or responded to his letters once he signed the contract, leaving him feeling swindled.[15] Trollope never pursued Newby but made sure to change publisher for his second novel the next year. He wrote later, 'It is probable that he did not sell fifty copies of the work; but of what he did sell he gave me no account ... After the publication I never said a word about the book, even to my wife.'[16]

Whatever Smith told Newby, it worked. Two days later everything was settled. Smith Elder would bring Emily and Anne's novels on board and relaunch them in new editions. To make them commercially preferable to Newby's copies, Charlotte appears to have struck a bargain with them to produce a remastered version of the texts that included an introduction by her and previously unpublished material by Emily and Anne, and accepting all editing and proof-reading, keeping the costs to George negligible. Within a week, and in credit to Smith Elder's efficiency, they were discussing layouts.

With a view to correcting errors, she started rereading the novels for the first time since her sisters' deaths. Anne's *The Tenant of Wildfell Hall*, her account of a woman fleeing her abusive alcoholic husband, had been a 'mistake'[17] she decided, frustratingly unrepresentative of the 'gentle, retiring, inexperienced' woman who had written poems of religious melancholy since girlhood and was 'blameless in deed and almost in thought'.[18] In this we can read her intention, not to rehabilitate their work for critical judgement but to preserve what was more fleeting, their personalities. More palatable to the public, she suggested, was Anne's first novel *Agnes Grey*. Furthermore, it could be reissued with *Wuthering Heights* in the same set they were originally published in by Newby, another less expensive option for George.

Equally unrepresentative for Charlotte, though inescapably impressive, was Emily's *Wuthering Heights*. Its power, she told Williams:

fills me with renewed admiration – but yet I am oppressed – the reader is scarcely ever permitted a taste of unalloyed pleasure – every beam of sunshine is poured down through black bars of threatening cloud – every page is surcharged with a sort of moral electricity; and the writer was unconscious of all this – nothing could make her conscious of it. And this makes me reflect – perhaps I too am incapable of perceiving the faults and peculiarities of my own style.[19]

It connects with Elizabeth's observation in Windermere of Charlotte being unaware of what was regarded vulgar in her novels. She may have put it to her, prompting a reconsideration of her own and her sisters' works and leading her to question Emily and Anne's objectivity too.

Even before the reissues were agreed and, indicating how much her past was preoccupying her, she told Williams she had begun to write a short memoir they could use as an introduction. Submerged in her sisters' papers to transcribe their poems and edit proofs so everything could be reset and printed properly, she became so obsessed and so upset that she forgot to write to Ellen. Sensing Charlotte's distraction, Ellen sent her a light-hearted note asking if the rumours were true: did she have a boyfriend? Was she getting married? With weary-sounding humour Charlotte replied that of course she was still alone, and regardless of having 'scarcely seen a single man ... since I left London' had 'many obstacles' to even consider the possibility of leaving her father.[20] The discordance between Ellen's tone and Charlotte's troubling private task opened a three-week lapse in their correspondence that only ended when Charlotte responded to another note from her, assuring her nothing was wrong, only that she was busy trying to finish her edits before the deadline. 'I found the task at first exquisitely painful and depressing but regarding it in the light of a sacred duty I went on and now can bear it better,' she explained, 'It is work, however, that I cannot do in the evening for if I did, I should have no sleep at night.'[21]

As the early autumn twilights closed the days too early, this ambivalence between close reading her sisters' words to recapture their voices and adjust their texts in silence and solitude, risked crushing her completely. Her revisions to the poetry were clumsy and damaged their rhythm and punctuation and she told Ellen the task brought a 'heavy burden' of depression. 'Some days and nights have been cruel ... my loathing of solitude grew extreme; my recollection of my sisters intolerably poignant.'[22] She completed the revisions and added a coda of seventeen unpublished poems she drew from two of Emily's notebooks and six from Anne's, including two she published in the August and December 1848 issues of *Fraser's Magazine*.[23]

She reflected:

> In looking over my sister Anne's papers I find mournful evidence that religious feeling had … subdued her mood and bearing to a perpetual pensiveness: the pillar of a cloud glided constantly before her eyes: she ever waited at the foot of a secret Sinai, listening in her heart to the voice of a trumpet sounding long and waxing louder.[24]

Anne had, she told Williams, 'from her very childhood a tinge of religious melancholy in her mind – this I ever suspected – and I have found, among her papers, mournful proofs that such was the case.'[25]

While a degree of piety might be admirable, Charlotte thought its excess depressed Anne 'as if her whole innocent life had been passed under the martyrdom of an unconfessed physical pain'. Only as she died in a Scarborough hotel room did Anne's religious melancholia disperse and:

> in her last moments this tyranny of a too tender conscience was overcome; the pomp of terrors broke up and, passing away, left her dying hour unclouded. Her belief in God did not then bring her dread, as of a stern Judge, but hope as in a Creator and Saviour: and no faltering hope was it, but a pure and steadfast conviction, on which in the rude passage from Time to Eternity, she threw the weight of her human weakness, and by which she was enabled to bear what was to be borne, patiently – serenely – victoriously.[26]

Charlotte mentions this twice in her introductions: 'She was a very sincere and practical Christian, but the tinge of religious melancholy communicated a sad shade to her brief, blameless life.'

The distance between their personalities created by Anne's religious morbidity had its equivalent in Emily's introversion. Charlotte wrote, 'My sister Emily was not a person of demonstrative character, nor one, on the recesses of whose mind and feelings, even those nearest and dearest to her could, with impunity, intrude unlicensed.' Hers was a life of contemplative seclusion, deliberately cleared of complications to allow her to make full the commitment of her expression:

> The extremes of vigour and simplicity seemed to meet. Under an unsophisticated culture, inartificial tastes, and an unpretending outside, lay a

secret power and fire that might have informed the brain and kindled the veins of a hero; but she had no worldly wisdom; her powers were unadapted to the practical business of life; she would fail to defend her most manifest rights, to consult her most legitimate advantage. An interpreter ought always to have stood between her and the world. Her will was not very flexible, and it generally opposed her interest. Her temper was magnanimous, but warm and sudden; her spirit altogether unbending.

As with Anne, Charlotte was keen to emphasise that the elements of Emily's fiction considered grotesque or vulgar demonstrated a faculty for unfiltered observation, rather than being the expressions of an unfit mind. Emily's:

> disposition was not naturally gregarious; circumstances favoured and fostered her tendency to seclusion; except to go to church or take a walk on the hills, she rarely crossed the threshold of home. Though her feeling for the people round was benevolent, intercourse with them she never sought; nor, with very few exceptions, ever experienced. And yet she knew them: knew their ways, their language, their family histories; she could hear of them with interest, and talk of them with detail, minute, graphic, and accurate; but *with* them, she rarely exchanged a word.[27]

Both were starved of support and encouragement, Charlotte reflected, but persisted to forge their novels by relying on internal reserves of self-perpetuating power: 'Energy nerved the one, and endurance upheld the other.' Despite being retiring, neither was deterred by hostile critics and with growing certainty in their own creative powers were prepared to start new novels. Only physical destruction stopped them; Emily and Anne were cut down 'in the very heat and burden of the day'.

Conscious of how other people had seen them all as insignificant women without power, status or influence, Charlotte was confronting the world that overlooked her sisters. Now it must look again at their personal nobility and their industry in perfecting the expression of original and volcanic talents: 'For strangers they were nothing, for superficial observers less than nothing; but for those who had known them all their lives in the intimacy of close relationship, they were genuinely good and truly great.'[28]

Writing candidly in a way their reticence once prohibited, this was not only Charlotte's love letter to the past but her plea for it to end. Without agency or breath Emily and Anne, who chose to live in realms of their own invention, would be forever characters in a new story started by their sister.

Setting the boundary between their shared past and her singular future, between protection and whatever was to follow, Charlotte positioned herself alone. Independent in name and identity from them now all three were necessarily separated, she resolved to cleave away from their creative and emotional counsel and take her first steps into an as yet unwritten future.

At the start of October, Charlotte received a letter from her school friend Mary Taylor, posted from New Zealand the previous April. As it took six months for mail to travel from England to Wellington, where Mary had emigrated, and another six months for a reply to come back, Mary was responding to a desperately unhappy note Charlotte sent her a year before in the wake of Anne's death. Even so, her advice could not have been better timed. It urged Charlotte to fight for professional success. 'You ought to care as much for that as you do about going to Heaven,' she told her sharply. She said she must believe in her own talent and its possibilities to bring friends and financial security. Mary wrote:

> It seems to me hard indeed that you who would succeed better than anyone in making friends and keeping them should be so condemned to solitude from your poverty. To no one would money bring more happiness, for no one would use it better than you would … I am convinced it would give you great and noble pleasures. Look out then for success in writing … Your books will sell and you will acquire influence and power.[29]

Soon after, the new editions of Emily and Anne's novels were published. Deliberately or not, yet with the same conviction with which she directed their book of poems only four years earlier, Charlotte had created their final joint venture. As a prose opposite to that first book, a fulfilment of the promise of the earlier, she knew this would be scrutinised by those who ignored the other. And with it, she concluded their collaborative enterprises and brought their work full circle. Copies arrived just before her second Christmas without them.

CHAPTER 3

1850

A Passionate Life

'What is this new book of Miss Brontë's, do you know?' Elizabeth asked Janet. 'It will be very interesting to hear more of her sisters but rather difficult for her to do it well and discreetly.'[1]

After hearing Charlotte was depressed, Elizabeth, Janet and Harriet Martineau discussed their concerns. Harriet told Charlotte to come stay with her in Ambleside, having heard 'from one of her acquaintance in London that she is in a very unsatisfactory state of health ... I shall do my best to take care of her.'[2] The day before Charlotte went, Harriet explained why she was so accommodating to one so notorious. '*I like Currer Bell's letters: but then, I knew herself before I knew her letters; & that makes much difference ...*'[3]

They had been writing since Harriet deciphered the note that came with *Shirley*. A few weeks after it, she was finishing dessert with her cousin Richard and his wife, Lucy, in their house near Hyde Park, when a messenger burst in with a suave-sounding note signed by Currer Bell: 'It would grieve me to lose this chance of seeing one whose works have so often made her the subject of my thoughts.'[4]

Having come from an address only a half-mile away, where Charlotte was staying with George Smith's family, Harriet sent a reply on foot offering tea the following evening. The next morning, a footman brought back an acceptance.[5] 'I shall try now to be patient till six o'clock comes,' Currer Bell had written. 'That is a woman's note,' Harriet decided. In a matter of hours, the face of Currer Bell would be revealed. Lucy wrote breathlessly to her teenage son in the country, 'We were wondering what sort of a being this same Currer Bell would turn out to be; whether a tall moustached man 6 feet high, or an aged female, or a girl, or altogether a ghost, a hoax or a swindler!'[6] As six o'clock approached, Lucy filled the darkening parlour with lighted candles to get the best view. They watched the door and the clock hands ticking towards six. There was a thunderous rap and the door burst open to reveal an impressively tall man. He announced he was collecting donations for homeless hostels. They sent him away and five minutes later a carriage drew up outside, the bell rang and after a moment of suspense the footman announced their guest. Being partially deaf and using an ear-trumpet, Harriet misheard it as 'Miss Brodgen' and had Lucy clarify that it was 'Miss Brontë', one of the names she heard in London gossip. 'In came a neat little woman, a very little sprite of a creature nicely dressed; & with nice tidy bright hair,' wrote Lucy. 'I thought her the smallest creature I had ever seen (except at a fair),' Harriet remembered, 'and her eyes blazed, as it seemed to me. She glanced quickly round; and my trumpet pointing me out, she held out her hand frankly and pleasantly.'[7] Charlotte told William Smith Williams, 'When I walked into the room and put my hand into Miss Martineau's the action of saluting her and the fact of her presence seemed visionary.'[8]

After introductions, she sat next to Harriet and looked at her with an expression of such open vulnerability and gratitude it caught Harriet off guard:

> Such a look – so loving, so appealing – that, in connection with her deep mourning dress, and the knowledge that she was the sole survivor of her family, I could with the utmost difficulty return her smile, or keep my composure. I should have been heartily glad to cry.[9]

After tea, they were left alone to talk. Harriet remembered there was something:

> inexpressibly affecting in the aspect of the frail little creature who had done such wonderful things, and who was able to bear up, with so bright an eye and so composed a countenance, under not only such a weight of sorrow, but such a prospect of solitude. In her deep mourning dress (neat as a Quaker's), with her beautiful hair, smooth and brown, her fine eyes, and her sensible face indicating a habit of self-control.[10]

When Harriet assured her *Jane Eyre* was among the best novels of their time, Charlotte glowed with pleasure and relief. Harriet remembered how:

> Jane Eyre was naturally and universally supposed to be Charlotte herself; but she always denied it calmly, cheerfully, and with the obvious sincerity

which characterised all she said. She declared that there was no more ground for the assertion than this: she once told her sisters that they were wrong – even morally wrong – in making their heroines beautiful, as a matter of course. They replied that it was impossible to make a heroine interesting on other terms. Her answer was: 'I will prove to you that you are wrong. I will show to you a heroine as small and as plain as myself, who shall be as interesting as any of yours.' 'Hence *Jane Eyre*,' said she, in telling the anecdote, 'but she is not myself any further than that.'[11]

She described writing feverishly in pencil in little square notebooks held close to her eyes, producing over 120,000 words in three weeks, until Jane left Rochester and Thornfield. She paused then finished it with more deliberation.[12] She had to be conscientious in fiction, she told Harriet, to constrain invented scenes with the integrity of her own experience. Harriet recalled she insisted:

> the account of the school in *Jane Eyre* is only too true. The 'Helen' of that tale is – not precisely the eldest sister ... but more like her than any other real person. She is that sister 'with a difference'. Another sister died at home soon after leaving the school and in consequence of its hardships ... Charlotte Brontë was never free ... from the gnawing sensation or consequent feebleness of downright hunger; and she never grew an inch from that time. She was the smallest of women and it was that school which stunted her growth.[13]

Charlotte said she read all her reviews calmly, taking praise with a grain of salt and intelligent criticism as instruction, but was mystified by comments made about *Jane Eyre* and asked if they made sense to her. Harriet knew it had been controversial because of Charlotte's exploration of the ambivalences of love, which she thought uncommonly well written, but did not consider that vulgar. However, she admitted, if she reread it she might understand criticisms better.[14] Charlotte begged her to do that and always share her honest opinions about her writing. Harriet agreed. It was a promise that would ultimately poison their friendship. But at that moment, the women were new friends and rejoined the rest of the household to talk with them in the candlelight.[15]

Knowing she was amongst sympathetic listeners that night, Charlotte recounted the sad story of her life of grief and isolation, just as she would go on to do with Janet and Elizabeth. Meeting Charlotte for the first time after no previous contact, even a stranger like Lucy Martineau could recount a thumbnail sketch of Charlotte's autobiography the next day:

> She lives in a most retired part of England, never seeing *any* body, & her Father has not slept out of his own house for the last 20 years. She is the only child left to him, 3 others having died of rapid decline within the last year.[16]

The life of Charlotte Brontë, as narrated by Charlotte Brontë herself, was reaching the ears of anyone willing to listen.

'Remember, the Windermere Station is your railway goal. Then 6 miles of omnibus or coach; and a word to the driver will bring you on to my gate.'[17] Harriet's command led to The Knoll, the house in Ambleside she built solely for herself and to her own specifications. 'I am living in a paradise,' she announced at the time, 'and I feel it impossible to step out of it.'[18] To her, the area's beauty made the locals thrive. 'Nobody seems ever ill here,' she observed, 'I never saw such a place for robustness, for all the quantity of rain that comes down. As for me, I have not had one day of ailment the whole year.'[19] She invited friends to join her. 'From my little terrace, I will show you paradise spread before us … If the weather is bad, never mind, I find it beautiful to stand at my window & see it rain.'[20]

That December week was marked by cold days, alternating cloud and sharp sunshine, frosting to clear-skied nights. When snow came, it only whitened the fell tops.[21] 'All this December, almost without intermission, we have had this yellow glow the whole day long,' Harriet wrote the day before Charlotte arrived, 'and the most splendid skies at night. My starlight walks before my early breakfast are delicious. The rushing River Rotha seems to carry down gushes of stars to the lake.'[22] Harriet rose early for an ice-cold bath then a walk in the dawn before she started writing at seven. She did not expect guests to join her and left them to follow their own routines. Charlotte told Ellen:

> Her visitors enjoy the most perfect liberty; what she claims for herself she allows them. I rise at my own hour, breakfast alone … I pass the morning in the drawing-room – she in her study. At two o'clock we meet, work, talk, and walk together till five – her dinner-hour – spend the evening

together, when she converses fluently, abundantly, and with the most complete frankness. I go to my own room soon after ten – she sits up writing letters till twelve. She appears exhaustless in strength and spirits, and indefatigable in the faculty of labour.[23]

The next day, she took Charlotte to her lecture about the Battle of Crecy at the local mechanics' institute. She noticed Charlotte could not take her eyes off her and became visibly moved as she described how Edward III demanded to know if his son had been injured or killed. Being told he was neither, Edward famously replied the boy was mighty enough to fight on to victory alone. Afterwards, the women walked back to The Knoll in silence. 'In the drawing room the first thing I did was to light the lamp, and the first flare showed Charlotte Brontë with large eyes, staring at me, and repeating "Is my son dead?"'[24]

Charlotte found Harriet impressive, marvelling at her self-reliance and independence, certain both would guard against grief or loneliness. To Ellen she described her as:

a great and a good woman; of course not without peculiarities but I have seen none as yet that annoy me. She is both hard and warm-hearted, abrupt and affectionate – liberal and despotic. I believe she is not at all conscious of her own absolutism. When I tell her of it, she denies the charge warmly; then I laugh at her. I believe she almost rules Ambleside. Some of the gentry dislike her, but the lower orders have a great regard for her.[25]

Nearby, the Kay-Shuttleworths returned to Briery Close and with the same relentless insistence that characterised all their interactions with Charlotte, pressed her to spend a few days with them. Seeking the excuse of alternative plans, she begged Ellen to come to hers instead of going straight home. Despite putting them off, James brought his carriage to take her on more of his sightseeing drives. Expecting to be exasperated, she was shocked when she saw him. Pallid and gaunt, he explained that his wife's health had collapsed and left her bedridden. 'I grieve to say he looks to me as if wasting away,' she confided to Ellen.[26] His vulnerability broke her irritation and she let herself admit he had always been kind to her. His friendship, Charlotte concluded, must have been sincere after all.

At the weekend, Harriet took Charlotte to dinner at the home of Edward Quillinan, an elderly minor poet and widower of Wordsworth's daughter

Dora. Keen to integrate Harriet into the community she kept at a distance; he told her he might invite a crowd of eligible men. Where Charlotte might have flustered, Harriet gave him a flat 'No' and told him she would neither change her lifestyle nor meet any locals.[27] Quillinan acquiesced and told her he would only include one neighbour, Matthew Arnold, as long as she brought her guest too. Harriet was satisfied.[28] After a couple of hours of conversation, the men bid them goodnight. Arnold described them:

> At seven came Miss Martineau and Miss Brontë (Jane Eyre); talked to Miss Martineau (who blasphemes frightfully) about the prospects of the Church of England … I talked to Miss Brontë (past thirty and plain …) of her curates, of French novels, and her education in a school at Brussels, and sent the lions roaring to their dens at half past nine.[29]

The underwhelming feeling was mutual. Charlotte thought him superficial but was told he would improve on acquaintance, like his mother. They never met again but within a few years he would come back to the memory of this supper to recycle it into an elegy. In it, he presents Harriet as a 'steadfast soul … unflinching and keen … which dared/ Trust its own thoughts' beside Charlotte, who 'young, unpractised, had told/ With a master's accent her feign'd / Story of passionate life.'[30]

Superficially, he was referring to her writing but obliquely he was considering what Charlotte told him that evening. Her education in Brussels was one of the turning points in her life, initiating deeply conflicting private emotions and an unrequited love that took her years to recover from, its influence bleeding into all her books and transmuting into her currently gestating novel, *Villette*. Yet here with two strangers, she talked about it all. Shy as she could be, Charlotte relied on a social persona emboldened by anecdotes she coined for strangers and confidantes alike that could not fail to win their hearts, hitting their mark with Arnold, as they had in London with Harriet, at Gawthorpe with Janet, and with Elizabeth at Briery Close.

She left Ambleside for the Bradford train the day before Christmas Eve, took a cab to Birstall and Ellen, and stayed for Christmas. She got back to the parsonage and her father on New Year's Eve. Before the end of that week, newspaper columns reporting morsels about the emperor of Austria moving into the London hotel later known as Claridge's, of Spain's scandalous Queen Isabella finding herself 'again in an interesting state', and the patenting of the world's first dishwasher in New York, also announced 'the authoress of *Jane Eyre*, Miss Brontë, has been on a visit lately to Miss

Martineau at Ambleside.'[31] Furthermore, as the new editions of *Wuthering Heights* and *Agnes Grey* were picked up, the press presented Charlotte's prefaces as an exposé: 'The unknown authors! The Bells! At length, the veil has been drawn aside that shrouded the mystery of the relationship of Currer, Acton and Ellis Bell. They were three sisters ...'[32]

Charlotte's life as an anonymous woman ended with the year 1850, which began with her neighbours' whispers, and ended with her name in the press. Currer Bell, birthed for print, was effectively killed by it. Unmasked, Charlotte stepped into 1851 a public figure and a celebrity, known to all by her own name – and for her own talents.

CHAPTER 4

1851
A Tigress Before Calamity

Charlotte and Elizabeth next met six months later, in the hot summer of 1851. Charlotte offered to stop off for the weekend on her way back from a month with her publisher's family in London. 'Just when we can't take her in,' worried Elizabeth.[1]

In London, everyone around her made plans for her rather than with her, showing her Richmond, Westminster and the newly opened Great Exhibition, all between incursions from Sir James, who considered Charlotte a living attraction to whom he guided clusters of fans. Any respite she salvaged was eroded by her unconquerable sense of obligation. 'Can I throw all these people overboard – derange all plans, break all promises?' she asked Ellen. 'Would it be rational to do this? Would it be right? Could it be done?'[2]

Despite staying with George, she had to wait until her last week before he had a day off. He was so overloaded with work without his manager, who was overseeing their new office in India, that he often stayed back until three or four in the morning, sometimes working all night, through the next day and into the evening doing thirty-two hours of continuous dictation to clerks.[3] Feeling similarly in demand, Charlotte felt buried by invitations even as she was packing to leave. With George otherwise engaged, his mother saw her off on the Manchester train on the morning of Friday, 27 June.

Elizabeth lived 2 miles south-east of Manchester's heavily industrialised centre in a large house she had taken a few months before she met Charlotte in Windermere. Balancing anxieties about renting such an expensive place against potential benefits, she was philosophical. 'Well! I must try and make the house give as much pleasure to others as I can and make it as little a selfish thing as I can ... I dare say we shall be ruined.'[4] Over all, it looked and felt perfect for a prosperous modern family and, as planned, it became a salon, hosting Charles Dickens, Thomas Carlyle and John Ruskin. 'Haworth parsonage is rather a contrast,' Charlotte observed.[5]

A path curved off Plymouth Grove to the front door, through a garden of shrubs and flowers planted by Elizabeth herself. It bordered open fields she rented for vegetables, for a cow, pigs and chickens like the cottage gardens of her Knutsford childhood. From the front door, a broad entrance hall opened into a music room on the immediate left, a library on the right and at the foot of the stairs at the end of the hall facing the front door, the dining room. A large parlour behind the music room led into the dining room, which in turn had two other doors that opened into a pantry and a scullery. The parlour windows looked into a side street, and at the back, next to the door to the dining room, Elizabeth set her writing desk before a large window. Upstairs were five bedrooms, three dressing rooms, a bathroom and two lavatories; more rooms than in Charlotte's entire home, which lacked both plumbing and inside lavatories. The house was run by a redoubtable housekeeper, Ann Hearn,[6] and two housemaids, one on leave the weekend Charlotte stayed, with such clockwork efficiency that 'the rooms are always tidy & one never sees any tidying'.[7] She was given the large guest bedroom a subsequent visitor described as perfect for those who appreciate homeliness; 'a charming room ... sofa, writing table etc. all so comfortable.'[8] Being far enough from the pollution of the city centre allowed for the windows to be left open that summer, filling the large square rooms with 'a whispering of leaves and perfume of flowers'.[9]

Here Elizabeth could introduce Charlotte to her family for the first time: her cleric husband of eighteen years, William ('a good and kind man too,' decided Charlotte[10]), and all but the eldest of their four daughters; 14-year-old Margaret, 8-year-old Florence and 4-year-old Julia, or as Elizabeth called them, 'Meta, Flossie and Baby'.[11] Missing was 16-year-old Marianne, at boarding school in London.[12] All the girls were inheritors of their mother's intelligence and charm and filled the house with liveliness and laughter.[13] Charlotte was enchanted by their exuberance and unselfconscious affection. Almost uncomprehendingly, she accepted it as an unexpected blessing. She thought they were as generous with their love as their mother, asking her, 'To what children am I not a stranger?'[14] Little Julia especially took to her, slipping her hand into Charlotte's and taking her about the house.[15] Charlotte would carry the memory of the child's tenderness back to her empty rooms in Haworth, writing a month later to Elizabeth, 'Could you manage to convey a small kiss to that dear but dangerous little person – Julia?

She surreptitiously possessed herself of a minute fraction of my heart, which has been missing ever since I saw her.'[16] This, Charlotte knew, was how a home should feel, with a partner and children and friends orbiting 'a woman whose conversation and company I should not soon tire. She seems to me kind, clever, animated and unaffected.'[17]

On the first evening, Charlotte asked for black tea, saying green gave her insomnia.[18] Elizabeth agreed but served her their premixed black and green tea anyway. The next morning when asked how she slept, Charlotte replied, 'Splendidly', sending knowing smiles around the table, and the same mixture was served the rest of the weekend. Had Elizabeth ever wondered whether Charlotte knew what was best for herself, she now had an inkling. She remembered this two years later when writing the seventh instalment of *Cranford*:

> If she was made aware that she had been drinking green tea at any time, she always thought it her duty to lie awake half through the night afterward (I have known her take it in ignorance many a time without such effects).[19]

June's long hot days intensified Charlotte's exhaustion after London, so they sat indoors at open windows and talked.[20] Without the interjections of Sir James, they could discuss their writing freely. Over the last decade, Elizabeth had produced articles and stories before her anonymous first novel *Mary Barton* in October 1848 and for the last year had been writing stories for Dickens' weekly magazine, *Household Words*. She suggested Charlotte consider it for a regular income but Charlotte told her she could not write to order, or without inspiration. Elizabeth was surprised when she added, 'If I had to earn my living, I would go out as a governess again, much as I dislike the life. But I think one should only write out of the fullness of one's heart, spontaneously.'[21]

A few weeks later when she was asked about it again, this time by George, she reiterated her position in an answer that indicated the remarkable difference between these relationships. While comfortable enough with Elizabeth to be frank about a back-up plan, with George she still needed evasions. Rather than simply telling him she might consider it, she performed a rigmarole, asking him to imagine Currer Bell's reaction, saying 'he' would not be willing: 'I will publish no serial of which the last number is not written before the first comes out.'[22] She often ventriloquised Currer Bell's voice when put on the spot, deferring to 'him' as a separate agency declining for her and absorbing any culpability for disappointment. One can imagine how such a reply was received by a man so short of time as George Smith. Nevertheless, sensing her embarrassment, he gallantly withdrew any unintended impertinence. Abashed, she rushed to assure him he had only ever been kind and considerate, claiming those the chief reasons for their friendship and not, as George saw it, for their professional relationship.[23] Relying on instinct over objectivity, Charlotte was occasionally misdirected into such naïve and unfortunate lapses.

She told Elizabeth about encounters with two individuals in recent weeks that struck her off an even course: arguing with William Thackeray and seeing scandalous live performances by a Jewish-French actress, Rachel Felix. The Thackeray incident challenged her public identity as an author while Felix disturbed depths in her private emotional self. Both eviscerated her lifelong feelings of physical, social and intellectual inadequacy.

For years she had hero-worshipped Thackeray as England's greatest living writer, telling William Smith Williams he would still be read in a century, guaranteed by:

> the thing that came into the world with *him* – his inherent genius: the thing that made him – I doubt not different as a child from other children, that caused him, perhaps, peculiar griefs and struggles in life – and that now makes him a writer unlike other writers.[24]

With admiration came identification. Seeing him as a born writer attracting challenges unique to the gifted, she pictured a man both elemental and earthy, an eternal talent amongst mortals; the kind of magisterial male author in fact she imagined Currer Bell to be. Conversely, Thackeray felt no divine origin story was needed to explain his success. He saw himself as a grafter, toiling in the mines of periodicals and journals, and scoring better deals wherever he could.

Despite being only five years older, he had been writing commercially for a decade longer than Charlotte. From the age of 26 he earned his living from unsigned articles and stories, and by 1851 had published fourteen books under different names. It was his satire, *Vanity Fair*, issued under his real name from January 1847 to July 1848 that brought him national recognition as a rival to Dickens. In the middle of that he, along with everyone else, heard about the mystery surrounding Currer Bell. When he read *Jane Eyre*, he told Williams it brought his writing to a standstill. 'It interested me so much that I have lost (or won if you like) a whole day in reading it …

Who the author can be I can't guess – if a woman she knows her language better than most ladies.'[25] Without further explanation, he added that the plot at least was familiar to him. When Williams quoted this in a letter to Charlotte she answered in the high-handed voice she was still assuming as Currer Bell. 'I feel honoured in being approved by Mr Thackeray because I approve Mr Thackeray.'[26] Nevertheless, she was defensive about his reservations: 'The plot of *Jane Eyre* may be a hackneyed one; Mr Thackeray remarks that it is familiar to him, but having read comparatively few novels, I never chanced to meet with it, and thought it original.'[27]

Two months later, she chose to make her praise public and dedicated the second edition of *Jane Eyre* to him. In her acknowledgements she thanks the public, the press and her publishers (in that order) but reserves especial thanks for the writer she celebrates with Biblical precedence who 'comes before the great ones of society, much as the son of Imlah came before the throned Kings of Judah and Israel'.[28] It elevated Thackeray to impossible Messianic status, reimagining him a divinely anointed master whose wit, intellect and talent were beyond dispute as timeless. But as a man who simply wrote for money, Thackeray was bemused.

Williams sent him a copy of the new edition but got no reply. Eventually, Thackeray acknowledged 'Currer Bell's enormous compliment' as the 'greatest … I have ever received in my life', but was still nonplussed, writing, 'I didn't know what to say in reply; it quite flustered and upset me.'[29] He wrote separately to Charlotte – without knowing her real name or identity – to both thank her and take her to task. He explained she had embarrassed him. Both she and Williams were oblivious to one of the most popular *Jane Eyre* theories doing the rounds of the Mayfair coteries that, being effectively separated from his institutionalised wife, Thackeray was none other than the original of Mr Rochester, and *Jane Eyre* a thinly disguised memoir by his disgruntled ex-lover, a governess who inspired *Vanity Fair*'s Becky Sharp. Charlotte was mortified. Now it was obvious what he meant about the familiar plot: it was his life and her preface and dedication appeared to confirm it. She protested:

Of course, I knew nothing whatever of Mr Thackeray's domestic concerns: he existed for me only as an author: of all regarding his personality, station, connections, private history – I was (and am still in a great measure) totally in the dark: but I am *very*, *very* sorry that my inadvertent blunder should have made his name and affairs a subject for common gossip.[30]

Her rationale was telling. Behind the title 'author' could be no complications or ambiguities. Naturally, she did not fully believe that, but it reveals how she idealised famous writers as being beyond the fallibilities of ordinary people. When she agreed to meet him for the first time, she did not expect him to be as resistant to definition as she, or that extravagant flattery might provoke more sarcasm than gratitude. George remembered:

> He insisted on discussing his books very much as a clerk in a bank would discuss the ledgers, but this was, on Thackeray's part, an affectation; an affectation into which he was provoked by what he considered Charlotte Brontë's high falutin'. Miss Brontë wanted to persuade him that he was a great man with a 'mission'; and Thackeray, with many wicked jests, declined to recognise the 'mission'.[31]

Their collision course was set.

George first brought them together at a London dinner party in December 1849, and then in the two summers that followed. Each time provoked a confrontation, escalating to their final argument in 1851. He knew they were consumed by curiosity to meet each other but kept quiet that he too was keen, for his own reasons. While Charlotte desired an audience with her idol and Thackeray burned to know who had written *Jane Eyre*, George's intentions were commercial. He had been ambitious to sign Thackeray for over ten years, since he was apprenticed to his father in the early 1840s. Once, when sent to a book auction, he became so engrossed by Thackeray's *Paris Sketch Book* that he missed it all and vowed to sign up the writer who could distract so powerfully. When he took over Smith Elder and brought on William Smith Williams, one of the first things he checked was if he knew Thackeray. Williams did, slightly, so George told him to offer Thackeray any terms he wished to name for anything he wished to write. By then, through George's tireless direction, the publisher was becoming one of London's most successful, yet his offer made Thackeray sceptical, thinking they were not in the business of improving anyone's lives but their own and dismissed it as too altruistic to be sincere.

He forgot about it and George was too awed to pursue him. It was not until he heard how much Charlotte worshipped Thackeray that he realised he could turn her to his own advantage. Introducing them was so prominent in his mind he suggested it as soon as they first met in the summer of 1848 when she and Anne launched themselves into his office to reveal their true identities. When Charlotte showed him a letter addressed to Currer Bell as proof of who she was, George said she must allow him to introduce them to his family, and that, 'Mr Thackeray would be pleased to see you.' She admitted she would like to meet him but was not ready to give up their disguises as Currer and Acton Bell yet.[32] Remarkably, George did not know Thackeray personally at that point. However, now he knew how he could make it happen.

A year later when Charlotte came back to London alone, he tried again. Reluctant to make another proposal she could defer or Thackeray could ignore, George went to Thackeray's home with an offer no one could refuse. He told him he was hosting the author of *Jane Eyre* and could introduce them on one condition: Thackeray must play along and not mention he knew who she was. 'I see! It will be all right, you are speaking to a man of the world,' Thackeray assured him. 'But,' George later observed, 'unhappily it was not all right.'[33]

Charlotte had come to London for a fortnight, arriving on Thursday, 29 November, her first time back since her life had been changed by publication, and her household irrevocably damaged by death. On all five of her visits she stayed with George at his invitation in the houses he shared with his mother, brother and three sisters, first at 4 Westbourne Place (in 1848 and 1849) and then after they moved to 76 Gloucester Terrace (in 1850, 1851 and 1853). Affable and genteel, the Smiths surrounded her with the protective band of family unity they sensed she lacked. Charlotte described their warmth and hospitality to Elizabeth, from the unaccustomed luxury of having a fire and candles in her room at night to the care of Mrs Smith, who, 'watched me very narrowly when surrounded by strangers; she never took her eyes from me. I liked the surveillance; it seemed to keep guard over me.'[34] Later, she would mine these visits for *Villette*, casting George as Dr John and his mother as Mrs Bretton, remembering how her 'many, many questions about past times' provoked her to tell the story of her 'single-handed conflict with Life, with Death, with Grief, with Fate'.[35]

The Smiths had not been without their tragedies. George's father had died prematurely a few years earlier, resigning Smith Elder entirely to him, 'But so courageous a mother, with such a champion in her son, was well fitted to fight a good fight with the world, and to prevail ultimately.'[36] To Charlotte, George was a blessed agent of heroism 'on whose birth benign planets have certainly smiled … Strong and cheerful, and firm and courteous; not rash, yet valiant.'[37] While kind to her, George knew Charlotte could be trying. He admitted:

> My mother and sisters found her a somewhat difficult guest, and I am afraid she was never perfectly at ease with them. Strangers used to say that they were afraid of her. She was very quiet and self-absorbed and gave the impression that she was always engaged in observing and analysing the people she met. She was sometimes tempted to confide her analysis to the victim.[38]

From the moment he brought Thackeray and Charlotte together, she was star-struck. 'I saw him enter, looked up at his tall figure, heard his voice, the whole incident was truly dreamlike – I was only certain it was true because I became miserably destitute of self-possession.'[39] Although not formally introduced, she saw him study her and once they stood to go to dinner he asked to shake her hand.[40] It was so momentous all she could tell Ellen was she had seen him in person, then later explained she made a fool of herself because she was overcome and exhausted.[41] Thackeray recalled 'the trembling little frame, the little hand, the great honest eyes. An impetuous honesty seemed to me to characterise the woman.'[42]

After dinner, the ladies retired to the drawing room, soon followed by George and Thackeray, smoking cigars. Thackeray strolled over to Charlotte and, letting the smoke coil around them, asked if she understood its meaning.[43] She was puzzled until she saw everyone's expressions change as he started to quote from *Jane Eyre*: 'This new scent is neither of shrub nor flower; it is – I know it well – it is Mr Rochester's cigar.'[44] His uncomfortable joke equated them both to the respective roles of Rochester and Jane in a nod to the gossip her unfortunate dedication confirmed. If he had felt publicly mortified by her, now it was his turn to make a joke at her expense. It was an act of dominance to make it clear her posture of anonymity was fooling no one and she could not expect strangers to indulge it. George caught her expression: 'Miss Brontë's face showed her discomfiture and in a chilly fashion she turned off the allusion. But I was almost as much discomposed … She cast an accusing look at me.'

Soon, Thackeray gave up on the evening and left for the Garrick Club, telling friends he had just met Jane Eyre personally.[45] Charlotte never describes this in any of her letters but during her stay with Elizabeth told her 'how difficult she found it, this first time of meeting Mr Thackeray, to decide whether he was speaking in jest or in earnest'.[46] Despite her embarrassment, she was reluctant to revise her opinion of him or of her own sense of inadequacy and relegated the evening's failure to her own shortcomings. She would not see him again until her next London visit in the summer of 1850. By then, she was ready for him.

This time, George accepted Thackeray's reciprocal dinner invitation and agreed to bring Charlotte to his house on Young Street, off Kensington High Street. When Thackeray dropped by in the morning to regale them as an appetiser, it was a more assertive woman he found. Confident of her fan adulation, he bragged, as he always did, about himself and his own writing but now she questioned everything he said, interrogating his anecdotes to show them as banal and witless in front of George, his potential paymaster. Once mocked or taken for granted, Charlotte turned her devotion into laser-like scrutiny, making others more uncomfortable than they felt free to make her. It was a side neither man had seen before. Neither knew what to do.

'I was moved to speak to him of some of his shortcomings,' she coolly reported to Ellen, in what George described as the 'queer scene' of the rising tensions between them. 'One by one the faults came into my mind and one by one I brought them out and sought some explanation or defence.'[47]

She left both men in no doubt she had launched a pre-emptive strike. If Thackeray chose tonight to make a spectacle of her again, he would not come out unscathed. Privately, George was becoming alert to Thackeray's discomfort now Charlotte's growing boldness enabled her to question his writing, as she felt he had done when he recited the section from *Jane Eyre*. George knew that as a priggishly self-confident man, Thackeray was no match for a sharp-witted woman.

> For that reason he did not like Charlotte Brontë, and the two did not get on well together. She was vexed because he, in his talk with her, would never be serious about his literature. He would talk in a bantering and burlesque way, as though he was ashamed of it. But this was only by way of defence against Charlotte Brontë's earnest and heroic views of the 'sacredness' and 'dignity' of literature.[48]

Regardless of their discomfort and his own reservations, George was undaunted. Certain his persistence to sign Thackeray would pay off and expand Smith Elder's profit and prestige, he accepted that might require unpleasantness for Charlotte.

On the evening of Wednesday, 12 June he drove her to Young Street, where Thackeray was pacing in anticipation. For his two daughters,

13-year-old Anne and 10-year-old Minny, the prospect of meeting the real Jane Eyre herself, as he told them to expect, was overwhelming. Both had read the novel surreptitiously like many young girls and expected someone magnificent. 'She enters in mittens, in silence, in seriousness,' Anne remembered, 'Our hearts are beating with wild excitement. This thing is the authoress, the unknown power whose books have set all London talking, reading, speculating.'[49] They gazed with as much fascination as she had at their father. Here, under their very roof was:

> the great Jane Eyre – the tiny little lady. The moment is so breathless that dinner comes as a relief to the solemnity of the occasion, and we all smile as my father stoops to offer his arm; for genius though she may be, Miss Brontë can barely reach his elbow.[50]

As dinner was served, they noticed how Charlotte gazed at their father, 'lighting up with a sort of illumination every now and then as she answered him'.[51] They interrupted and babbled to each other and the adults until they grew bored, incurring a remonstrative look from Charlotte that left a permanent impression with Anne of someone 'somewhat grave and stern, specially to forward little girls'. Charlotte was as severe as her appearance, she thought. 'She had no curls or loops such as ladies wore them – she did not look pleasant … and I remember how she frowned at me whenever I looked at her.'[52]

Later they were joined by the sort of clever women who intimidated Thackeray: the Spiritualist writer Catherine Crowe; young poet Adelaide Proctor with her American mother Anne (whose husband was the dedicatee of *Vanity Fair*) and Thomas and Jane Carlyle who dropped by uninvited, all of whom knew the Gaskells, along with some of Thackeray's close confidantes – Jane Elliot, her sister Kate Perry and the literary hostess Jane Brookfield. All were as interested and excited to meet Charlotte as Thackeray's daughters, and all expected her conversation to be as entertaining as her writing. George knew she was capable of dazzling in the right company; however, as with the Arnolds, she recoiled. He was no raconteur and without the vivacity of an Elizabeth to conduct the conversation, Charlotte withdrew. At one point, Thackeray provocatively addressed her as 'Currer Bell' loudly enough for the others to hear. Jane Brookfield saw her annoyance and heard her snap that, 'the person he was talking to was Miss Brontë and she saw no connection between the two.'[53] She concluded Charlotte was out of her depth and as the drawing-room lamps began to dim and smoke, boredom made them sarcastic.[54]

Refusing to perform conversational tricks for Thackeray, Charlotte turned away to make small talk with another governess on the side-lines, a Miss Trulock. Jane Brookfield interrupted to ask Charlotte if she liked London. After an expectant pause Charlotte said curtly, 'Yes and no.' Brookfield would dine out on this for years to come, turning 'My Conversation with Charlotte Brontë' into a party piece that characterised Charlotte as the most unsociable woman she had ever met. When listeners waited for a punchline after 'Yes and no', Brookfield would laugh, 'That is all!' She was not alone. Anne Proctor took every opportunity to amuse others with what she called the dullest evening of her life. Charlotte was unsuited to socialising she decided and told Thackeray she thought she 'turns everyone "the seamy side out" – so plain a person as Miss Brontë must see all things darkly'.[55]

Later that night, after George took Charlotte home, Anne watched her father sneaking out to his club again and soon the others dispersed and took their own carriages. In theirs, Charlotte startled George by touching his knee. 'She would make you a very nice wife,' she said. He asked who she meant. 'Oh, you know who I mean,' she replied. He did not. 'And we relapsed into silence,' George wrote. He assumed she meant Adelaide Proctor because he had been talking to her all night.[56] While it is impossible to determine Charlotte's feelings for him, it is revealing this should be the first thing she mentioned once they were alone.

A few weeks later, Thackeray mentioned his next Christmas-themed novella to George. His own publisher turned it down because they were disappointed with sales of the previous, he said, so must have been surprised when George told him to name his price for it. Never one to miss an opportunity, Thackeray said he wanted £150, the equivalent of £17,000 in 2023. George wrote him a cheque on the spot. The deal to secure Thackeray's first book with Smith Elder was done.[57]

Their final clash came in the summer of 1851 when Charlotte attended one of Thackeray's lectures in London. Beginning on 22 May, he held them on Thursday afternoons at the King Street assembly rooms behind Pall Mall. Tickets of 2s 6d were sold from the offices of Smith Elder.[58] Thackeray told Thomas Carlyle he needed stooges in the audience to lead the applause but need not have feared.[59] Positive reviews drew unexpected crowds, leaving standing room only.[60] George, again hosting Charlotte for her annual

London break, prompted her to come a day early to catch the second one, on Thursday, 29 May. A reporter from the *Morning Chronicle* attended it and was impressed by the audience. The first few rows, Charlotte told Ellen, were completely filled by the elderly duchesses and countesses who won the best of Thackeray's attention.[61] She locked eyes with him as soon as she arrived. He came down from the platform and took her to his mother, announcing for half the audience to hear, in jest but with a barb, 'Mother, you must allow me to introduce you to Jane Eyre!'

In a hall bustling with aristocrats, he was calling her out as the most famously uncouth domestic servant in England. If he needed an opportunity to remind her of her position as a lower-class subject, without defence against the scrutiny of social superiors, and to restate his own as the effortless commander of patronage, here it was. 'Everybody near turned round and stared at the disconcerted little lady, who grew confused and angry when she realised that every eye was fixed upon her,' George added. 'My mother got her away as quickly as possible.'[62] As they took their seats, Mrs Smith saw Thackeray continuing to point them out until heads began to turn and opera glasses were raised. 'I am afraid Mr Thackeray has been playing me a trick,' Charlotte told her as whispers rose around them.[63]

Some, including the Earl of Carlisle, thrust out their hands in introduction. She told Ellen that another 'turned out to be Mr Monckton Milnes. Then came Dr Forbes whom I was sincerely glad to see.'[64] These men had loose connections to her and all knew more than she would have chosen to share. Carlisle remembered her father's preaching at Haworth; Monckton Milnes was friends with Thackeray, the Gaskells, Harriet Martineau and the Arnolds; and Forbes had advised on her sister Anne's decline.[65] But in private, after displays of courtesy, Carlisle and Monckton Milnes were derisory: 'Her person was insignificant, her dress somewhat rustic, her language quaintly precise and formal, her manner odd and constrained. Altogether this was a woman whom even London could not lionise; somebody outwardly altogether too plain, simple, unpretending.'[66]

Thackeray drew the attention back to himself and began. The reporter thought he captivated 'the brilliant audience and was warmly applauded despite differences of opinion (which must exist among all who read or think at all)'.[67] Charlotte told Elizabeth how he left the podium at the end and asked her for her opinion. 'This she mentioned to me not many days afterwards, adding remarks almost identical with those which I subsequently read in *Villette* where a similar action on the part of M. Paul Emanuel is related.'[68]

As Charlotte and Mrs Smith got up to leave, those in the rows around them jumped to their feet and rushed to the aisle. They jostled to peer at Charlotte and parted into two lines on either side as she started for the exit. Mrs Smith firmly took her arm:

> and they went along the avenue of eager and admiring faces. During this passage through the 'cream of society', Miss Brontë's hand trembled to such a degree, that her companion feared lest she should turn faint and be unable to proceed; and she dared not express her sympathy or try to give her strength by any touch or word, lest it might bring on the crisis she dreaded.[69]

Once back at the Smiths' house, Charlotte wrote to her father and Ellen that she enjoyed the lecture but did not mention she was smouldering with rage. Thackeray, Smith knew, had 'roused the hidden fire in Charlotte Brontë's soul' by causing a rush to her and risked being 'badly scorched himself as the result'.[70] Sensing an apology was due, Thackeray's mother called in the next morning with her granddaughter Anne. Charlotte knew they were testing the water. Later in the afternoon, Thackeray himself turned up. When George got home, he heard raised voices. Charlotte and Thackeray were arguing:

> Only these two were in the room. Thackeray was standing on the hearth-rug, looking anything but happy. Charlotte Brontë stood close to him, with head thrown back and face white with anger. The first words I heard were, 'No Sir! If you had come to our part of the country in Yorkshire, what would you have thought of me if I had introduced you to my father, before a mixed company of strangers, as Mr Warrington?' Thackeray replied, 'No, you mean Arthur Pendennis.' 'No, I *don't* mean Arthur Pendennis!' retorted Miss Brontë, 'I mean Mr Warrington and Mr Warrington would not have behaved as you behaved to me yesterday.' The spectacle of this little woman, hardly reaching to Thackeray's elbow, but somehow looking stronger and fiercer than himself, and casting her incisive words at his head, resembled the dropping of shells into a fortress. By this time, I had recovered my presence of mind, and hastened to interpose. Thackeray made the necessary and half humorous apologies, and the parting was a friendly one.[71]

The hypocrisy of Thackeray's indiscretion, which could not have been lost on Charlotte, was that he too was publishing under assumed names. While he released *Vanity Fair* under his own, he gave himself the freedom to use other invented ones; the Christmas book George bought from him came out under one of his favourites, M.A. Titmarsh. Yet she never considered unmasking him in public. She told Ellen, 'I had a long talk with him and I think he knows me now a little better than he did.'[72] A year later, Thackeray wrote it off as being down to Charlotte's bitterness, telling a friend:

> You see by Jane Eyre's letter don't you why we can't be very great friends? We had a correspondence – a little one; and met, very eagerly on her part. But there's a fire and fury raging in that little woman, a rage scorching her heart which doesn't suit me. She has had a story and a great grief that has gone badly with her. 'Tis better to have loved & lost than never to have loved at all.' I said the same thing before I read it in Tennyson.[73]

Charlotte told Elizabeth all this in their long conversations that warm airless weekend in Manchester. 'Thackeray's lectures and Rachel's acting are two things in this great Babylon which have stirred and interested me most,' she told her, 'simply because in them I found most of what was genuine, whether good or evil.'[74]

Elizabeth's daughters remembered how passionately she spoke about seeing Rachel Felix a few weeks before. Interviewed in the twentieth century, they recalled how, 'Her eyes fairly blazed, and she clenched her fists as she tried to give them her impressions of the great French actress.'[75]

George and his mother had taken her to St James's Theatre near the assembly rooms, where Felix had a summer residency playing the doomed heroines of French plays: the title role in *Adrienne Lecouvreur* by Ernest Legouvé and Eugène Scribe, about an actress who dies in mysterious circumstances; and as Camille, a woman murdered by her brother, in Pierre Corneille's *Les Horaces*. She saw both a week apart and was electrified. 'Her acting was something apart from any other acting it has come my way to witness,' she told a friend about *Adrienne Lecouvreur*, 'her soul was in it – and a strange soul she has – I shall not discuss it.'[76] She curtailed her thoughts in that moment but could not suppress the disturbance it caused her. The second time, Charlotte called her performance:

> a wonderful sight – terrible as if the earth had cracked deep at your feet and revealed a glimpse of hell – I shall never forget it – she made me

shudder to the marrow of my bones: in her some fiend has certainly taken up an incarnate home. She is not a woman – she is a snake.[77]

In another letter she called Felix a demon who would haunt her dreams:

Fiends can hate, scorn, rave, writhe, and *agonise* as she does, not mere men and women. I neither love, esteem, nor admire this strange being but (if I could bear the high mental stimulus so long) I would go every night for three months and watch and study its manifestations.[78]

Unnerved yet magnetised by Felix's emotional and physical abandon, Charlotte returned to it in other letters, to relive the experience in detail later in *Villette*, written with painful, sporadic progress late into the next year. 'I had seen acting before, but never anything like this: never anything which astonished Hope and hushed Desire.'[79] In *Villette*, she describes a theatre visit that composites her own, where her narrator, Lucy Snowe, is transfixed by a renowned actress 'whose powers I had heard reports which made me conceive peculiar anticipations.'[80] Charlotte chooses to describe her as a physically unremarkable woman; 'plain' – the word she used for herself and Jane Eyre – a 'frail creature' of 'feeble strength', whose true power eclipses her appearance and burns its titanic, elemental form in physical expression, an ungoverned will rising from invisibility like a planet above the horizon, transgressing male and female, good and evil to incarnate carnal and unashamed passions for consumption by all who witness her:

Before calamity she is a tigress; she rends her woes, shivers them in convulsed abhorrence. Pain, for her, has no result in good; tears water no harvest of wisdom: on sickness, on death itself, she looks with the eye of a rebel. Wicked, perhaps she is, but she is strong and her strength has conquered beauty, has overcome grace and bound both at her side.[81]

Here was the conqueror as female; defiant, self-determining, and eviscerating her restraints to triumph. Charlotte was staggered. There, on stage, was an expression of her own buried fire, her resilience continually tested by tragedy, and there – magnificent and insubordinate – was the woman as artist. From the anonymity of the audience, Lucy Snowe turns to her male companion – later identified by George as based on himself – to ask his thoughts. 'He judged her as a woman, not an artist: it was a branding judgement.'[82]

In fiction, Charlotte climaxes the scene with a collapse into anarchy as the theatre is engulfed in flames. She was recalling the time George was evacuated from a burning theatre but may have known how one of Felix's own performances was also interrupted by an emergency. Instead of an inferno, the reality was more peculiar than dramatic. Exhausted, Felix collapsed one night on stage. According to *The Standard*, she fainted when, in a pivotal moment of silence, a lapdog someone had smuggled into the audience leapt out of the darkness and started barking at her.[83]

On Sunday morning, the Gaskell household parted company to attend different church services, the Gaskells to the Unitarian chapel in Cross Street where William was minister, leaving Charlotte to attend an Anglican service. As soon as she returned, a servant said a letter had come for her. She opened it and found a jubilant George writing that he had finally and properly signed Thackeray by commissioning him to write a new novel.[84] It seemed that two days earlier, as George's mother waved Charlotte off on the Manchester train, George had stuffed his pockets with banknotes and gone to Thackeray's house, astonishing him with an offer of the present-day equivalent of £110,000, which he theatrically counted into Thackeray's hands.[85]

'I am glad,' Charlotte replied, before she commented that he had better imprison Thackeray in the basement to make sure he wrote it.[86] George set a deadline and expected Thackeray to start immediately. Within days, however, he heard Thackeray decided to put his windfall to better use and had taken his daughters off on a European tour.

When *The History of Henry Esmond* was released to glorious reviews the following year, George marked the occasion by commissioning Samuel Lawrence to draw Thackeray's portrait. George was as proud of it as hunters were of mounted kill. He sent an engraving to Charlotte. She examined it closely and showed her father. It was good the artist had softened Thackeray's spiteful expression, she teased. She hung it up on the parlour wall across from her own portrait. As in life, she noticed, 'Thackeray looks away from this latter character with a grand scorn, edifying to witness.'[87]

CHAPTER 5

1852–53
Eclipse

Charlotte ruminated on those two powers, those reflections of her hidden selves – the masterly man of letters and the carnal woman incarnate – and gave them form in the novel she started writing that summer, *Villette*. Duality, doubles, alternates haunted her through her waking hours and into the dreams she had through winter.

By February 1852, she explained to Elizabeth she was recovering from being seriously ill. With her seasonal depression around the anniversary of her brother's death came pains in her side, a 'frequent burning and aching in my chest. Sleep almost forsook me or would never come except accompanied by ghastly dreams.'[1] She was seen by a doctor at the end of December who confirmed her lungs were clear but, suspecting she had an inflamed liver, prescribed mercury pills to be taken at night, followed in the morning by drinking a black purgative of Epsom salts, liquorice, cardamom, ammonia and senna. She had symptoms of poisoning within twenty-four hours. The following week she was so ill, with slack teeth and a swollen ulcerated tongue, she could not eat or drink more than a few teaspoons of liquid. Her father was alarmed enough to want to send for the doctor who had diagnosed Anne's tuberculosis as terminal. Instead, the doctor who saw Charlotte in December came back and was horrified when he realised he had made her worse.[2] He told Charlotte he 'never in his whole practice knew the same effect produced by the same dose on man, woman or child and avows it is owing to an altogether peculiar sensitiveness of constitution'.[3] Alternative medicine was administered and Charlotte, for all her delicacy, started to recover straight away.

On reflection she said if it happened again, she would pray 'let this cup pass from me'. Tellingly, her phrasing connects with a passage she had already written in *Villette*, describing the bereaved Lucy Snowe:

torn, racked and oppressed in mind. Amidst the horrors of that dream I think the worst lay here. Methought the well-loved dead, who had loved *me* well in life, met me elsewhere, alienated: galled was my inmost spirit with an unutterable sense of despair about the future.[4]

In her loneliness, Charlotte wondered how anyone, living or dead, could find their way to her, to restore her to the kind of company of love she lost when her siblings died.

Her sickness had passed, she told Elizabeth, and now she was benefiting from what she had been missing: 'the kind attentions and cheerful society' of friends. Once well enough, she went to stay with Ellen and her family in Birstall, observing that her mother and sisters cared for her as Charlotte Brontë not Currer Bell, indicating perhaps only Ellen knew the truth, allowing her to flit between their levels of knowledge.

In March, she began the long task of producing a final draft but was interrupted by revisions for the second edition of *Shirley*, scheduled for the autumn, and told George she hoped both could be released together but asked him not to announce *Villette* until she was closer to finishing it. She put it aside in the summer then resumed in October, sending him the first two thirds on the 26th. Four weeks later, near the end of November, she sent the final part and began a nervous wait for his response.

Despite concerns George might be lukewarm, she told Ellen she was praying for approval and begged for his opinion and for Williams to be 'unsparing', with a caveat that she was unlikely to alter anything further.[5] For once, she thought, she had succeeded in producing something modest and uncontroversial. 'Whether it is well or ill done I don't know … The book, I think will not be considered pretentious nor is it of a character to excite hostility.'[6]

Williams read it quickly and replied with reservations about an absence of the narrator's life history and the inconclusive ending. Charlotte left both ambiguous to force readers to make unqualified judgements about Lucy Snowe and her destiny. Here she could reproduce, for the reader, the experience of judging one who remains in the shadows without understanding what put her there. Her reply about her artistic decisions, sounds like self-defence:

> You say that she may be thought morbid and weak unless the history of her life be more fully given. I consider that she *is* both morbid and weak at times – the character sets up no pretensions to unmixed strength

– and anybody living her life would necessarily become morbid. It was no impetus of healthy feeling which urged her to the confessional for instance – it was the semi-delirium of solitary grief and sickness.[7]

Her anxiety over George's silence had another cause. As with her previous novels, she had refashioned incidents and people from her own life, some with so little disguise they could be recognised by acquaintances and included unmistakable portraits of him and his mother as the narrator's benign godmother and her handsome son for whom Lucy Snowe has a secret love she eventually abandons when she accepts it will never be reciprocated. In the final part was an elegy to that near-love: 'What was become of that curious one-sided friendship which was half marble and half life; only on one hand truth, and on the other perhaps a jest? Was this feeling dead? I do not know, but it was buried.'[8]

If he ever suspected she had more than a professional respect for him, George now had confirmation. For Charlotte, it was a confession made from behind a mask. As she intended it to be read by him and everyone who knew him, as well as by the wider public, it was a risky act of self-exposure. Refracted through the double medium of Lucy Snowe and then Currer Bell, she could declare herself a woman who had loved a man while accepting he was never hers to lose. As well as confessing a secret love, she was affirming her determination to move on from it.

Naturally, her truth was less definite than a fiction that regenerated elements of her relationships to extend their possibilities. But alert to the comparisons, George felt too much had been recycled from her life and those of others to make it a commercial and critical success. '*Villette* is full of scenes which one can trace to incidents which occurred during Miss Brontë's visits to us,' he reflected. 'Several of her expressions are given *verbatim*.'[9]

Recognising all the autobiographical components, George felt they misfired Charlotte's talent and made the book depressing. Too much French alienated the English reader he thought, and the whole was too dull and narrow, too lacking in scale or incident to be anything other than disappointing. He accepted she might not be able to create otherwise or that, if her imagination had peaked, she was draining her dreadful past and meagre present for material. He concluded she and her sisters never found better circumstances to nurture their imaginations and had been starved by Haworth.[10]

He appears to have requested rewrites, for Charlotte to release her characters and readers from suffering by taking some liberties with romance. In response, Charlotte reminded him of her devotion to truth; unless someone was going to propose a happy ending, she suggested, there could be none for characters like Lucy Snowe, or by inference for herself. As such things did not happen in her reality, she would not allow them in her fiction. 'Lucy must not marry Dr John,' she insisted, discarding any fulfilment between their fictional counterparts as blithely as she might have felt he had done between them in actuality:

> he must draw a prize in life's lottery; his wife must be young, rich and pretty; he must be made very happy indeed. If Lucy marries anybody – it must be the Professor – a man in whom there is much to forgive, much to 'put up with'.[11]

George may have interpreted her inflexibility as strategic, her method of bargaining with him. By offering an absurd counterargument she might test how he would dissuade her. He declined to embark on an editorial seduction and expressed his reservations as he expressed his hopes: with money. While he had thousands for Thackeray, he made her fee lower, only £479 (the equivalent of £53,000 in 2023), sent as a draft without any covering note, convincing her she had so upset him he had terminated their discussion. When his letter appeared the next day, she replied in uneasy relief that she had been on the verge of leaving for London:

> to see what was the matter and what had struck my publisher mute ... you have thus been spared the visitation of the unannounced and unsummoned apparition of Currer Bell in Cornhill. Inexplicable delays should be avoided when possible, for they are apt to urge those subjected to their harassment to sudden and impulsive steps.[12]

Conspicuously for Charlotte, the usefulness of Currer Bell was expiring. The false name she once defended to critics and to George and Williams as a flesh-and-blood man of impetuous decisions and heaven-struck inspiration now paled to what he had always truly been, an insubstantial ghost, an 'apparition' that might materialise without warning, and potentially without welcome. Despite agreeing with George that *Villette* should be published and advertised as being by Currer Bell, the persona was finally dead. Charlotte Brontë never signed that name again.

In the middle of December, Charlotte asked Ellen if she had noticed her father's curate, Arthur Nicholls:

> I know not whether you have ever observed him specially when staying here: your perception in these matters is generally quick enough – *too* quick I have sometimes thought – yet as you never said anything – I restrained my own dim misgivings – which could not claim the sure guide of vision.[13]

She knew her father thought Arthur was weak and heard him ridicule his health complaints, dismissing comments Arthur made about leaving Haworth to start elsewhere, perhaps abroad, with remonstrances to be a man and pull himself together. Arthur visited the parsonage every day to discuss parochial duties with Patrick, and receive his allocation of the week's services of masses, Christenings, marriages and funerals. Arthur had seen Charlotte daily for years, Elizabeth later recalled, 'seen her as a daughter, a sister, a mistress and a friend.'[14] His discomfiture and stolen looks suggested there was something her father was missing. Charlotte wrote, 'I vaguely felt – without clearly seeing – as without seeing, I have felt for some time – the meaning of his constant looks – and strange, feverish restraint.' She may have recognised symptoms she had felt before for others.

A week before Christmas, she heard him stay late with Patrick in his study, while she sat in the parlour across the passage. On his way out, Arthur paused outside the door:

> He tapped: like lightning it flashed on me what was coming. He entered – he stood before me. What his words were – you can guess; his manner – you can hardly realize – nor can I forget it – Shaking from head to foot, looking deadly pale, speaking low, vehemently yet with difficulty – he made me for the first time feel what it costs a man to declare affection where he doubts response.
>
> The spectacle of one ordinarily so statue-like – thus trembling, stirred, and overcome gave me a kind of strange shock. He spoke of sufferings he had borne for months – of sufferings he could endure no longer – and craved leave for some hope. I could only entreat him to leave me then and promise a reply on the morrow.[15]

She asked if he told her father and Arthur said he had not dared. She escorted him out of the house then went back to tell Patrick. He exploded with rage, 'into a state not to be trifled with – the veins on his temples started up like whip-cord – and his eyes became suddenly blood-shot'. In his fury, he shouted insults about Arthur that Charlotte said made her blood boil. 'If I had loved Mr N and had heard such epithets applied to him as were used – it would have transported me past my patience.'

The next morning, she sent a note across the lane to Arthur declining his proposal. Her father's vehement opposition to both the idea of her marrying and to Arthur specifically infuriated her, but as ever she felt she had no choice but to pacify him. Although not attracted to him, she explained to Ellen, she was haunted by how Arthur had been willing to lay his feelings open to rejection by her and to ridicule from her father, sacrificing any dignity he had. 'That he cared something for me,' she told Ellen sadly, 'and wanted me to care for him. I have long suspected, but I did not know the degree or strength of his feelings.'

Arthur replied directly. He accepted her decision and promised to leave both his job and Haworth as soon as he could. Dejected, he did not come back that week and stayed in his room, refusing all meals. While she did not want to encourage Arthur, Charlotte tried to stop her father sending Martha over with what she called 'a most cruel note' of his own and sent another distancing herself from his fury, urging Arthur to maintain his courage and spirits. Shocked, Ellen asked Charlotte how Patrick could behave so badly. Charlotte told her, 'I only wish you were here to see Papa in his present mood: you would know something of him. He just treats him with a hardness not to be bent – and a contempt not to be propitiated.'[16] She repeated what Patrick told her; that he felt Arthur had been disingenuous in keeping his intentions secret for so long, and that as Arthur earned so little 'the match would be a degradation – that I should be throwing myself away – that he expects me, if I marry at all – to do very differently.' Her own objections, she noted, had nothing to do with Arthur's income or his silence, but only that she could not match his ardour.

Feeling it was impossible to stay on, Arthur sent Patrick his resignation and moved out of the Brown family home to lodge with colleagues elsewhere in the district whom he drafted in to cover his duties. A cloud of antagonism hung in the rooms of the parsonage into the new year with the subject both forbidden and unavoidable. Around Charlotte, everyone had an opinion. Patrick remained infuriated; Martha was bitter and said her father wanted to shoot Arthur. Their combined hostility only heightened Charlotte's sympathy:

They don't understand the nature of his feelings – but I see now what they are. Mr N is one of those who attach themselves to very few, whose sensations are close and deep – like an underground stream, running strong but in a narrow channel.[17]

Before the end of the month, Arthur had written back to Patrick to withdraw his resignation. Patrick replied that he may on one condition: that he send a written declaration that he would never mention his proposal to either him or Charlotte again. As Arthur did not, Charlotte assumed he was following his original plan to emigrate and told Ellen in the first days of 1853 how she could not help being affected by this. 'Without loving him, I don't like to think of him suffering in solitude and wish him anywhere so that he were happier. He and Papa have never met or spoken yet.'[18]

Charlotte may have applied her father's own condition to him and told him she did not want to hear about it either, and nothing more was said until after she travelled to London to stay with the Smiths again, 'very quietly' this time, as *Villette* was due to be published in the second week of January, around the same time as Elizabeth's second novel, *Ruth*. Provisionally, she went to check and correct printed proofs without the difficulties at home or the demands of visits and parties of an otherwise usual holiday in London. 'Being allowed to have my own choice of sights this time I selected rather the *real* than the *decorative* side of life,' she told Ellen and was amused that Mrs Smith and her daughters were 'a little amazed at my gloomy tastes' in wanting to visit hospitals and prisons, 'but I take no notice.'[19]

She had ten days of diligent revision of *Villette* before a letter came from her father describing yet more difficulties with Arthur now he was back in Haworth. 'You thought me too severe,' Patrick told her, 'but I was not candid enough. His conduct might have been excused by the world in a confirmed rake or unprincipled army officer, but in a Clergyman, it is justly chargeable, with base design and inconsistency.' Neither man was talking to the other, with Arthur shunning Patrick in church, 'turning his head from the quarter where I was and hustling away amongst the crowd, to avoid contact.'[20] Members of the congregation noticed the friction and what Patrick thought was Arthur's expression of wounded pride and were starting to whisper in the pews. His closing remarks that he could never trust Arthur again and wished he would move to Australia and avoid all women forever may have secured a silence from Charlotte, for a few days later another letter came from him trying a different approach. This one sought to undermine Arthur with humour, being purportedly dictated by Flossy, the family dog:

I observe those manoeuvres, and am permitted to observe many of them, which if I could speak, would never be done before me. I see people cheating one another, and yet appearing to be friends – many are the disagreeable discoveries which I make which you could hardly believe if I were to tell them.

Patrick made sure to characterise Arthur in the assumed voice of Flossy as disloyal and fickle, having:

lost all his apparent kindness, scolds me, and looks black upon me – I tell my master all this, by looking grave, and puzzled, holding up one side of my head … Ah! my dear Mistress, trust dogs rather than men. They are very selfish, and when they have the power, (which no wise person will readily give them) very tyrannical …[21]

Incredulous, Charlotte sent both to Ellen, who noted on one of them 'Poor C!'

Along with these, Patrick forwarded another letter from home. This one was from a fan, writing in appreciation of *Jane Eyre*.[22] Her reply is the first surviving response to a member of the public signed as 'C. Brontë', rather than Currer Bell.

As soon as Elizabeth saw their novels risked competing for press space, she realised she had not heard from Charlotte since the previous spring. She sent concerns that critics would either review one over the other or spin a false competition between them, then asked why she had not heard from her. Charlotte replied that the last communication between them was from her to Elizabeth, leaving the ball in her court and assumed she was busy. She agreed it was sensible to avoid a clash and asked George to postpone *Villette* by a week but thought it might be inevitable they would be framed as rivals. 'But we need not care: we can set them at defiance: they *shall* not make us foes.'[23]

The *Manchester Times* reviewer called *Ruth* one of the best novels since Jane Austen's.[24] Charlotte sent congratulations but thought *Villette* was not worthy to be pushed ahead of a novel that had 'social use' in advocating for empathy for those considered 'fallen women' in civilised society.[25] *Villette* was largely well received, with more than one reviewer saying it would have made the author famous had she no other accolades. Its 'extraordinary literary power' was 'everywhere original, everywhere shrewd, and at heart everywhere kindly' with lifelike characters drawn in 'a keen spirit of observation'.[26] Other critics felt it too sombre to leave an entirely favourable impression and recommended Charlotte redraft the unsatisfactory ending and cut its most melancholy passages to 'save readers the pains of skipping which they will inevitably do'.[27]

The day before it was published, Charlotte asked Smith Elder to send complimentary copies out to her friends. Excited by the prospect of positive reviews, she told Margaret Wooler and Ellen to expect theirs imminently and reminded Harriet of the promise she made when they first met: that she should be as truthful with her as a sister. She could not bear being condemned, she wrote, 'but I love, I honour, I kneel to Truth. Let her smite me on one cheek – good! The tears may spring to the eyes; but courage! There is the other side – hit again, right sharply!'[28]

Harriet thought Charlotte was sincere, an opinion she would later reverse. She remembered:

> This was the genuine spirit of the woman. She might be weak for once; but her permanent temper was one of humility, candour, integrity and conscientiousness. She was not only unspoiled by her sudden and prodigious fame, but obviously un-spoilable. She was somewhat amused by her fame, but oftener annoyed; – at least, when obliged to come out into the world to meet it, instead of its reaching her in her secluded home, in the wilds of Yorkshire.[29]

Harriet knew Charlotte would get her opinion whether she asked for it or not. She had already read *Villette* and hated it, and was drafting a long critique she planned to publish anonymously. Since Charlotte 'so desired to know' what she thought, as Harriet put it, she would tell her. *Villette*'s sobriety and unrequited love were irritating and justified previous criticisms of her work, she told her:

> I do deeply regret the reasons given to suppose your mind full of the subject of one passion – love. I think there is unconscionably too much of it (giving an untrue picture of life) and speaking with the frankness you desire I do not like its kind – I anticipate the renewal of the sort of objection which you mentioned to me as inexplicable to you the first evening we met; and this time, I think it will not be wholly unfounded.[30]

Charlotte underlined this with red ink and sent her letter back to her. 'I protest against this passage,' she told her, 'it struck me dumb.' Wounded by her implication that she was obsessed with something she had no knowledge of – a normal relationship between two people in love – she objected, 'I know what love is as I understand it and if a man or woman should feel ashamed of feeling such love then there is nothing right, noble, faithful, truthful, unselfish on this earth.'[31]

Disregarding this response, Harriet published her anonymous article in the *Daily News*. George saw it and included it with press cuttings he sent to Charlotte. She read:

> The book is almost intolerably painful … 'Currer Bell' here afflicts us with an amount of subjective misery which we may fairly remonstrate against; and she allows us no respite – even while treating us with humour … An atmosphere of pain hangs about the whole … All the female characters, in all their thoughts and lives, are full of one thing, or are regarded by the reader in the light of that one thought – love … so dominant is the idea – so incessant is the writer's tendency to describe the need of being loved, that the heroine, who tells her own story, leaves the reader at last under the uncomfortable impression of her having either entertained a double love, or allowed one to supersede another without notification of the transition.[32]

Charlotte was stupefied with shock. She told him it was undoubtedly by Harriet. 'I have received a letter from her precisely to the same effect marking the same points and urging the same objections … Her letter only differs from the review in being severe to the point of injustice.'[33] Her feeling of betrayal was made greater for having been a staunch defender of Harriet's individualism, staying loyal when others criticised her. Only days before, she had been protesting to the steadfast Margaret Wooler – who urged her to distance herself from someone so unashamedly irreligious – that she was too loyal and forgiving to drop her. Now she wondered how she could have been so willing to give her the benefit of the doubt and reassessed how much she had invested in their friendship, accepting that surrendering her hard-won trust had been a mistake.

This was not the first time Charlotte felt her loyalty and trust were not valued. Throughout her life, she would later tell Elizabeth, she had never been able to inspire the esteem she felt for others, always stranding her on the losing side of love. She wrote again to Margaret telling her that at least the good reviews of *Villette* pleased her 'for the sake of those few *real* friends who take so sincere an interest in my welfare as to be happy in my happiness.'[34]

Harriet never admitted to Charlotte she had written the review, but after making enquiries, George knew she was behind it. Nothing could calm Charlotte as her disappointment seared to fury then implacable coldness. She stopped writing to her. As the weeks passed, the personal costs of the growing rift preyed on her mind ('she says everything does prey on it, in the solitude in which she lives,' Elizabeth observed)[35] while for Harriet, embroiled in the affairs of Ambleside, there was little impact. She continued to be active and 'merry as a gig' when she bumped into one of Elizabeth's friends, Susanna Winkworth, who described how although Harriet 'talked very nicely to her about Miss Brontë' they agreed about disliking *Villette*. Her sister Katie said it left her feeling 'eerie' to be forced to see the world through the eyes of a woman so yearning for reconciliation in her personal relationships. 'I wonder whether Miss B is so, and I wonder, too, whether she ever was in love; surely she could never herself have made love to anyone, as all her heroines, even Lucy Snowe, do.'[36] She thought the novel sounded like a confession:

> She comes out of utter darkness, and vanishes into it again, and there is no sort of solution to all the miserable riddles of her life ... it tells one a great deal about Miss Brontë herself; and what a sad story it tells! ... Poor creature, how she must have suffered in that lonely Yorkshire life, and when she was a governess![37]

In London, Thackeray came to the same conclusions, and laughed with friends over how such a confession of love could come from someone so unattractive as Charlotte:

> It amuses me to read the author's naïve confession of being in love with two men at the same time; and her readiness to fall in love at any time. The poor little woman of genius! The fiery little eager brave tremulous homely-faced creature! I can read a great deal of her life as I fancy in her book and see that rather than have fame, rather than have any other earthly good or mayhap heavenly one, she wants some Tomkins or another to love her and be in love with. But you see she is a little bit of a creature without a penny worth of good looks, 30 years old I should think, buried in the country, and eating up her own heart there, and no Tomkins will come ... destined to wither away into old maidenhood with no chance to fulfil the burning desire.[38]

In mid-March, having heard nothing from Charlotte for a month, Harriet inquired of her through George. He knew Charlotte had cut her off so made a point of assuring her that Charlotte's silence was not because she was unwell. In fact, he told her, Charlotte was better than he had ever seen her. As a businessman protective of sales first and his authors second, he could not resist the opportunity to take a swipe at her: 'You will be glad to learn that *Villette* has had a very fair success and it appears to be better liked by the public than by the 'Critics' and the latter have, *on the whole*, been merciful …'[39] At last, Harriet made the connection between her critique and Charlotte's withdrawal and confronted her directly to ask why her letters had stopped. Charlotte confided to Ellen:

> Miss Martineau wrote to ask why she did not hear from me – and to press me to go to Ambleside. Explanations ensued – the notes on each side were quite civil – but having deliberately formed my resolution on substantial grounds – I adhered to it. I have declined being her visitor – and bid her good-bye. Of course, some bitterness remains in her heart. It is best so, however; the antagonism of our natures and principles was too serious a thing to be trifled with.[40]

She told Margaret that Harriet had shown her:

> a spirit so strangely and unexpectedly acrimonious that I have gathered courage to tell her that the gulf of mutual divergence between her and me is so wide and deep – the bridge of union so slight and uncertain – I have come to the conclusion that frequent intercourse would be most perilous and unadvisable and have begged to adjourn *sine die* my long-projected visit to her. Of course, she is now very angry and I know her bitterness will not be short-lived, but it cannot be helped.[41]

The gulf was not bridged and they never spoke again.

'You ask about Mr N,' Charlotte wrote to Ellen on 6 April. 'I hear he has got a curacy but do not yet know where – I trust the news is true.' She said Arthur and Patrick were still not speaking despite still working together. 'Papa has a perfect antipathy to him – and he, I fear, to papa. Martha hates him. I think he might almost be dying and they would not speak a friendly word to or of him.' Charlotte heard that when other vicars visited Arthur he was so withdrawn and silent they never returned:

He scarcely speaks. I find he tells them nothing, seeks no confidant, rebuffs all attempts to penetrate his mind. I own I respect him for this. He still lets Flossy go to his rooms and takes him to walk … He looks ill and miserable. I think and trust in Heaven he will be better as soon as he fairly gets away from Haworth. I pity him inexpressibly. We never meet nor speak, nor dare I look at him. Silent pity is just all I can give him and as he knows nothing about that, it does not comfort. He is now grown so gloomy and reserved that nobody seems to like him. His fellow-curates shun trouble in that shape, the lower orders dislike it.[42]

Having for most of her life been the one who loved others without being loved in return and with a new novel whose principal theme was unrequited love, Charlotte unexpectedly found herself on the other side of that dynamic, as the rejector rather than the rejected, the one who closed the door on someone else, to refuse them the affection they were desperate to express. An impossible-to-avoid imaginative sympathy that sprung up in defence of Arthur from the moment her father first forbade their marriage, resurfaced again as she began to reconsider him with kindness and some growing credit:

How much of all this he deserves I can't tell. Certainly, he never was agreeable or amiable and is less so now than ever and alas! I do not know him well enough to be sure that there is truth and true affection – or only rancour and corroding disappointment at the bottom of his chagrin. In this state of things I must be and I am entirely passive.[43]

Despite having declined, she still weighed up his proposal. She struck out a sentence in a letter to Ellen, 'I know if I were near him', then started again:

I may be losing the purest gem – and to me far the most precious life can give – genuine attachment. Or I may be escaping the yoke of a morose temper. In this doubt conscience will not suffer me to take one step in opposition to Papa's will, blended as that will is with the most bitter and unreasonable prejudices. So I just leave the matter where we must leave all important matters.[44]

She decided to leave it with God and turned to prayer in her quandary. She could either permanently reject someone she did not love and risk losing her last chance at marriage or accept him and whatever life that would bring, one where she might receive love but never feel it for a man who was either sincere or not. The parsonage consensus was that Arthur was an impoverished opportunist seeking to take advantage of a woman desperate for love. Yet, she wondered, would anyone with those intentions truly be willing to sacrifice his well-being and livelihood to deceive her?

As conjecture was all her unmarried friends could offer, she turned to her married confidante. 'Would it suit you if I were to come next Thursday?' she asked Elizabeth in the middle of April, 'I know of no engagement on my part which need compel me longer to defer the pleasure of seeing you.' She seemed to have forgotten it would be her thirty-seventh birthday. Picturing an escape into Elizabeth's happy domestic haven, she went on, 'I always like evening for an arrival; it seems more cosy and pleasant than coming in about the busy middle of the day. I think if I stay a week that will be a very long visit; it will give you time to get well tired of me.'[45]

As soon as she got to Plymouth Grove the prospect of being embraced by familiarity was shattered. To her horror the Gaskells were already entertaining someone else. Elizabeth recalled:

> Our friend was gentle and sensible after Miss Brontë's own heart, yet her presence was enough to create a nervous tremor. I was aware that both of our guests were unusually silent; and I saw a little shiver run from time to time over Miss Brontë's frame … the next day Miss Brontë told me how the unexpected sight of a strange face had affected her.[46]

Elizabeth remembered how two years on from meeting the Arnolds and after many more introductions in London, 'the physical sensations produced by shyness were still the same; and on the following day she laboured under severe headache.'[47] Charlotte's nervousness, Elizabeth thought, was so unshakeable it must be ingrained in her constitution. Yet she saw how Charlotte refused to surrender to it, forcing her hand back into the fire of social activity against her instinct to withdraw, regardless of 'how acutely she suffered in striving to overcome it'.[48]

The visitor was Marianne's music teacher, Miss Maggie Bell, one of the three sisters of an Edinburgh physician living in Manchester.[49] By Elizabeth's account, Maggie persevered with Charlotte and even volunteered to come back to play the piano and sing for them. Elizabeth sent her a note the next day to reschedule and thank her 'exceedingly for your kindness but I find that Miss Brontë would rather enjoy going to the amateur performance; at least such is the feeling in the quiet repose of today.'[50] This last clause is suggestive of how sensitive Elizabeth was becoming to Charlotte's mercurial inclination to change her mind depending on an instantaneous diagnosis of mood and circumstances.

The weekend passed and on the Monday evening the Gaskells took Charlotte to the Theatre Royal in Peter Street for the local Shakespearian society's library fundraising production of *Twelfth Night*. Charlotte knew the play well but left no impressions of the performance in her letters, recording only her amusement at watching the Gaskell girls leave. Her favourite, 6-year-old Julia, was 'stepping supreme from the portico towards the carriage … I believe in Julia's future; I like what speaks in her movements, and what is written upon her face.' To Charlotte she was a 'little wild-flower' too young and capricious to care for the likes of her. 'She *does* not, and *cannot*, for she does not know me; but no matter. In my reminiscences she is a person of a certain distinction. I think hers a fine little nature, frank and of genuine promise.'[51] Fifty-five years on, Julia would remember Charlotte Brontë affectionately in an interview where she described another example of her morbid shyness when a visitor dropped by:

> Mrs Gaskell rose to greet her visitor and turned to introduce her to Miss Brontë, but she had vanished. Mrs Gaskell thought she had left the room by the other door leading to the dining room; but after Mrs Sydney Potter's departure, she emerged from behind one of the heavy curtains, excused herself by saying 'I felt I could not meet a stranger.'[52]

Had she time to prepare herself, Charlotte might have been open to meeting the lady, a remarkable Manchester character. The wife of a calico printer, Louisa Potter published nostalgic sketches in the *Manchester Guardian* about life at the start of the century. Two generations later in the 1890s, she reflected on how bewildering it was to lose her rural landscape twice, when country settlements were subsumed into industrial villages that in turn were swept off by larger factories, more tenements, and wider roads devouring what had once been the future.[53]

On Tuesday evening, Maggie Bell returned with one of her sisters to play and sing old Jacobite ballads at Elizabeth's piano. They used a collection likely familiar to Charlotte, released in her childhood by one of her early heroes, James Hogg. As Charlotte's sisters had sung and played the piano, she may even have remembered them singing from it. If so, the irony of having these two living Bell sisters singing the songs of her own lost Ellis and Acton Bell could not have been lost on her. Elizabeth noticed how

Charlotte was affected by the music and the lyrics, roused to anguished power by the women's voices. 'Miss Brontë had been sitting quiet and constrained till they began *The Bonnie House of Airlie*, but the effect of that and *Carlisle Yetts*, which followed, was … irresistible.'[54] The women sang of grief, lost love, remembrance:

> My father's blood's in that flower tap,
> My brother's in that harebell's blossom;
> This white rose was steeped in my luve's blood,
> And I'll aye wear it in my bosom.[55]

Watching Charlotte, Elizabeth saw how 'the beautiful clear light came into her eyes; her lips quivered with emotion; she forgot herself, rose, and crossed the room to the piano, where she asked eagerly for song after song.'[56] The sisters invited her to their home the next morning to hear more and Charlotte gratefully agreed. Flattered to have won her over, the Bells looked forward to Elizabeth bringing her to their house less than 2 miles away in Mosley Street. But the next day, just as they arrived at the gate, Elizabeth told Charlotte something that made her freeze: inside she would introduce her to the third Bell sister. Charlotte could go no further:

> Her courage failed. We walked some time up and down the street; she upbraiding herself all the while for folly, and trying to dwell on the sweet echoes in her memory rather than on the thought of a third sister who would have to be faced if we went in. But it was of no use; and dreading lest this struggle with herself might bring on one of her trying headaches, I entered at last and made the best apology I could for her non-appearance.[57]

On another evening, Elizabeth invited two male friends to dinner. She told neither who Charlotte was but expected them to have enough shared interests for a conversation:

> To our disappointment she drew back with timid reserve from all their advances, replying to their questions and remarks in the briefest manner possible; till at last they gave up their efforts to draw her into conversation in despair, and talked to each other and my husband on subjects of recent local interest.[58]

Elizabeth understood part of Charlotte's reticence stemmed from her feeling of physical ugliness. She had always felt this, Charlotte told her, it having 'been strongly impressed upon her imagination early in life'. As an adult, as one relationship after another fell into estrangement, Charlotte exaggerated this sense of disadvantage, imagining her appearance rather than her unsociability put off strangers. She told Elizabeth, 'I notice that after a stranger has once looked at my face, he is careful not to let his eyes wander to that part of the room again!' Elizabeth countered that 'a more untrue idea never entered into any one's head.' The two men who came to dinner were, Elizabeth noticed, 'singularly attracted by her appearance; and this feeling of attraction towards a pleasant countenance, sweet voice, and gentle timid manners, was so strong in one as to conquer a dislike he had previously entertained to her works.' Detached and silent, Charlotte listened until one of them brought up Thackeray. 'The ice of her reserve was broken, and from that time she showed her interest in all that was said and contributed her share to any conversation.'[59]

The men thought Thackeray's character descriptions were affected by his moralising, something both Elizabeth and Charlotte recognised. Both expressed hidden aspects of their personalities in their novels and used them to exercise those aspects of their natures which found no outlet in daily life. Elizabeth explained:

> The difference between Miss Brontë and me is that she puts all her naughtiness into her books, and I put all my goodness. I am sure she works off a great deal that is morbid *into* her writing and out of her life; and my books are so far better than I am, but I often feel ashamed of having written them, as if I were a hypocrite.[60]

After dinner, they continued discussing their novels, as they had by letter. Before Charlotte got to Manchester, Elizabeth had already passed her reflections on *Villette* to Janet, disagreeing with her that it was too literary and suggested, appealing to her curiosity about Charlotte's personal life, that she should see it more as a confession than a work of art. She told her that as she understood it from Charlotte, *Villette* was virtually an autobiography, an admission of her conflicting passions and their necessary repression:

> I believe it to be a very correct account of one part of her life; which is very vivid and distinct in her remembrance, with all the feelings that

were called out at that period, forcibly present in her mind whenever she recurs to the recollection of it ... in looking back upon it all the passions and suffering and deep despondency of that old time come back upon her ... Many times over I recognised incidents of which she had told me as connected with that visit to Brussels ... there can be no doubt that the book is wonderfully clever; that it reveals depths in her mind, aye, and in her *heart* too which I doubt if ever anyone has fathomed.[61]

In their conversations, Elizabeth drew more glimpses of Charlotte's daily life, just as she hoped, hearing anecdotes of disappointment and emotional deprivation that made Elizabeth 'look up to her strength and (outward if you will) patience, with wonder and admiration'. Charlotte described the once-esteemed friendships in eclipse: the 'uncomfortable kind of coolness with Miss Martineau, on account of some *very* disagreeable remarks Miss M made on *Villette* and this had been playing on Miss Brontë's mind'; and her reassessment of Thackeray, ('My word!' wrote Elizabeth after hearing Charlotte's 'piercingly keen' observations of *Henry Esmond*, the book procured by George. 'He had reason when he said he was afraid of her.'). And yet, Elizabeth knew, despite Charlotte's instinct to light her way ahead by burning bridges, 'she is thoroughly good; only made bitter by some deep mortifications and feeling her plainness as "something almost repulsive".'

By her own account, Charlotte was a drudge to duty – 'duty to her father, to the poor around her, to the old servants (I have heard incidentally of such delicate kindness of hers towards them)'[62] – who thirsted for a sudden transformative experience into sophistication and excitement. Elizabeth thought this naive. 'If she can but give up her craving for keen enjoyment of life,' she told Janet, 'which after all comes only in *drams* to anyone, leaving the spaces between most dreary and depressing.' As delusional as it sounded, Elizabeth understood this ideal of escape could only have sprung from the irreproachable sense of helplessness Charlotte expressed. Without that hindrance, Elizabeth wondered, what could Charlotte be, or have for herself? What achievements could she have won had she been faced with only a fraction of her struggles?

What would have been her transcendent grandeur if she had been brought up in a healthy and happy atmosphere no one can tell ... I'm sure I could not have borne (even with my inferior vehemence of power and venture) her life of monotony, and privation of anyone to love.[63]

Elizabeth told her friend John Forster, editor of *The Examiner*, that Charlotte was grateful for his paper's sympathetic review of *Villette* and, after Charlotte left, continued to him:

I like her more and more. She is so true, she wins respect, deep respect from the very first – and then comes hearty liking – and last of all comes love. I thoroughly loved her before she left – and I was so sorry for her! She has had so little kindness and affection shown to her. She said that she was afraid of loving me as much as she could, because she had never been able to inspire the kind of love she felt.[64]

Charlotte left the Gaskells on the afternoon of Thursday, 28 April, travelling to Bradford and then on to Birstall to stay with Ellen and her family for the weekend. She gave an assurance to Elizabeth that her father wanted her to come to stay with them in return for her kindness, which Elizabeth accepted to take up at the start of autumn. Despite her stay with the Gaskells having been unremarkable and not without anxieties, once she was back in Haworth, back with her father, monotony and solitude, she told Elizabeth it 'impressed me as the very brightest and healthiest I have known these five years past'.[65]

That spring, Whitsunday fell on 15 May. Taking the sacrament in church brought Charlotte and Arthur face to face:

I got a lesson not to be repeated. He struggled – faltered – then lost command over himself – stood before my eyes and in the sight of all the communicants white, shaking, voiceless – Papa was not there – thank God! Joseph Redman spoke some words to him – he made a great effort – but could only with difficulty whisper and falter through the service. I suppose he thought; this would be the last time; he goes either this week or the next. I heard the women sobbing round – and I could not quite check my own tears.[66]

Gossip got back to her father on the lips of Redman, the parish clerk, and John Brown. Charlotte heard Patrick scoff, calling Arthur an 'unmanly driveller'. It seems not to have occurred to the men who derided Arthur and made sarcastic jokes about his lovesickness that they denigrated her by association – if his feelings were to be laughed at, then she was too. She was appalled by her father's lack of compassion and haunted by how much Arthur must have suffered for loving her without hope of it being returned, commenting:

I never saw a battle more sternly fought with the feelings than Mr N …
and when he yields momentarily you are almost sickened by the sense of
the strain upon him. However, he is to go – and I cannot speak to him
or look at him or comfort him a whit – and I must submit. Providence is
over all – that is the only consolation.[67]

A few days later, the church wardens collected money to buy him a leaving present and asked what led him to go, was it down to Patrick? Arthur
denied it. Trying to determine if he had been pushed, they asked if he had
been willing to leave. He said he was not and it caused him great pain.
At a tea for him in the Sunday School he deliberately cut Patrick off in
the middle of his formal tribute to him. 'This sort of treatment offered in
public is what Papa never will forget or forgive,' Charlotte told Ellen. 'It
inspires him with a silent bitterness not to be expressed. I am afraid both are
unchristian in their mutual feelings: Nor do I know which of them is least
accessible to reason or least likely to forgive. It is a dismal state of things.'[68]

On Wednesday, 25 May, some representatives of the church and Sunday
School held a leaving party for Arthur. They gave him a gold watch and
made an appreciative speech about his community work. Everyone present
would have expected Patrick, as Arthur's superior, to deliver both. In a
deliberate and very public snub, he chose not to go despite the party being
held only a matter of feet from his front door. 'I dare not mention Mr
N's name to him,' Charlotte said. 'He speaks of him quietly and without
opprobrium to others – but to me he is implacable.' She went in defiance
and told them her father was ill again.[69]

The next evening, Arthur came to the parsonage to formally say goodbye
to Patrick and hand over the deeds of the school. Charlotte felt she could
not speak to him either in her father's presence, or alone:

He went out thinking he was not to see me. And indeed till the very last
moment I thought it best not. But perceiving that he stayed long before
going out at the gate and remembering his long grief I took courage and
went out trembling and miserable. I found him leaning against the garden-
door in a paroxysm of anguish, sobbing as women never sob. Of course
I went straight to him. Very few words were interchanged – those few
barely articulate: several things I should have liked to ask him were swept
entirely from my memory. Poor fellow! but he wanted such hope and such
encouragement as I could not give him. Still I trust he must know now that
I am not cruelly blind and indifferent to his constancy and grief.[70]

He left Haworth at six the next morning. 'He is gone – gone – and there's an end of it,' Charlotte wrote:

> I see no chance of hearing a word about him in future – unless some stray shred of intelligence comes through Mr Grant or some other second-hand source. In all this it is not *I* who am to be pitied at all and of course nobody pities me. They all think in Haworth that I have disdainfully refused him &c. If pity would do Mr N any good he ought to have, and I believe has it. They may abuse me, if they will. Whether they do or not, I can't tell.[71]

A month later, when Ellen came to stay for the weekend, she found the subject was still contentious. Patrick lectured them both in his supercilious way about how one must adapt to changing circumstances and happily accept the vagaries of fate. 'The consummate vanity of the man made him equal to any artifice,' she recalled years later when her memory was still vivid of how Charlotte 'turned upon him with rage as we breakfasted, when he made some kind of hypocritical remark to me on the vicissitudes of life.'[72] As both she and Charlotte knew, there would have been no loss for Charlotte to resign herself to, had it not been for Patrick's interference and hostility.

That weekend, Charlotte was free to discuss the situation in private. Unexpectedly, Arthur had been reluctant to turn his back on her permanently, Ellen learned, and surprised her by continuing to write. Torn, Charlotte felt unable to commit to any kind of reply. Now in his absence she was reassessing whether she should have accepted his proposal after all. This puzzled and concerned Ellen. Led by Charlotte's own ambivalence about Arthur, she feared she was starting to cave under the strain of her own loneliness, reducing her to such desperation she was now considering marrying anyone in a last attempt to avoid the spinsterhood Ellen felt was Charlotte's inescapable destiny. To Charlotte's astonishment, Ellen appears to have tried to explain this to her. Instead of drawing friendly sympathy, her admission of vulnerability about Arthur had only drawn castigation. The women argued and Ellen left.

Seeking backup when she got home, Ellen reported to their mutual friend Mary Taylor that Charlotte was betraying herself and her commitment to solitariness, that she and Mary must persuade her not to waver from the path of self-denial and duty she had always walked, as Ellen herself had, and that both she and Charlotte must dedicate themselves to bearing their lot, 'whatever that is'.[73] The long journey of the letter and its reply to and from the southern hemisphere meant Ellen did not get Mary's answer until a year later. Nevertheless, Mary's words about the matter must have carried enough indignant ire to still scald her:

> You talk wonderful nonsense about Charlotte Brontë ... What do you mean about 'bearing her position so long and enduring to the end'? ... If it's C's lot to be married shouldn't she bear that too? Or does your strange morality mean that she should refuse to ameliorate her lot when it lies in her power? How would she be inconsistent with herself in marrying? Because she considers her own pleasure? If this is so new for her to do, it is high time she began to make it more common. It is an outrageous exaction to expect her to give up her choice in a matter so important, and I think her to blame in having been hitherto so yielding that her friends can think of making such an impudent demand.[74]

All communication between Charlotte and Ellen stopped. Silence fell between them for the first time in two decades and their letters to each other ceased, throwing both back on the resources of their other less-engaged and less-sustaining friendships. As Charlotte's disinclination for Arthur reversed, so did her affection for Ellen.

On Sunday, 3 July, the likely day Ellen left to go home, Charlotte turned to George and wrote, with a sense of conclusion in her tone, 'Let me just say, though I say it not without pain, a correspondence which has not interest enough in itself to sustain life *ought* to die.' Shaken by her argument with Ellen, she chose this moment to acknowledge another failing relationship. George had been writing less often than he used to – only seven letters from her to him survive from the first seven months of 1853, indicating how few she was responding to – and a distance had opened between them as she feared his personal and professional interest waned after the mixed reviews of *Villette*. Having not heard from him for two months she played it safe and sympathised with the horrendous workload he hinted at in his last letter and urged him to rest. All the same, she gingerly suggested, he sounded too busy to want to speak to her now, detaching from their once companionable exchanges as he turned 'with distaste from the task of answering a friendly letter'. He was indeed overworked, but his distractions were not solely those of business. Unknown to Charlotte, and in telling contrast to the convulsions of her anxious and obstructed relationship with Arthur,

George had fallen in love simply and unreservedly with a woman who felt the same. He would propose to her before the end of the year.[75]

Charlotte told Elizabeth again how keen she was to bring her to Haworth. Through the early months of summer, they proposed and rescheduled dates around the obstacles of domestic commitments for Elizabeth and as illness in Haworth parsonage made alternate invalids of Charlotte and her father. One night in June, while she was in bed with flu, she heard her father hesitate on his way upstairs. From the darkened stairwell he called her name. She hurried out and found him unable to find his step or see the light of the candle he was carrying. He seemed to have lost his sight. 'He was in total darkness. Medical aid was immediately summoned but nothing could be done. It was feared a slight stroke of paralysis had occurred.'[76] While his speech and movements were not affected Charlotte naturally feared those would come next, to leave him paralysed by the next day. By morning, he was gradually able to distinguish daylight and his sight slowly restored imperfectly over the next few hours, as though a curtain was rising.[77]

After the uneasiness this fright gave her, Charlotte looked forward to seeing Elizabeth again as a reviving source of warmth, approaching like a welcome season, telling her, 'You and the bright heath and ripe corn shall all be classed together in my expectations.'[78]

As her father recuperated and his sight recovered, she read him Elizabeth's serial *Cranford*, newly published as a single-volume novel which she received as a gift from Elizabeth on 9 June, one of the days Charlotte had hoped Elizabeth would be able to visit. 'I have read it over twice,' she told her, 'once to myself and once aloud to my father. I find it pleasurable reading – graphic, pithy, penetrating, shrewd, yet kind and indulgent.'[79]

These were the very qualities Charlotte told Elizabeth she admired in her letters. They came to her in the silence and stillness of the parsonage, that deepened now without Ellen's involvement, 'as pleasant as a quiet chat, as welcome as spring showers, as reviving as a friend's visit; in short … very like a page of *Cranford*.'[80] To Charlotte's mind, Elizabeth approached her fiction as she approached the unobtrusive domestic details of a woman's life: with care, scrutiny and with a memory for the telling detail.

CHAPTER 6

1853

Debatable Land

'I am spoken of as an alien,' Charlotte protested to the editor of *The Christian Remembrancer* that summer.[1] She was responding to the latest in a spate of articles contending the bitterness in her fiction had a root in her life. As reviewers noted similarities between Jane Eyre and Lucy Snowe, they speculated on how such characters were produced. Being so indifferent to 'moral perversity, the toleration of, nay indifference to, vice' they said, their creator should have been improved by money since she first appeared to the world as 'soured, coarse and grumbling; an alien, it might seem from society, and amenable to none of its laws'.

Villette's moral campaign, they proposed, was to arouse sympathy for a debased class of woman that must 'embody much of the authoress's own feelings and experience'. No personal disadvantages can hinder the unentitled sense of superiority this kind of woman expresses, they insisted, to demand 'room to expand, love, tenderness, and a place in happy domestic life. But in truth she draws a character unfit for this home which she yearns for.' 'Without feelings of humble reverence for men, female characters such as Lucy Snowe, and by implication Charlotte Brontë, cannot deserve the respect of a man,' the reviewer concluded firmly.[2]

Extraordinarily, for one who had been recently so protective of her personal identity as to hide behind an assumed identity, Charlotte wrote to them under her own name to set the record straight, to explain precisely what kind of circumstances produced women in revolt like Jane Eyre and Lucy Snowe. With a frankness she would at one time have only spoken through her characters, Charlotte spelled it out:

> Providence so regulated my destiny that I was born and have been reared
> in the seclusion of a country parsonage. I have never been rich enough

to go out into the world as a participator in its gaieties, though it early became my duty to leave home in order partly to diminish the many calls on a limited income. That income is lightened of claims in another sense now, for of a family of six I am the only survivor.

My father is now in his 77th year; his mind is clear as it ever was, and he is not infirm, but he suffers from partial privation and threatened loss of sight; as his general health is also delicate, he cannot be left often for long: my place consequently is at home. These are reasons which make retirement a plain duty; but were no such reasons in existence, were I bound by no such ties, it is very possible that seclusion might still appear to me, on the whole, more congenial than publicity; the brief and rare glimpses I have had of the world do not incline me to think I should seek its circles with very keen zest – nor can I consider such a disinclination a just subject for reproach.

This is the truth. The careless, rather than malevolent insinuations of reviewers have, it seems, widely spread another impression. It would be weak to complain, but I feel that it is only right to place the real in opposition to the unreal.[3]

With Harriet's broadside still weighing on her mind, she asked the editor to show this to their critic and remind them of their distinctly unchristian behaviour in disregarding the 'golden rule' of St Matthew's gospel; of doing only what we would have done to ourselves. It is possible the editor replied, for in the next issue he published a sanctimonious notice acknowledging her complaint while excusing his reviewer as Charlotte's 'original and some-what warped mode of viewing things must excite speculation' about the mind that was guilty of 'some grave faults in her earliest work'. It was, he continued, natural to suppose she had been 'embittered by the want of congenial enjoyment'. In conclusion, he wrote, they were satisfied to hear she was now devoting herself to looking after her elderly father.[4]

If Charlotte thought they were uncharitable in public and disingenuous in their reply, she had good reason. While the editor claimed ignorance as a defence, some earlier articles show how much he did know about Charlotte's life. Reviewing *Jane Eyre* in 1848, the critics restrained themselves from the unmediated contempt reserved for recalcitrant women as 'the name and sex of the writer are still a mystery'.[5] But three years later in an 1851 article entitled 'Minor Poets of the Day' they now knew Currer, Ellis and Acton Bell were not just women, but could refer to them as 'sisters' only a matter of months after Charlotte confirmed it in her biographical preface for the new edition of *Wuthering Heights* and *Agnes Grey*. Her account of how Emily and Anne perished from hardship and ill health before their time seems not to have moved the critics at *The Christian Remembrancer*. Far from being sympathetic, they felt it was unwarranted exceptionalism that did not excuse the moral degradation of their novels. The Brontës' tragedies, they suggested, were nothing more than the necessary consequences women faced if they protested against a natural order of injustice:

> The experience of the three sisters must have thrown them among men more than commonly selfish, overbearing, and debased, to give them such impressions of woman's evil fate among them; and indeed their works have throughout vague hints of a certain brutal monstrous oppression, from which women have suffered and died … All have to bear some of this world's trials; many have borne whatever amount of disappointment, weariness, and uncongenial labour may have pressed upon these sisters, and in their resignation have profited by trials which impatient and rebellious spirits have struggled and beat against in impotent resistance.[6]

In short, it would have been better for everybody if the Brontës had put up and shut up: 'We think it is clear that in so far as these writers had been humbler, purer, of a more submissive faith, they would have been better poets.'[7]

After what must have felt like the irreparable conclusion of her twenty-two-year friendship with Ellen, Charlotte was at a loss. According to Elizabeth:

> No one comes to the house; nothing disturbs the deep repose; hardly a voice is heard; you catch the ticking of the clock in the kitchen, or the buzzing of a fly in the parlour, all over the house. Miss Brontë sits alone in her parlour; breakfasting with her father in his study at nine o'clock. She helps in the housework; for one of their servants, Tabby, is nearly ninety and the other only a girl.[8]

Adrift without near-daily contact with Ellen, without the nourishment of her letters or the equally sustaining outlet of replying, Charlotte appealed to other, less close friends for company. 'All the summer I have felt the wish and cherished the intention to join you for a brief period at the seaside,' she told Margaret Wooler.[9] And to Elizabeth, 'Ever since I was at Manchester, I have been anticipating your visit.'[10]

She also contacted Mary Taylor's brother Joe, whom she had known for more than twenty years – as long as she had been friends with Mary – as well as his wife Amelia Ringrose, once one of Ellen's close friends. They had married a few years before and had a 2-year-old daughter in fragile health. They invited her to join them on their trip to Scotland. Fostered by a love of its literature from half a century before, Charlotte romanticised the country. She and her siblings had devoured the poetry of Burns and the novels of Scott and the issues of *Blackwood's Edinburgh Magazine* edited by James Hogg. After visiting for the first time in July 1850 with George and his family, she found Scotland impossible to forget during waking hours or sleep. She and the Taylors travelled from Yorkshire via Carlisle, arriving at Dumfries where they stayed overnight, before taking a stagecoach 40 scenic miles to Kirkcudbright. As soon as they arrived, the Taylors thought their daughter was sick from the change of diet or coastal air. While Charlotte admired their devotion, she thought they were indulging her but said nothing when they decided to turn around. They got the train back to Yorkshire and found somewhere to stay in Ilkley, but in their haste lost Charlotte's trunk, leaving her without a change of clothes. After a round trip of more than 300 miles to stay less than 30 from Haworth, she headed home where she found her father 'far from well' as she often did when away for even a few days.[11] Respite from domestic concerns was, as ever, barred by obstacles and impossible to achieve.

As Elizabeth's stay looked less likely to be disrupted, Charlotte cautioned her to lower her expectations and joked nervously that Haworth was a social and cultural desert, 'Leaving behind your husband, children and civilisation, you must come out to barbarism, loneliness, and liberty.'[12] As the summer waned, she wrote to her again. 'Come to Haworth as soon as you can: the heath is in bloom now. I have waited and watched for its purple signal as the forerunner of your coming.'[13]

On a drab September Monday, after five months of plans and cancellations, Elizabeth made her way to Haworth for the first time. She described her journey up from Manchester, taking a morning train, to be collected outside Keighley station by a cab Charlotte booked, that took her 'four tough, steep, scrambling miles, the road winding between the wavelike hills that rose and fell on every side of the horizon.'[14] After rows of factories and cottages as lead-coloured as the sky, they reached 'a long, straggling village; one steep narrow street – so steep that the flag stones with which it is paved are placed end-ways, that the horses' feet may have something to cling to, and not slip down backwards.'[15] The sharp left turn off Main Street into Church Street took them past the house where Arthur lodged with the Browns, up past the school-house on one side and the graveyard wall on the other, over which blew intolerable fumes. Elizabeth was shocked. 'I had to keep my handkerchief to my nose always,' she wrote. 'Miss Brontë says she can tell which way the wind is in the morning before she gets up, by the smell which fills her bedroom if it blows from the churchyard.'[16]

She got to the front steps not long after midday, just as another visitor was coming down them, 'a ruddy tired-looking man of no great refinement',[17] a tycoon and hobby poet named Francis Bennoch who contacted Charlotte as an opportunistic fan to ask for a few hours of her time and set off before she could decline. Nevertheless, after Bennoch had a preliminary conversation with Patrick she had to accommodate him. Like Charlotte, he had published a poetry collection when he was 30 and also sought the solicitations of the greats. He went as far as to dedicate his 1841 collection to Wordsworth only to be told by him not to give up his day job.[18]

After two years of hearing about her grim home on the moors, Elizabeth could now check how Charlotte's observations corresponded with her own. The square Georgian house stood without shelter on a tree-less grass rise behind the church of St Michael and All Angels, whose churchyard pooled towards and around it. At the front was a drying green, bordered with a few low brambles, and round the back the household's privy stood near a single-storey wash house and scullery extending from the kitchen into a yard that opened on to the lane. The front windows looked out across the pavement of graves towards the rain-blackened church tower. Behind the church, Main Street's pitched and crooked slate rooftops dropped below the line of moors swelling up on the other side of the valley. 'Moors everywhere beyond and above,' Elizabeth noted.[19]

While the parsonage's smallness and position at the top of the village could not have been further from the expanse of Plymouth Grove, Elizabeth was charmed. Charlotte brought her into 'an exquisitely clean passage, to the left into a square parlour looking out on the grass plot, the tall headstones beyond, the tower end of the church, the village houses and the brown moors.' The parlour was:

> the perfection of warmth, smartness and comfort, crimson predominating in the furniture, which did well with the bleak, cold colours without. There was her likeness by Richmond, given to her father by Messrs Smith

and Elder, the later print of Thackeray, and a good likeness of the Duke of Wellington, hanging up.[20]

A 'high, narrow, old-fashioned mantelpiece' stood between two recesses 'filled with books; books given to her, books she has bought and which tell of her individual pursuits and tastes; *not* standard books.'[21] Elizabeth thought the furnishings looked mostly new:

> evidently refurnished within the last few years, since Miss Brontë's suc-
> cess has enabled her to have a little more money to spend. Everything fits
> into, and is in harmony with, the idea of a country parsonage, possessed
> by people of very moderate means.[22]

There were nine rooms over two floors; four on the ground and five upstairs, with a hallway and staircase through the middle. On either side of the front door were the parlour and Patrick's study. Behind the parlour was a small pantry; behind Patrick's study the kitchen. Above that was Charlotte's room, behind Patrick's room directly above his study. Above the pantry was the room shared by Martha and Tabby, and above the parlour was a large spare room first occupied by Patrick and his late wife and then by Patrick's sister-in-law when she joined the household after his wife's death. 'Where the rest of the household slept when they were all one large family, I can't imagine,' Elizabeth wondered. Here she found a fire lit for her in the grate and the same view as from the parlour windows below, over the churchyard and across a valley that over the next four days she would find not at all barbaric but 'really beautiful in certain lights, moonlight especially'.

They had dinner at two in the afternoon, with Martha serving Patrick separately in his study 'according to his *invariable* custom (fancy it! Only they two left)' Elizabeth wrote, appalled that even death's reduction of his children to a solitary one would not vary his routine.

Afterwards, Charlotte took her out through the back fields and over the lower slopes of the moors where she used to walk with her sisters. The pasture behind the parsonage reached into drystone sheep fields lying across the rise, up to a low green hillock. A little way over brought them to an uneven and tree-less plateau of gorse and heather and rock. 'The heather-bloom had been blighted by a thunder-storm a day or two before,' wrote Elizabeth, 'and was all of a livid brown colour, instead of the blaze of purple glory it ought to have been. Oh, those high, wild, desolate moors, up above the whole world, and the very realms of silence!'[23] The two women walked against the wind into the sweeps of moorland, towards where Charlotte told her Lancashire started, 'but the sinuous hills seemed to girdle the world like the great Norse serpent, and for my part I don't know if they don't stretch up to the North Pole,' Elizabeth wrote. They turned to look down on the distant valley, towards the spread of mill houses and smoking chimneys of Keighley in the distance, where:

> here and there from the high moorland summit we saw newly built churches – which her Irish curates see after – every one of those being literal copies of different curates in the neighbourhood, whose amusement has ever since to call each other by the name she gave them in *Shirley*.[24]

They walked down to the house for tea, to be told that Patrick would join them for once, 'an honour to me I believe,'[25] Elizabeth commented. She found the 76-year-old vicar 'a tall fine looking old man, with silver bristles all over his head; nearly blind'[26] who spoke with a strong Northern Irish accent. He had 'a sort of grand and stately way of describing past times, which tallied well with his striking appearance,'[27] but she noticed how his gentility gave way to acerbity when it came to the personal, and how inflexibly he exerted his authority over Charlotte, making her acquiesce in a way Elizabeth had never seen before:

> He was very polite and agreeable to me, paying rather elaborate old-fashioned compliments, but I was sadly afraid of him in my inmost soul; for I caught a glare of his stern eyes over his spectacles at Miss Brontë once or twice which made me know my man; and he talked *at* her sometimes.[28]

Watching them together confirmed everything Elizabeth heard from Charlotte and others. Here was the implacable and distant Irishman she had been warned about, a father yet to find a cause good enough to bend from cold formality with his only surviving child. Whenever away from him, Charlotte spoke dejectedly about their relationship, describing a kind of ransom that made it suffocating to stay but escape impossible. It was clear Patrick thought Charlotte must be managed and restrained, having never surrendered 'the feeling that Charlotte was a child to be guided and ruled … and she herself submitted to this with a quiet docility that half amused, half astonished me.'[29] Elizabeth described how when Charlotte left the room:

then all his pride in her genius and fame came out. He eagerly listened to everything I could tell him of the high admiration I had at any time heard expressed for her works. He would ask for certain speeches over and over again, as if he desired to impress them on his memory.[30]

Another visitor had the same experience. When alone with visitors Patrick asked them if they had read and admired Charlotte's novels:

He seemed to have a three-fold feeling; regret that novels should have proceeded from his daughters; paternal pride, evident and sometimes garrulously demonstrative pride; and a wandering inability altogether to believe it.[31]

Over tea, Charlotte mentioned Bennoch's intrusion, telling Elizabeth how he suggested himself as a patron for writers short of funds. Elizabeth scoffed that if the price was interference, it was too high. Patrick was dismissive and 'abused us both for a couple of proud minxes'.[32] She thought he sounded unaffected by others' opinions, one who sided with 'men against the masters, and vice versa just as he thought fit and right; and is consequently much respected and to be respected. But he ought never to have married. He did not like children.'[33]

He went to smoke a pipe in his study, leaving them to sew and talk by the fire, turning the conversation to 'long ago when that very same room was full of children and how one by one they had dropped off into the churchyard close to the windows'.[34] Charlotte explained how her parents 'had six in six years, and the subsequent pinching and family disorder which can't be helped, and noise etc. made him shut himself up and want no companionship nay be positively annoyed by it'.[35]

At eight thirty, they rejoined Patrick for prayers. His study was small with a narrow iron grate and, Elizabeth noticed, little indication of a cleric's contemplative or academic activities, with 'not a sign of engraving, map, writing materials etc. beyond a desk, no books but those contained on two hanging shelves between the windows, his two pipes and a spittoon.'[36] On the wall above them hung a shotgun Charlotte told her was loaded, as was a pistol she said he always carried in his pocket like a watch. Both added to Elizabeth's 'fear, rather than admiring fear' of Patrick, to treat loaded firearms so casually as to bring 'this little deadly pistol sitting down to breakfast with us, kneeling down to prayers at night to say nothing of our loaded gun hanging up on high, ready to pop off on the slightest emergency.'[37]

Patrick and the servants retired to their bedrooms by nine. Charlotte and Elizabeth stayed up for another hour or so and 'talked over the clear, bright fire; it is a cold country, and the fires were a pretty warm dancing light all over the house.'[38] Without company, Charlotte said, she normally sat there 'quite alone thinking over the past; for her eyesight prevents her reading or writing by candlelight, and knitting is but very mechanical and does not keep the thoughts from wandering.'[39] When Elizabeth went to her room she heard her pacing for the next hour until she too came upstairs.

The next morning started at breakfast with Patrick in his study at nine, and then:

> the letters come; not many, sometimes for days none at all. About twelve we went out to walk. At two we dined, about four we went out again; at six we had tea; by nine everyone was in bed but ourselves. Monotonous enough in sound, but not a bit in reality.[40]

Martha brought meals from the small kitchen where Elizabeth saw an almost fairy-tale tableau of crone and harassed young woman, with Tabitha Aykroyd, 'sitting in an armchair by the kitchen fire and Martha, the real active serving maiden'.[41] Tabby had been cook and general housekeeper with the family for nearly thirty years, joining them when she was a widow in her fifties, and now partly deaf and partly lame, acting as instructress to the 25-year-old Martha.

Elizabeth gauged Tabby's maternal power within the house. 'To a visitor at the parsonage, it was a great thing to have Tabby's good word. She had a Yorkshire keenness of perception into character, and it was not everybody she liked.'[42] She struck Elizabeth as 'a thorough specimen of a Yorkshire woman of her class, in dialect, in appearance, and in character.'[43] She put her age at over 90, indicating the family's or Tabby's own miscalculation (she was roughly 82). As the oldest person in the house, older even than the seemingly Biblically ancient Patrick, she came from an earlier pastoral age, remembering Haworth of the late 1770s before mills chased away the fairies, in the sunset of the Jacobean manors ruined in neighbouring fields.[44]

At one point, Elizabeth asked Martha to show her the family tomb. They waited until Charlotte was busy and stole out to the church, where Martha showed her the memorial, listing the names of Charlotte's mother and all her siblings:

'Yes!' said Martha. 'They were all well when Mr Branwell was buried; but Miss Emily broke down the next week. We saw she was ill, but she never would own it, never would have a doctor near her, never would breakfast in bed. The last morning she got up, and she was dying all the time, the rattle in her throat while she *would* dress herself: and neither Miss Brontë nor I dared offered to help her. She died just before Christmas – you'll see the date there – and we all went to her funeral. Master and Keeper, her dog walking first side by side and then Miss Brontë and Miss Anne and then Tabby and me. Next day Miss Anne took ill just in the same way and it was 'Oh if it was but spring and I could go to the sea, Oh if it was but spring.' And at last spring came and Miss Brontë took her to Scarborough. They got there on the Saturday and on the Monday she died. She is buried in the old church at Scarborough. For as long as I can remember, Tabby says since they were little bairns, Miss Brontë and Miss Emily and Miss Anne used to put away their sewing after prayers and walk all three one after the other round the table in the parlour till near 11 o'clock. Miss Emily walked as long as she could and when she died Miss Anne and Miss Brontë took it up and now my heart aches to hear Miss Brontë walking, walking, on alone.[45]

This, Elizabeth realised, was how Charlotte spent her last hour every night, making:

that slow monotonous incessant walk in which I am sure I should fancy I heard the steps of the dead following … She said she could not sleep without it, that she and her sisters talked over the plans and projects of their whole lives at such times.[46]

The austerity of the house appeared to have its expression in Charlotte's very body and in her compulsion to control and order everything around her. Disruption was enough to interrupt her train of thought and 'her habits of order were such that she could not go on with the conversation if a chair was out of its place; everything was arranged with delicate regularity.'[47]

During the day they read, sewed and talked. They reflected on their differences and similarities, and their lives' divergent paths, despite shared ambitions. Charlotte felt a divine ordinance marked her out for sorrow, setting her apart and barring the way to happiness, not just for life's larger desires and plans, but for any insignificant pleasure others took without exertion. The thwarted holiday with the Taylors was an example, how they had 'set out joyfully; she with especial gladness' only to pay with inconvenience, expense and lost property.[48] Elizabeth countered that all lives are touched by grief and only perceptions set people apart:

> I thought that human lots were more equal than she imagined; that to some happiness and sorrow came in strong patches of light and shadow, (so to speak), while in the lives of others they were pretty equally blended throughout. She smiled, and shook her head, and said she was trying to school herself against ever anticipating any pleasure; that it was better to be brave and submit faithfully; there was some good reason, which we should know in time, why sorrow and disappointment were to be the lot of some on earth.[49]

Storms embittered the week's damp beginning into gales. In its exposed position, the parsonage became like a rock in a river. Rain lashed the windows, wind swept round the gables and plunged down the chimneys into its hearths, 'piping and wailing and sobbing round the square unsheltered house in a very strange unearthly way', Elizabeth wrote.[50] Nevertheless, she and Charlotte continued taking twice daily walks across the moors even after the weather turned. When they stopped at strangers' houses for shelter, Elizabeth found Charlotte's reserve vanished. 'Her quiet, gentle words, few though they might be, were evidently grateful to those Yorkshire ears. Their welcome to her, though rough and curt, was sincere and hearty.'[51]

Patrick took separate walks and refused to let Charlotte treat him as the invalid he insisted he was whenever she was away from home, making her appear over-protective. Elizabeth saw him go out 'in defiance of her gentle attempts to restrain him, speaking as if she thought him in his second childhood; and comes home moaning and tired having lost his way. "Where is my strength gone?" is his cry then. "I used to walk 40 miles a day".'[52]

He was saving face, unaware how much she knew. Charlotte had confided details of not only their shared past, but his present moods and behaviour. Privately, she discussed the Arthur situation, how it created enmity with Patrick and killed her friendship with Ellen. Knowing how much Charlotte sacrificed for her father and how his moods and fluctuating health terrorised her, Elizabeth was appalled by him and awed by the 'patient docility' of her care.[53]

After an afternoon walk then tea in the evening, Elizabeth developed long discursive conversations with Charlotte about her fiction and its wellsprings in her past. With no intermediary between them now, she pressed her for as much information as she could bear to share:

> We talked over the old times of her childhood; of her elder sister's (Maria's) death, – just like that of Helen Burns in *Jane Eyre*; of those strange, starved days at school; of the desire (almost amounting to illness) of expressing herself in some way, – writing or drawing; of her weak-ened eyesight, which prevented her doing anything for two years, from the age of seventeen to nineteen; of her being a governess; of her going to Brussels; whereupon I said I disliked Lucy Snowe, and we discussed M. Paul Emanuel.[54]

Charlotte's 'wild, strange facts' about herself and her sisters were inexhaust-ible, and as limitless as the retreating waves of moorland around the house. She told Elizabeth she modelled the headstrong titular character of *Shirley* on Emily, 'about whom she is never tired of talking, nor I of listening. Emily must have been a remnant of the Titans – great-grand-daughter of the giants who used to inhabit earth.'[55] Charlotte described her in terms of a raw, self-perpetuating power untempered by consistent formal education or an assimilation into a wider family or community. A personality formed in relative isolation among like-minded siblings made her staunch with them and averse to strangers. If *Wuthering Heights* formed her letter to the world, the reviews were its reply:

> Emily, poor Emily, the pangs of disappointment as review after review came out about *Wuthering Heights* were terrible. Miss Brontë said she had no recollection of pleasure or gladness about *Jane Eyre*, every such feeling was lost in seeing Emily's resolute endurance yet knowing what she felt.[56]

A month after Anne died Charlotte described how, stripped of their solidar-ity, she was left in a companionless void:

> The great trial is when evening closes as night approaches. At that hour we used to assemble in the dining room – we used to talk. Now I sit by myself. Necessarily I am silent. I cannot help thinking of their last days – remembering their sufferings and what they said and did and how they looked in mortal affliction. Perhaps all this will become less poignant in time.[57]

She talked about her brother and his disintegration from the family's great hope to its shame. Elizabeth was reluctant to repeat details of his alcoholism and drug dependence to correspondents and thought 'the less said the better, poor fellow. He never knew *Jane Eyre* was written although he lived for a year afterwards; but that year passed in the shadow of the coming death, with the consciousness of his wasted life.'[58] As Branwell brought home opium and the scene in *Villette* where Lucy Snowe takes an accidental overdose matched Elizabeth's own experience of taking it, she asked if it was written from experience. Charlotte said no, she used a technique when describing anything she had not personally experienced. She concentrated on something before she fell asleep to trigger sensory dreams she could subsequently describe. Even although that sounded less credible, Charlotte had no cause to deny it as opium was not illegal. Given her worship of truth, as she put it, Elizabeth accepted her explanation.[59]

At one point when describing her siblings she broke off, perhaps in response to a question about what they looked like, went upstairs and came back with an oil painting, unframed and still on its stretcher. A muddy piece from Branwell's late teenage years as an aspiring portraitist, it struck Elizabeth as 'rough, common-looking'. It showed the three sisters on either side of a column: Anne and Emily on one side, ('girls of sixteen and fourteen with cropped hair and sad, dreamy-looking eyes'); and Charlotte on the other, 'a little, rather prim-looking girl of eighteen.'[60] Originally, Branwell sketched a self-portrait between them but painted it over with the pillar as soon as he saw how four figures overcrowded the composition. He abandoned it before he finished his representations of Emily and Anne and started another family group in a landscape format to accommodate all four spaced further apart. Elizabeth never mentions this second painting, suggesting she never saw it. As she thought the resemblance to Charlotte was accurate, she decided the others must be too.[61] Others who remembered Emily and Anne thought Branwell had so failed to capture them that his paintings were worthless. Ellen thought them 'very poor', and Arthur would later say he could only find the trace of a resemblance in Branwell's depiction of Anne in one painting and of Emily in the other and Charlotte in neither. That Charlotte makes no reference to either painting in any of her extant letters is significant, especially given that she was asked for a photograph or a painting of Emily and Anne by William Smith Williams to be engraved as a frontispiece for the new edition of *Wuthering Heights* and *Agnes Grey*. She was unequivocal. 'I grieve to say that I possess no portrait of either of my sisters.'[62] As she possessed both paintings, we may infer she thought both so unlike her sisters they could be disqualified as likenesses in the literal sense.

The only professional portrait of herself hung in the parlour, a drawing by George Richmond made at George Smith's request when she was in London in the summer of 1850. She sat for Richmond at his studio near Regent's Park over three sessions that went from mortification to distress. She was embarrassed when he asked her to remove an obvious hairpiece, thinking it the detached lining of her bonnet, and when he showed her the completed portrait, she wept for its resemblance to her sisters. Her father thought it made her look old but praised Richmond's 'admirable tact and delicacy'.[63] On balance, Elizabeth considered it accurate, 'though, of course, there is some difference of opinion on the subject; and, as usual, those best acquainted with the original were least satisfied with the resemblance.'[64]

Had a more definitive likeness existed of them, such as a photograph, as has been theorised since the middle of the twentieth century with a regularity that belies the desire for one more than the historical suggestion of its existence, it is impossible to explain why Charlotte would not have mentioned it to William Smith Williams, or at least shown it to Elizabeth in place of the Pillar Portrait, instead of privileging the faulty above anything more accurate. Depictions then, of Emily and Anne, became the posthumous responsibility of their brother, construed through his murky paintings, but more importantly through Charlotte's narration of their lives as characters in her prefaces of 1850, and now in conversations with Elizabeth, which she in turn would blend and make anew.

By the time Elizabeth prepared to leave on the morning of Friday, 23 September, she and Charlotte knew their growing friendship could provide what the other lacked; Elizabeth had a place in Haworth when she needed solitude and simplicity, and for Charlotte the warm, vivacious opposite in Manchester.[65] Elizabeth wrote:

> We parted with many intentions, on both sides, of renewing very frequently the pleasure we had had in being together. We agreed that when she wanted bustle, or when I wanted quiet, we were to let each other know, and exchange visits as occasion required.[66]

Departing for the train from Keighley, Elizabeth took with her the cheerful affability that lifted everyone in her company. 'After you left, the house felt very much as if the shutters had been suddenly closed and the blinds let down.' Charlotte wrote she tried to stay sensible for the rest of the day – the eve of the anniversary of Branwell's death – but could not ignore the return of the 'depressing silence, shadow, loss, and want' Elizabeth left in her wake. The effect of her stay, however, was not diminished by her absence. She told her it 'did permanent good. Papa, I am sure, derived real benefit from your visit; he has been better ever since.'[67]

On the train, Elizabeth must have considered everything she had seen and felt at the parsonage, for once home she hurriedly described the trip to friends. Two specific conversations with Charlotte gave her food for thought, about her rejecting two offers made to her: Arthur's proposal and Bennoch's patronage. While they had laughed off the latter, it seemed to Elizabeth that marriage and money were all that was missing from Charlotte's life. She began to wonder if something of the two could be combined and presented in a form more acceptable to her. Love and financial stability could propel her out of the morbidity and self-reflection that made her so desperate, and both could only come through the intervention of a well-meaning friend like her.

By the end of October, she had a plan.

CHAPTER 7

1853
Treachery

Elizabeth wrote to one of her friends, the former Conservative member for Pontefract and one-time poet, Richard Monckton Milnes.[1] He had introduced himself to Charlotte at the London lecture where Thackeray called her out as Jane Eyre. Having heard he had procured a state pension for Tennyson, Elizabeth wondered if he could do something similar for Charlotte. She knew from Charlotte's response to Bennoch that she would reject a blatant offer but, in a stroke of ingenious inspiration, wondered if they could provide it indirectly by securing Arthur a better income and making him a more attractive potential son-in-law to Patrick. 'Her father's only reason for his violent and virulent opposition is Mr Nicholls's utter want of money or friends to help him to any professional advancement,' she explained. 'I felt sure you would keep the story secret. If my well-meant treachery becomes known to her, I shall lose her friendship, which I prize most highly.'[2]

Her 'treachery' while well intentioned was undeniably cunning. Having picked up from Charlotte that Arthur was still in Yorkshire and had, as recently as July, been staying a couple of miles away with one of his vicar friends, Elizabeth contacted the Haworth postmaster, William Hartley, to ask for Arthur's mailing address. As the wife of a minister, wishing to write to another member of the clergy she should not arouse any suspicion, yet she still had to use what she called her 'skilful diplomacy' to get it. Upon receiving a reply from Hartley that Arthur was now the curate to the Rev. Thomas Cator in Kirk Smeaton near Pontefract she congratulated herself and told Milnes that a supplement of £100 a year to Arthur would give Charlotte ten times the pleasure that twice the amount would if offered to her. If Milnes could make enquiries, she suggested, a boost to Arthur's income, or even better a new curacy, would change more than one life. Three months later, Monckton Milnes reported back to her that he had found Arthur in Pontefract and met him in person. Having asked the vicar of Leeds to pull some strings, he could offer him a curacy in either Lancashire or Scotland. To his surprise, Arthur flatly declined both. He seemed to Milnes to be completely burned out emotionally. Despite appearing to be a hearty representative of the strongly built Celtic stock of Northern Irishmen, he found Arthur 'sadly broken in health and spirits'.[3] Milnes made sure not to mention Elizabeth to him ('or my head would not have been safe on my shoulders' commented Elizabeth) but told her how respectfully Arthur spoke of Patrick Brontë and that he had talked of Charlotte 'simply and unreservedly'. Evidently, Arthur's thoughts were still immovably in Haworth.[4]

Charlotte was restless after Elizabeth left. She read inconsistently and made a few starts at writing fiction but abandoned them. Less than a fortnight after her visit, she fled to join Margaret Wooler at her home in Hornsea on the east coast for a 'happy and a pleasant week', thanking her for 'the true kindness which gave it its chief charm' and telling her when she came home how she would miss her company in the long winter evenings ahead whenever she went for walks on the moors alone.[5] She brooded on the loss of what little intimacy she once had with others and how impossible she found compromise. Where Elizabeth felt diplomacy, tact and an imperceptible bending of the facts might produce the best outcome for all, Charlotte felt the only sincerity in relationships could be absolute honesty, regardless of what it brought her or others. She told Elizabeth in November that, 'honest, porcupine sensitiveness is worth millions more than the smoothest and most polished ice of apathy over which the foot of friendship ever slid to its downfall.'[6]

By mid-November, she was cheering herself by planning another break away from home with a week in London. It had been a year since she told George she was so piqued by his silence she might just 'materialise' in his office. Back then, she still felt confident enough of a welcome to propose visits at short notice. Now she said nothing. She did not tell him or anyone else at Smith Elder that she had already arranged to stay in lodgings rather than with his family as she always had in the past, presumably to allow her to turn up as unexpectedly as on her first momentous visit with Anne in the summer of 1848. That occasion heralded the beginning of her London celebrity. We may conjecture whether she felt recreating the circumstances might reignite that thrilling success, to let her retrace those steps and begin, perhaps, again.

Towards the end of the month, having not heard from George for four months, she was alarmed to receive a note from him that she thought expressed 'a good deal of uneasiness and disturbance of mind'. Gauging that a momentous step was imminent she wrote to his mother to ask what was wrong. Charlotte may have thought George was contemplating the future of Smith Elder. She knew his workload was taking a toll on his health and was conscious of how things had changed between them. The heat and industry she had enjoyed with him and William Smith Williams in the six years between *Jane Eyre* and *Villette* had evaporated and the letters that once flooded between them had dried up. Charlotte may have wondered if Williams and Smith were coming to the natural end of their careers and whether George was about to put the company up for sale. Assuming his decision was professional rather than personal she asked his mother, 'if he is going to take any important step in life – as some of his expressions would seem to imply – is it one likely to conduce to his happiness and welfare?'[7] The next day the tight-lipped Mrs Smith wrote back that her son was 'quite well and very happy' and would tell her in due course that he was about to take 'a very important step in life, the most important – and I know with every prospect of happiness'.[8]

Charlotte did not need to hear more. In that instant she understood George's silence had been because he was more interested in talking to another woman than to her, just as he had been that night at Thackeray's dinner party. He was so unmistakably involved with someone that he was ready to propose to her. Despite being on the verge of packing to leave, she cancelled her visit immediately. She wrote to the landlady of the Bloomsbury boarding house and told her she would compensate her for the late cancellation. She contacted one of the friends she planned to meet to tell her it was off because 'man proposes but another disposes'. She said 'circumstances have taken a turn' but did not explain further.[9] A week later, she gathered all the books Smith Elder had sent her, boxed them up and posted them back, telling Williams, in what would transpire to be her last message to him, never to send her anything else. 'Do not trouble yourself … these courtesies must cease some day and I would rather give them up than wear them out.'[10] On Saturday, 10 December she contacted George. Carefully, and with exceptional coldness she wrote, 'In great happiness as in great grief words of sympathy should be few. Accept my meed of congratulation.'[11]

Charlotte always weighed her words with great deliberation. 'Meed' is an Old English term describing a payment made from obligation, a transaction without feeling. Having made it clear to Williams she felt she was being managed with courtesy she took the same approach with George. In some ways her reaction to discovering he was in a relationship matched Ellen's reaction to her own with Arthur – which she had never mentioned to George. The 'grief' and 'sympathy' in her congratulation must have alerted George she was mourning an ending for her, rather than celebrating a beginning for him. Now stripped of all their generosity and joy, his gifts, once received by Charlotte as unrivalled indulgences, were degraded in this new light into generalised 'courtesies', those meaningless concessions given out of professional necessity rather than from any sincerely held affection. Returning them suggests she now thought Williams and Smith had finished with her and she was being handled with a kind of officiousness that cancelled out the certainty she once cherished, that theirs was genuine friendship.

By now Arthur had written six unhappy letters to her in six months, appealing for her response. Having written similarly heartbroken letters in the past that were met with an equally unendurable silence from the object of her love, Charlotte stopped ignoring him and replied that he must accept his lot and submit to it. He wrote back that her advice had comforted him greatly and begged for more. Soon they were corresponding, with Charlotte offering the kind words no one gave to her when she was distraught.[12] He wrote to her from Oxenhope, barely a mile from Haworth, pleading with her to meet him. Where before she had refused, this time she went, and kept it secret from her father.

She turned to Margaret Wooler:

I wonder how you are spending these long winter evenings. Alone – probably – like me. The thought often crosses me, as I sit by myself, how pleasant it would be if you lived within a walking distance and I could go to you sometimes or have you come and spend a day and night with me.

She must have talked to her about having fallen out with Ellen, for Margaret offered counsel to her about bridging the gulf. 'Do not think that your kind wish respecting E Nussey and myself does not touch or influence me,' Charlotte replied, 'it does both; yet I hardly know how to take the step you recommend. My heart —' The thought is interrupted: the next page of the letter was destroyed.[13]

Through December, Arthur continued to send Charlotte letters that she read and replied to in secret. As he had sworn to Patrick that he would never mention his proposal to her or him again, she may also have promised not to have any contact with him either, in order to keep what little peace Patrick permitted. As the injuries of his vituperative abuse of Arthur still burned Charlotte, she said nothing about their correspondence and compromised her own paramount sense of integrity by volunteering to conceal the truth. In the course of this limping, half-hearted romance, she must have felt that she and Arthur were becoming not lovers but liars together.

While Charlotte's spirits were being decimated by a loneliness deeper – unthinkably – than in previous years, at Plymouth Grove the Gaskell family's rooms were filling with warmth, laughter and festivity. Jubilant and industrious, Elizabeth had been writing and publishing fortnightly stories in *Household Words*, finalising family trips to London for Christmas then Paris in the new year while teasing out present ideas from her children, asking 19-year-old Marianne to find out what her sisters wanted, before reminding her to help their housekeeper fetch a hundred cards and more sprays of ivy to decorate the house.[14]

'If ever it should befall you to live a very still lonely life,' Charlotte practically cried to her after Christmas, 'which I believe it never will, for you are too genial to sink to the obscure lot, you will find once and again that the post shall bring you a letter … which warms you and makes you grateful to the heart's core.'[15]

Starved of all of that, of voices, affections, opinions, of news in letters to and from Ellen, George and William Smith Williams, of wit from Thackeray and Harriet, bereft of the company of Anne, Emily and Branwell and stymied into a painful truce with her father that cost her Arthur's love, Charlotte drifted into a stasis that winter, stranding her in a deeper solitude that was partly her tragedy and partly her fault.

The new year bells had barely stopped tolling before snow began to fall across England. Gales from the south-east battered the coast, sinking ships and drowning all on board. Further inland, relentless snow fell into nighttime, frosting at dawn before the next blizzard built drifts knee-deep in the streets and higher than a man in the country lanes. By the end of the first week of January 1854, the *Bradford Observer* recorded snowdrifts in Leeds 10 feet high and rising, warning that men had sunk to their chin in the shallower parts. Roads became impassable and trains were cancelled, postponing the mail coaches. Buried at the parsonage, Charlotte watched for a signal of human contact, the extension of any hand that could draw her out of the enveloping blankness of loneliness, as all around her England became, the papers said, 'cold as charity'.[16]

CHAPTER 8

1854

Providence

'Her thoughts and affections must really need control. It is an example of the dangerous gift such a mind as hers must be.'[1] One of Ellen's friends was gossiping to her about Charlotte.

They had not spoken since their argument the previous summer. Convinced Charlotte was betraying her own romantic ideals by settling for less than she deserved, Ellen thought she was making decisions out of desperation, whose consequences would bring her more problems than solutions. While justified, she should have known that Charlotte would not be easily defied. Charlotte, feeling Ellen should give up on insisting what was best for her and find a way to support her, saw Ellen's concerns as expressions of the same self-interested possessiveness as that of her father, interpreting her advice as a controlling desire to keep her at a disadvantage and obstruct what could be her last chance at marriage and motherhood. Both women were correct in their own ways, but their uncompromising refusal to listen to the other destroyed the equanimity of their lifelong friendship. By extending their points into arguments they made any reconciliation impossible without surrender.

Charlotte could disagree with both Ellen and her father, be disappointed by both, but she refused to continually argue with both so she cut off Ellen, an action Ellen's friends saw as the sad and reprehensible act of a desperate woman. 'You have suffered so much pain about her evidently,' one of Ellen's friends consoled her, 'now you are ready to forget all, I can see, and this is kind and right.'[2]

In January, seizing an opportunity to heal the rift, Margaret Wooler told Charlotte that Ellen was ill and urged her to reach out. Charlotte thanked her for using kind words which, as she put it, turned away her wrath, and wrote to her. Ellen's friends cautioned her about being too forgiving. 'It seemed unnatural that she could so throw off all her old friendship,' one told her, 'but she will not quite forget I hope, but will remember enough to see how your true friendship was shown.'[3] They began a cautious exchange of letters through February and into March. Charlotte asked after Ellen's mother and sisters. Ellen told her about her sister-in-law's sudden ill health. Charlotte described how Patrick had fared that winter and mentioned she had been to stay with Margaret. Neither raised the cause of their estrangement – Arthur – and performed a genteel dance, stepping carefully around the inflammatory subject to avoid another falling out. But an accident revealed everything.

On the last Monday in March, Charlotte opened an envelope from Ellen, expecting another move in this careful reconciliation. Instead, there was a note along with another letter in Charlotte's own handwriting. It was a personal letter she thought she had sent to Arthur. In a moment of distraction, she must have put it into an envelope already addressed to Ellen and sent it to her by mistake. Ellen read it before she realised it was for someone else and to Charlotte's mortification sent it back. The letter has not been preserved, but Charlotte explained, 'it was intended to relieve him from great anxiety.' She had been writing to both at the same time, she told her sheepishly, 'which I suppose accounts for the confusion'.[4] Neither would have been convinced by that as Charlotte was no stranger to writing to multiple correspondents on the same day. She said she had been suffering 'some days of indisposition and uneasiness … when I felt weak and unfit to write'. She was being guarded about the causes of what must have seemed to Ellen an inexplicable lapse by someone who had always been meticulous about her correspondence.

In truth, she was upset from the stress of arguing with her father about Arthur and her right to see him. Now she had been exposed, she could tell Ellen almost everything and divulged what happened since they last spoke and how Arthur had written to her all winter:

> The correspondence pressed on my mind. I grew very miserable in keeping it from Papa. At last sheer pain made me gather courage to break it – I told all. It was very hard and rough work at the time – but the issue after a few days was that I obtained leave to continue the communication.[5]

Arthur visited Haworth after Christmas, she explained, and having been granted permission by her father to meet and speak with him 'all I learnt inclined me to esteem and, if not love – at least affection. Still Papa was very, *very* hostile – bitterly unjust.'[6]

After relenting and giving her permission to meet Arthur, Patrick taunted Charlotte in private for demeaning herself with someone so impoverished. She protested:

> Father, I am not a young girl, not a young woman even. I never was pretty. I now am ugly. At your death I shall have £300 besides the little I have earned myself. Do you think there are many men who would serve seven years for me?[7]

Patrick let it drop until, unable to let his aggression subside, he asked why she had to marry a curate. She told him, 'Yes, I must marry a curate if I marry at all; not merely a curate but your curate; not merely your curate but he must live in the house with you, for I cannot leave you.' Patrick stood up to look down on her. 'Never,' he said, 'I will never have another man in this house.' He stalked out of the room and refused to speak to her for all the next week.[8]

The fights distressed her enough to leave her unable to write or even think coherently, resulting in her sending Arthur's letter to Ellen. Seeing Charlotte's anguish, Tabby confronted Patrick and asked him bluntly if he was trying to kill his daughter. He went past her, up to Charlotte's room and shouted at her for not wanting a man with 'more brass' in his pockets than Arthur.[9]

When they met again, Charlotte told Arthur all this and of the obstacles to extracting her from her life. He refused to be put off. It started to dawn on Charlotte, a woman used to creating walls around her that she had finally met someone willing to scale them. Arthur was proving to be a man who saw her defences and accepted their challenge, who refused to be intimidated by her father or be ruled by him. He was more stubborn and resolute than Charlotte herself. She told Ellen:

> He has persevered. The result of this, his last visit, is that Papa's consent is gained, that his respect, I believe, is won, for Mr Nicholls has in all things proved himself disinterested and forbearing. He has shown too that while his feelings are exquisitely keen he can freely forgive. Certainly I must respect him – nor can I withhold from him more than mere cool respect.[10]

She had one final thing for Ellen, a detail of great magnitude told with the brevity she used once before, when Jane Eyre revealed something similar for her reader: 'In fact, dear Ellen, I am engaged.'[11]

She asked her not to tell anyone and wrote to Margaret the next day that her father had not only been won round to having Arthur as his son-in-law but had offered him his old job back. Arthur wanted to marry in three months, she told her, then would move in with them. 'It gives me unspeakable content to see that now my Father has once admitted this new view of the case – he dwells on it complacently.' And Patrick's first priority – himself – would be met to such a degree that their marriage should barely trouble him. 'In all arrangements his convenience and seclusion will be scrupulously respected,' she told Margaret with more relief than pleasure.[12] 'Providence offers me this destiny,' she concluded. 'Doubtless then it is best for me.'[13] Four weeks later, she told Elizabeth she 'found herself' engaged. 'Things have progressed, I don't know how. It is of no use going into detail.' Other people were very glad about it, she said, and even her father and Arthur had been improved by her bringing them through the impasse in their relationship. Out of gratitude for being accepted, Arthur made a promise to Patrick that he would do everything he could to support him personally and professionally in his declining years. That made Patrick:

> cheerful and satisfied; he says he has been far too stern; he even admits that he was unjust – terribly unjust he certainly was for a time, but now all this is effaced from memory – now that he is kind again and declares himself happy and talks reasonably and without invective. I could almost cry sometimes[14]

Now she had made everyone else happy, Charlotte had to ask if she was too. In her novels, she imagined the transformative power romance had to pacify truculent spirits. Where Jane Eyre and Rochester brokered an equality between them, her own courtship had been essentially a battle of principles between her and those she was closest to; opposing her father to assert her right to self-determination and a relationship outside the duties he demanded of her, and beyond the limited perceptions both he and Ellen had of her as a daughter and a companion. She told Ellen, 'There is a strange half sad feeling in making these announcements. The whole thing is something other than imagination paints it beforehand: cares, fears, come mixed inextricably with hopes.'[15] Her victory of self-assertion proved only the iron of her perseverance and that, ultimately, she could prevail. More than anyone else, Charlotte Brontë already knew that.

'My destiny will not be brilliant,' she told both Ellen and Elizabeth, but quickly checked herself with a reminder that Arthur was 'conscientious, affectionate, pure in heart and life'.[16] Alerted by her tone of reservation Elizabeth turned to a friend, 'I have half a mind not to tell you ...' and nevertheless repeated everything Charlotte had told her. She wondered if, by agreeing to marry him, Charlotte was emboldening Arthur's less agree-able characteristics. 'I fancy him very good, but *very* stern and bigoted; but I daresay that is partly fancy. Still it arises from what she has told me.' His austere religious principles could ostracise Charlotte from her more liberal friends, Elizabeth worried. 'I am terribly afraid he won't let her go on being as intimate with us heretics. I see she is, too, a little.'[17] In another respect, she thought it good Charlotte would marry someone who knew Branwell, Emily and Anne. It would give them a shared history together that made planning their future less of an act of severance from her past. 'He sounds vehemently in love with her,' Elizabeth concluded, having supposed the alternative could have been someone momentarily dazzled by her genius. 'With all his bigotry and sternness it must be charming to be loved with all the strength of his heart as she sounds to be.' And that, she thought, might be exactly what Charlotte needed. 'She would never have been happy but with an exacting, rigid, law-giving, passionate man. Only, you see, I'm afraid one of his laws will be to shut us out.'[18] She wrote to Charlotte and told her to come stay with her for a few days the following week.

As news of her engagement got out, letters of congratulation began to arrive. Unexpectedly, one came from George Smith. Charlotte thanked him with a long awkward letter written in a tone of lapsed intimacy. She said she was glad to hear he got married. 'You never told me any particulars about her – though I should have liked them much – but did not like to ask questions.' In her case, she said, she had been pursued for years, 'and I hope that in at last acceding to it – I am acting right.' She must have wondered if she had mentioned Arthur to George before, especially in connection with the character she based on him in *Shirley*, for 'I fear I must accuse myself of having formerly done him less than justice.' Even to someone whom she had decided had become a stranger again, she could not forget how close they had once been for long enough to withhold her worries:

> I believe I do right in marrying him. I mean to try to make him a good wife. There has been heavy anxiety, but I begin to hope all will end for the best. My expectations, however, are very subdued, very different I daresay to what yours were before you were married. Care and Fear stand so close to Hope I sometimes scarcely can see her for the Shadow

they cast. And yet I am thankful too and the doubtful Future must be left with Providence.[19]

In her final paragraph, Charlotte made what must have sounded like a farewell to the literary world that had slipped through her fingers. Neither she nor George could know it would be precisely that. She asked him in emotionless terms to give her best wishes to his mother and sisters then turned again to this unknown wife, whose invisible power levered him away from her. 'I hardly know in what form of greeting to include your wife's name as I have never seen her. Say to her whatever may seem to you most appropriate and most expressive of good-will.' She sometimes thought of William Smith Williams, she said, and wondered if he was well, suggesting she had no expectations of hearing either about him or from him. In conclusion, she made it clear she thought her partnership with them was finished. 'In the course of the year that is gone Cornhill and London have receded a long way from me. The links of communication have waxed very frail and few. It must be so in this world.' If George got this far and wondered whether Charlotte was regretful, she made sure her final words were sharp enough to make him think twice. 'All things considered I don't wish it otherwise.'[20] They would never speak again.

Charlotte took the train from Keighley to Manchester on Monday, 1 May. She could only stay three days as she planned to spend the next two weeks with Joe and Amelia Taylor in Hunsworth and then with Ellen in Birstall. The next evening, Elizabeth invited a few guests to supper. Among them her two confidantes, Katie and Emily Winkworth, who had been gossiping about Charlotte for years since they all read *Jane Eyre*. Emily arrived first and met Charlotte, then Katie came later. Elizabeth introduced them and left them to talk. Privately she had kept them up to date with Charlotte's news, leaving Katie to wonder how she could say anything without letting on they had been talking about her. They let Charlotte ask questions until Katie thought she looked tired and made to go. Charlotte told her she hoped she would see her again before she left, so Katie decided to come back the next day. When she did, Elizabeth whispered she should say something about the engagement. As soon as they were alone, Katie told Charlotte, 'I was very glad to hear something Mrs. Gaskell told me about you.'
    'What was it?' asked Charlotte.

'That you are not going to be alone any more.'

Charlotte put her head on her hand and said, 'Yes, I am going to be married in June.'

'It will be a great happiness for you to have someone to care for and make happy.'

'Yes, and it is a great thing to be the first object with any one.'

She told Katie how highly Arthur was regarded by parishioners who sounded happy to have him back. Although she knew he was a worthy Christian and an admirable man, neither meant they matched personally. 'I cannot conceal from myself that he is not intellectual. There are many places into which he could not follow me intellectually.' She thought his religious opinions might limit her friends further than she had done already, by repelling those he disagreed with. Katie suggested the opposite might happen, that Charlotte might guide him. She replied, 'That is what I hope; he has a most sincere love of goodness wherever he sees it. I think if he could come to know Mr Gaskell it would change his feeling.'

Charlotte questioned her about her sister Susanna's marriage and while Katie would later say she thought Arthur sounded like half the man her brother-in-law was, Charlotte wanted to know details: whether he was selfish about small things, shared their economies or appreciated Susanna's endeavours and self-denials. Regardless of her prospects, she told Katie, she had resolved Arthur's 'love was too good to be thrown away by one so lonely' as she. Privately, Katie thought that despite her reservations Charlotte was making the best choice for herself. She told one of her friends she could imagine Charlotte developing an enduring relationship with a man with a stable temperament like Arthur's than with any of the Byronic heroes of her imagination, who might make her *feel* she was more in love with them than she was. Whoever had been the original of Paul Emanuel in *Villette*, Katie speculated, must surely have been her true love. Perhaps they were not together because he had been lost at sea as the ending of that novel suggests. She wondered if Charlotte had ever told Elizabeth anything about him.[21]

Elizabeth continued the conversation when Katie went home, listening to Charlotte describe her preparations which 'as she said, could neither be expensive nor extensive; consisting chiefly in a modest replenishing of her wardrobe, some repapering and repainting in the parsonage'.[22] Now there would be two clergymen in the house, they had agreed to create a study for Arthur, by converting a store room, rather than have him take over or share the existing study with Patrick. The three great writers of that house were never equipped with a study for any or all of them. Even once Charlotte was a success, she continued to write her novels on scraps of paper leaning on a portable desk she could hold in her lap. Elizabeth reflected, 'on this idea, and plans for his comfort, as well as her father's, her mind dwelt a good deal; and we talked them over with the same unwearying happiness which, I suppose, all women feel in such discussions.'[23]

'I wish you were here,' Charlotte told Ellen in June. The month opened 'sultry and electric' and as the prospect of her wedding drew nearer, she, her father and Arthur all became ill from anxiety. Patrick complained of intermittent deafness and was depressed. 'It was all I could do to keep him up and I own I was sad and apprehensive myself,' she confided. He was well enough to preach one day, then not the next. 'It is strange how he varies – how soon he is depressed and how soon revived. It makes me so thankful when he is better.'[24]

Having seen how she indulged and placated her father, Arthur broke the news to her that he was so ill he had seen the same doctor who had diagnosed her sister Anne with terminal tuberculosis. Knowing how death could decimate a household with a single cough, Charlotte was 'thoroughly frightened' and interrogated him about his symptoms. Exasperated, she explained to Ellen:

> In the first place – he could give his ailment no name. He had not had one touch of rheumatism – that report was quite groundless. He was going to die, however, or something like it. I took heart on hearing this, which may seem paradoxical, but you know dear Nell when people are really going to die they don't come a distance of some fifty miles to tell you so.[25]

The doctor said he was perfectly healthy and suffering only from an over-excited mind. As Charlotte nurtured her father at the expense of her own peace, through his vacillations of mood and physical discomfort, it now appeared Arthur was readying to expect the same. He soon learned what others had before him, not to mistake Charlotte's selflessness for subservience. 'In short I soon discovered that my business was, instead of sympathising, to rate him soundly.' He was, she reported to Ellen:

> Perfectly unreasonable, however, on some points, as his fallible sex are not ashamed to be, groaning over the prospect of a few more weeks of bachelorhood as much as if it were an age of banishment or prison. It is probable he will fret himself thin again in the time but I certainly shall not pity him if he does.[26]

Expressing weaknesses in the certainty of consolation was a luxury never afforded to her. In all her long years of loneliness, no one had come with words of assurance or encouragement. To her father she was an automaton of mercy, forever useful to minister more kind words and consolation, to be overlooked afterwards. Now another man expected the same. She told Ellen:

> There is not a woman in England but would have more sense, more courage, more sustaining hope than to behave so. Man is indeed an amazing piece of mechanism when you see – so to speak – the full weakness of what he calls his strength. There is not a female child above the age of eight but might rebuke him for the spoilt petulance of his wilful nonsense.[27]

Women like her, she raged, regardless of their capabilities or needs, were coerced into the roles of unpaid nursemaids for men who enjoyed comforts impossible for women to imagine. What many men regarded as commonplace entitlements would be exceptional if made by women.

On Friday, 9 June a box tied shut with a cord came from a Halifax dressmaker. Inside was a white muslin wedding dress and a lavender and silver silk 'going away' dress. Charlotte, once so hungry for mail that she often read and responded to letters on the same day, knew as soon as she opened that box the material reality of her marriage would be quite literally in her hands. She could not do it. Two days later she was still staring at it, telling Ellen she had no idea what its contents looked like.[28] Jane Eyre had been similarly unsettled. Her wedding dress brought the double-edged prospect of rescue and divorce from the only things she owned, her past and the self she forged from it.[29]

As the date kept shifting with the church schedule and last duties of the outgoing curate Arthur was replacing, Charlotte drafted eighteen announcement cards for friends but invited only two, Ellen and Margaret, asking them to keep it all secret, and explaining that Arthur 'enters into my wishes about having the thing done quietly in a way which makes me grateful and if nobody interferes and spoils his arrangements, he will manage so that not a soul in Haworth shall be aware'.[30]

Eventually, she chose the earliest time the ceremony could be conducted, at eight in the morning on Thursday, 29 June. Ellen and Margaret arrived the morning before, laid out the wedding dress she had finally unpacked and tried to calm her nerves. She was anxious about leaving her father, as ever, and explained the arrangements for him while she was away. As the household retired to bed after evening prayers, she returned to his study to say goodnight. Instantly, he shattered any possibility of a tender happy moment. He announced he had decided not to come to her wedding, so would not be giving her away. As a man who conducted them for a living, he knew how this would thwart one due to start in eleven hours. Charlotte fled to Margaret and Ellen for a solution – one that Patrick knew and kept quiet – and while she later excused this as another episode of his ever-recurring debilitation, only cured by her cancelling plans, his heartlessness could not have been lost on them. They described the crisis to Elizabeth:

> What was to be done? Who was to give the bride away? There were only to be the officiating clergyman, the bride and bridegroom, the brides-maid, and Miss Wooler present. The Prayer Book was referred to; and there it was seen that the Rubric enjoins that the Minister shall receive 'the woman from her father's or *friend's* hands', and that nothing is speci-fied as to the sex of the 'friend'. So Miss Wooler, ever kind in emergency, volunteered to give her old pupil away.[31]

Their level-headedness to look for a solution in the *Book of Common Prayer* is testimony to their care and protectiveness of Charlotte, ensuring Patrick could not damage her plans now, no matter what he tried. In her only letter surviving from her wedding day, Charlotte does not mention her father to Ellen, as she normally did, but instead asks she give her 'kindest and most grateful love' to Margaret.[32]

The next morning, Charlotte, Ellen and Margaret waited in the par-lour for word the bridegroom was on his way. Arthur had to walk across the moors from Rev. Joseph Grant's house in Oxenhope where he stayed overnight with his only guest, Rev. Sutcliffe Sowden, who was perform-ing the ceremony. John Brown got a local teenager to wait on the hill top behind the parsonage until he saw them approach, then run to the parsonage to tell the women it was time to leave. While the boy fetched the parish clerk, the women walked down the lane to the church on what Charlotte described as 'that dim quiet June morning'. Within half an hour she went from Charlotte Brontë, a 'spinster' of 'no rank or profession', as she was described in the record, to clergyman's wife. She signed her new name, Charlotte Nicholls, in the vestry witnessed by Ellen and Margaret and left with Arthur by the back door. The party returned to the house where, at a table Ellen had decorated with posies of wildflowers gathered by Martha, they ate a reception breakfast of boiled ham. Martha remembered how

Patrick, now recovered from the debilitation that lasted until the moment the wedding ended, joined them and 'behaved well in his grandiloquent manner'.[33] Shortly afterwards, a coach pulled by a pair of horses arrived at the gate and took Charlotte and Arthur off for a train to North Wales and the start of their honeymoon.

By lunchtime, after the curates had gone, Patrick was left with his daughter's two friends. He lapsed into doubt about losing Charlotte to marriage, hoping to draw commiseration from Ellen. A week later, he wrote to thank her for offering him 'kind and considerate' counsel, a remarkable act of humility for the indomitable father of the village to an unmarried woman his daughter's age. Interestingly, no comparable note survives to Margaret, a shrewd woman of his own generation, possibly indicating she was less indulgent. He told Ellen, 'You are perfectly right in what you say respecting the usual effects of changes in regard to those far advanced in years.' The old, he wrote, are often burdened by minor transitory concerns about the present and future that time proves to be groundless.

Ellen would not have been surprised that Patrick agreed about having to adjust to changes and navigate the vicissitudes of life. Had he not been so vainly self-absorbed he might have recognised her words. They were, after all, his own. She was repeating the lecture he gave Charlotte the previous June when he thought he had dispatched Arthur from her life for good. Sweetly and with such impeccable courtesy that her sting was lost on him, Ellen gave this man who had felt no obligation to accompany his last child to her wedding, a sharp taste of his own medicine. 'The old villain!' she wrote years later, 'I can never think of this episode without the most contemptuous feeling.'[34]

Charlotte's new life, solemnised that morning and budding unseen by those who had until now been closest to her, gave both Patrick and Ellen much to think about and little, it seems, to celebrate. 'I hope that under Providence the change that has occurred, in my case, will be for the good of all parties concerned – in reference both to time,' Patrick told Ellen, 'And eternity.'[35]

Part Two

Departing

(1854–1857)

CHAPTER 9

1854

A Strange and Perilous Thing

A few days after the new Mr and Mrs Nicholls left Haworth, a remarkable misprint appeared in the local papers. The *Leeds Mercury* marriage announcements reported the Rev. Arthur Bell Nicholls had married Charlotte, the only daughter of 'Patrick Pronte'.[1] It also misreported the minister as 'Lowden' rather than Sowden, but misspelling 'Brontë' would have carried meaning for Patrick and Charlotte, inadvertently echoing their name to its earlier form, 'Prunty'. It is ironic that as Charlotte took her first uncertain steps into a contested future, traces of her long-buried family past still surfaced.

The couple left Keighley by train, travelling west through Lancashire then south to Conwy on the north coast of Wales. They had 'a pleasant enough journey' Charlotte reported when they arrived at a coaching inn round the corner from the station, even when the overcast day turned wet and wild. She and Arthur 'sheltered' together indoors, she said, in the first hint that intimacy was blossoming between them.[2] The next day they took the train to Bangor for the weekend. 'The weather was not very favourable there,' she wrote, 'yet by making the most of opportunity we contrived to see some splendid scenery. One drive indeed from Llanberis to Beddgelert surpassed anything I remember of the Lakes.'[3]

On Monday, 3 July they left for Anglesey, stayed overnight then went on to Holyhead harbour for the morning steamer across St George's Channel to Kingstown (called Dún Laoghaire after 1921) for a connecting train to Dublin. There they spent two days, with Arthur showing Charlotte around his alma mater, Trinity College, and its chapel where he started his ecclesiastical career. On the second day, they were joined by some of Arthur's family: his 38-year-old elder brother Alan and two cousins, Joseph Bell – a student in his final year at Trinity – and 24-year-old Mary Anna

Bell. Charlotte found them all to be pleasant and welcoming. The men, she said, seemed 'thoroughly educated gentlemen'.[4] She found Alan 'sagacious, well-informed and courteous', considered Joseph academically gifted and Mary Anna 'a pretty lady like girl with gentle English manners'. She made a similar observation about their widowed mother, the 53-year-old Mrs Harriette Adamson Bell, when she met her at the end of the week, expressing some relieved surprise that the whole family seemed more English than Irish, challenging an expectation she brought with her to Ireland. 'I had heard a great deal about Irish negligence,' she explained, suggesting someone had tried to discourage or unsettle her by telling her the Irish might be inhospitable to an Englishwoman like her. Trollope had noticed this when he brought his Yorkshire wife to Banagher ten years earlier. He lived and worked in southern Ireland until the end of the 1850s and thought his neighbours acted slighted by his choice of an English wife and warned him to choose either Catholic or Protestant associates but not a mixture of both. He was not a man to be intimated and wrote off the locals as generally 'perverse, irrational, and but little bound by the love of truth'.[5]

Charlotte experienced nothing comparable. Meeting her husband's family was remarkable in two respects. The first would only be realised by those who outlived her and was the kind of auspicious detail she herself would have appreciated in fiction: with Mary Anna she had shaken hands with the woman her husband would go on to marry years after her death. Memories of Charlotte would remain with Mary Anna until the end of her life, as did the excitement they all felt at meeting the renowned author of *Jane Eyre*.

The second was instantly noticeable to Charlotte: she had lost her shyness. Meeting strangers with her husband brought none of the turmoil it caused her in all the years of her solitude. The anxieties that plagued her on visits to London, Manchester and the Lake District in the last few years had completely disappeared. Her terror of new faces and new opportunities to be scrutinised, sidelined or ridiculed that crippled her all her adult life, that crushed days under the oppression of anxious anticipation about going amongst people, that made her recoil at parties and hide behind curtains, had vanished. Remarkably, from this point on, she never refers to it again in her letters. Only one change in her life had brought this: marriage. With Arthur standing between her and the world, being diligently attentive to her, she lost her vulnerability and terror of interacting with strangers. Her honeymoon brought Charlotte an intimacy and protection missing from her life until then and her only challenge was to accept it. Embraced by

Arthur's attentiveness, she felt drawn out of the introverted isolation she had passed most of her life. The barrier between her and the outer world had been breached in the way she had hoped, by love. Just not the kind she imagined for herself or her heroines.

Her husband was no Byronic hero like Edward Rochester or Paul Emanuel; he was real. Arthur was a dark, stoutly built man, pragmatic about details and impatient with irrelevancies. But amongst his family and out of the context of his officiating duties as her father's understudy at Haworth, she could see him as other unbiased people saw him. 'My dear husband,' Charlotte could call him now:

> appears in a new light here in his own country. More than once I have had deep pleasure in hearing his praises on all sides. Some of the old servants and followers of the family tell me I am a most fortunate person for that I have got one of the best gentlemen in the country. His aunt too speaks of him with a mixture of affection and respect most gratifying to hear.[6]

She saw and felt his devoted love for her and hoped she could nurture something similar in tribute, in gratitude for what sounded to her like an act of mercy. In the first week of her marriage, Charlotte found herself the primary focus, for the first time ever, of someone who loved her. Now she was called for, escorted, held, kissed, protected, guided – receiving the loving attention she had bestowed on others without any return of affection. Unused to the happy conclusion of fulfilled hopes, she did not know what to do next. She told Ellen, 'Much pleasure has sprung from all this, and more, perhaps, from the kind and ceaseless protection which has ever surrounded me, and made travelling a different matter to me from what it has heretofore been.'[7] Arthur had changed her perspective forever. While it pacified her, the experience also brought enough new impressions for reflection. She told Ellen that marriage – or rather being in an intimate relationship – had left her 'a good deal changed: I know more of the realities of life than I once did. I think many false ideas are propagated – perhaps unintentionally.'[8]

Two weeks into their marriage, she had lost the doubts she once had and grew in certainty that she had, by the grace of God, made the right choice 'and I pray to be enabled to repay as I ought, the affectionate devotion of a truthful, honourable, unboastful man'.[9] For the first time, she was becoming indebted to someone else's unselfish kindness. As its consolation transformed her, it drew new and unfamiliar feelings that helped begin to restore her sense of self. 'It is a solemn and strange and perilous thing for a woman to become a wife. Man's lot is far, far different,' she told Ellen. Out of habit she signed her surname as 'Brontë'. She scored it out and wrote 'Nicholls'.

Notes of congratulation followed the couple throughout their honeymoon, which Charlotte collected in packets from the nearest post offices. She intended to acknowledge them all but had so little time to herself she could only dash off one letter a week for the first three weeks, then caught up with three more in the days before they came back. 'I scribble one hasty line,' she told Ellen, and eleven days later told Margaret, 'I feel that it is time to give some account of myself,' as though she knew she had been missing.[10] If she wrote any other letters – to her father for example – they have been lost.

Typically, Katie Winkworth could not wait for Charlotte to get home from her honeymoon and used gossip about Elizabeth to resume their discussion from Plymouth Grove to see if Charlotte's feelings for Arthur had changed (presumably so she could broadcast it back to her friends). Katie knew Elizabeth thought Charlotte and Arthur were asymmetric and would be incompatible had it not been for Charlotte's need for companionship. 'I do fear a *little* for her happiness,' she told a friend, 'just because he is narrow and she is not. Good, true, pure and affectionate he is, but he is also narrow, and she can never be so.'[11] Charlotte admitted as much in her reply to Katie. 'My husband is not a poet or a poetical man,' she explained, 'and one of my grand doubts before marriage was about "congenial tastes" and so on.'[12] With no distance between her and Arthur now, she could have little doubt his devotion and protection were worth more than the poetical spirit she once imagined heroic lovers needed. Elizabeth thought about writing to Charlotte too but held back for fear her confidences would be compromised. 'Miss Brontë is married, and I ought to write to her,' she told one friend, 'but I've a panic about the husband seeing my letters. Bridegrooms are always curious; husbands are not.'[13]

From Dublin, Arthur's brother and the Bell cousins took Charlotte and Arthur back to their family home in Banagher, roughly in the centre of Southern Ireland, south of the Shannon. There, Arthur had grown up with his aunt and uncle and his cousins. Their house, Cuba Court, stood on land a couple of miles from the centre of town. It was a tall square neoclassical building dating from the 1730s with an orchard and outbuildings, looking to Charlotte like a gentleman's country seat.[14] On the long carriage drive through the grounds she – indeed both she and Arthur – might well have recalled her father's acrimony towards him. Patrick assumed Arthur was from a lower social rank than he, mocked his lack of 'brass' and standing and dismissed Arthur's meek rebuttals as lies to win over Charlotte, who he thought was demeaning herself with an opportunist. As Charlotte knew Patrick's childhood home had been an earth-floored farm cottage, she could see her husband's early life could not have been more different from his, or for that matter from the childhood her father had given her. Here was no plainer answer to Charlotte's doubt about her father's judgement. 'Most of the rooms are lofty and spacious,' Charlotte breathlessly described:

> and some, the drawing room, the dining room etc. – handsomely and commodiously furnished. The passages look desolate and bare. Our bedroom, a great room on the ground floor, would have looked gloomy when we were shown into it but for the turf fire that was burning in the wide old chimney.[15]

She had been suffering from a cold since the day of her wedding and was put to bed by Arthur's aunt Harriette, who nursed her with 'kindness and skill' until she recovered.

They stayed there a week ('I must say, I like my new relations') until Charlotte felt better, before embarking on a two-week tour. They travelled south-west along the Shannon to explore the area around the coastal town of Kilkee in County Clare. Quartered in an inadequate hotel, the couple found much they could have complained about but with a notably uncharacteristic lightness of spirit Charlotte reported, 'we laugh instead of grumbling.'[16] Sharing the experience with Arthur minimised any inconveniences they encountered into absurdities that amused them both and sent them outdoors on to the magnificent panorama of cliffs overhanging the Atlantic. They agreed the coast at Kilkee was the most magnificent they had ever seen. 'Completely girdled with stupendous cliffs,' wrote Arthur, 'it was most refreshing to sit on a rock and look out on the broad Atlantic boiling and foaming at our feet.'[17] When Charlotte edged away from him to absorb the scene alone, she noticed his respectful protection:

> We went out on to the cliffs and saw the Atlantic coming in all white foam, I did not know whether I should get leave or time to take the matter in my own way. I did not want to talk – but I *did* want to look and be silent. Having hinted a petition, licence was not refused – covered with a rug to keep off the spray I was allowed to sit where I chose – and he only interrupted me when he thought I crept too near the edge of the

cliff. So far he is always good in this way – and this protection which does not interfere 'or pretend – ' is I believe a thousand times better than any half sort of pseudo sympathy. I will try with God's help to be as indulgent to him wherever indulgence is needed.[18]

From Kilkee they travelled east, inland along the Shannon Estuary to Limerick and probably stayed there overnight, then west back along its opposite side to Tarbert. After another overnight stay they went south-west to Tralee, then in their last week went south-east again to Killarney. Its beauty so overwhelmed Charlotte, she found it impossible to describe.

Around Friday, 21 July, a guide took them riding through the Gap of Dunloe, a ravine of pools and streams between some of Ireland's highest mountains. When they approached a dangerously broken pass strewn with rocks, their guide advised them to dismount and proceed on foot. Arthur did but Charlotte stayed in the saddle, confident she could guide her horse step by step. The horse became increasingly nervous and slipped. Arthur came to its head to try to calm it, but it was too startled and reared up, throwing Charlotte off its back. As Arthur made to restrain the horse, Charlotte tumbled between its kicking legs. In the confusion of rocks and hooves she knew in that moment one kick would kill her:

> I had my thoughts about that moment – its consequences – my husband – my father. When my plight was seen, the struggling creature was let loose, she sprung over me. I was lifted off the stones neither bruised by the fall nor touched by the mare's hooves. Of course, the only feeling left was gratitude.[19]

Their next overnight stop was in the little harbour town of Glengarriff, then following the line of the coast south they diverted inland, eastwards to Cork. 'I shall make no effort to describe the scenery through which we have passed,' she told Ellen when she stole a moment to write. 'Some parts have exceeded all I ever imagined.'[20] After a few days, they took the train to Dublin for the weekend before they began the journey back to Haworth. Before they left, Charlotte wrote to tell Martha when they would get home and confide that her father had never been far from her thoughts. Her anxiety for him:

> followed me all through my journey and made me miserable sometimes when otherwise I should have been happy enough. I longed to come

home a fortnight since though perhaps it would not have done much good and I was sure that you would do your best for him.[21]

She told her they would get back on Tuesday night and asked if she could prepare a late supper for them. As the prospect of home loomed, Charlotte weighed up the conflict of homesickness with the desire for flight she had experienced for decades. Now, she knew she would return to a home changed permanently by her marriage.

Once back at the parsonage, they were plunged into the activities and duties of their newly combined lives. Charlotte thought her father looked thinner and older and considered him too weak to work, an opinion challenged by the vicar of Bradford when he visited a few weeks later and said Patrick had not aged a day since he last saw him a year before. Nevertheless, Arthur assumed Patrick's responsibilities and undertook all the church services until Charlotte contacted the curate of Skipton to ask if he could help. On top of this, Arthur gave religious instruction to the pupils of the weekday National School every morning between nine and ten thirty, gave midweek lectures at the Haworth Mechanics' Institute and spent his afternoons visiting the poor and sick of the parish. 'Each time I see Mr Nicholls put on gown or surplice – I feel comforted to think that this marriage has secured Papa good aid in his old age,' she wrote. Arthur's diligence and dedication demanded the same from her. 'My own life is more occupied than it used to be,' she told Margaret, 'I have not so much time for thinking: I am obliged to be more practical, for my dear Arthur is a very practical as well as a very punctual, methodical man.'[22]

Demands on their attention were immediate, with callers and stacks of letters. Wishing to thank the villagers, Charlotte and Arthur organised a supper in the schoolroom beside the parsonage. Pupils, teachers, bellringers, the choristers and other parishioners came and when one toasted Arthur as a 'true Christian and a kind gentleman', Charlotte was touched enough to conclude that such a husband was 'better than to earn either Wealth or Fame or Power'. Having him elevated beyond her expectations, she wondered if it was she who was not yet worthy of him.[23] As her contemplative solitary life ended, so did the luxury of scheduling her own time:

Marriage certainly makes a difference in some things and amongst others the disposition and consumption of time. I really seem to have had scarcely a spare moment ... Not that I have been hurried or oppressed but the fact is my time is not my own now; somebody else wants a good portion of it and says we must do so and so. We do 'so and so' accordingly, and it generally seems the right thing – only I sometimes wish that I could have written the letter as well as taken the walk.[24]

She told Ellen she was not troubled by having little time for herself now, as a wife's duties distracted her from the thinking that dogged her before:

My life is changed indeed: to be wanted continually, to be constantly called for and occupied seems so strange: yet it is a marvellously good thing. As yet I don't quite understand how some wives grow so selfish. As far as my experience of matrimony goes, I think it tends to draw you out of and away from yourself.[25]

A relationship, Charlotte came to conclude, was the curative for much that ailed her single female friends and began to intimate solutions to those she had previously admired as independent. Reviving the kind of matchmaking they did when they were younger, Charlotte told Ellen the brother of the vicar who married them was interested in her.[26] And to 62-year-old Margaret she wrote:

I wish, my dear Miss Wooler *you* had some kind, faithful companion to enliven your Solitude at Richmond, some friend to whom to communicate your pleasure in the Scenery, the fine weather, the pleasant walks. You never complain, never murmur, never seem otherwise than thankful, but I know you must miss a privilege none could more keenly appreciate than yourself.[27]

Charlotte wanted everyone to have the security she now felt, never considering that not everyone felt they lacked it. She invited Ellen to stay but cautioned her things had changed. 'Take warning, Ellen – the married woman can call but a very small portion of each day her own. Not that I complain ...'[28] Her husband was thriving, she said, and even her father's health had stabilised. About herself, she was as self-deprecating as she often was with Ellen when she felt light hearted. 'I think I am decent – better certainly than I was two months ago, but people don't compliment me as they do Arthur.' To ensure she did not alienate her too much, she added an evocative description of the moors, harking back to the setting of the familiar long ago, when Ellen joined her with Branwell, Emily and Anne on walks:

The moors are in glory. I never saw them fuller of purple bloom. I wanted you to see them at their best. They are just turning now and in another week I fear, will be faded and sere. As soon as ever you can leave home be sure to write and let me know.[29]

At the parsonage, Ellen encountered a different household from the one she was used to. Significantly, Charlotte was calmer and seemed happy. At one point in her fortnight with them, Ellen joined Charlotte and Arthur for a walk on the moors and asked Charlotte if she was writing anything. She may have known Charlotte had started a new novel provisionally entitled *Emma* the previous winter. Charlotte told her she was not. 'Arthur says I have no time for writing now, as I must attend to my duties as a clergyman's wife.' Catching up with Arthur, Ellen challenged him on how he could justify preventing her from writing. He told her, 'I did not marry Currer Bell, the novelist, but Charlotte Brontë, the clergyman's daughter. Currer Bell may fly to heaven tomorrow for anything I care.'[30] Arthur may have been trying to say his love for Charlotte was not influenced by her fame, or repelled by her notoriety, but went beyond public demonstrations of talent to meet the real woman she was. But his separation of the woman from the writer told Ellen he saw both as conflicting identities, and she feared Charlotte might have to agree with him. Having known her since she was a girl, she understood the woman and the writer were one and the same and that Arthur's assumptions ran contrary to her ambitions. She began to suspect, with more evidence yet to collect, that his inadequacy was turning into a need to control.

Though Ellen was shocked enough to remember his words for decades to come, she may have heard something similar from Charlotte herself, as Charlotte told Margaret she imagined marriage would necessarily end her years as a literary novelty and, believing her ration of happiness was balanced by Providence, must choose between fame or domestic contentment.[31] Yet this should not be interpreted as her retirement from writing. She had Elizabeth's example of managing roles as a cleric's wife and a mother with being a successful novelist, all the while publishing anonymously.

She returned to the draft of *Emma*. 'We all seek an ideal in life,' she began, narrating in the voice of not only a married woman, but a widow.[32] Arthur recalled:

One evening at the close of 1854 as we sat by the fire listening to the howling of the wind around the house my poor wife suddenly said, 'If you had not been with me I must have been writing now.' She then ran upstairs, brought down and read aloud the beginning of her New Tale. When she had finished, I remarked 'The Critics will accuse you of repetition, as you have again introduced a school.' She replied, 'O I shall alter that – I always begin two or three times before I can please myself.' But it was not to be.[33]

Decades later, he made an 'unqualified contradiction' of Ellen's anecdote about him not marrying Currer Bell and told this story again to demonstrate he did not stop Charlotte from writing. He said he had 'no recollection whatsoever of any such incident as that related … on the authority of Miss Nussey – it is quite untrue that I ever objected to another book being written by my wife.'[34] But his retelling has a significant difference to how he told it originally. In his attempt at self-defence, he left out something he knew would have agreed with Ellen's version of events: that Charlotte said she would have been writing had it not been for him.

A few weeks later, Charlotte and Ellen were exchanging gossipy letters about their mutual friends when Charlotte casually told her Arthur habitually read Ellen's letters over her shoulder and did not approve of how freely they wrote to one another:

> Men don't seem to understand making letters a vehicle of communication – they always seem to think us incautious. I'm sure I don't think I have said anything rash; however, you must *burn* it when read. Arthur says such letters as mine never ought to be kept – they are dangerous as lucifer matches, so be sure to follow a recommendation he has just given, 'fire them' or 'there will be no more.' Such is his resolve. I can't help laughing – this seems to me so funny, Arthur, however, says he is quite serious and looks it.[35]

Ellen was furious. When she fired back an incredulous response, Charlotte reiterated that Arthur was not joking and needed an unambiguous promise from her to burn her letters. 'He says you must give him a plain pledge to that effect, or he will read every line I write and elect himself censor of our correspondence.' She said Arthur was worried her letters might end up in others' hands, evidently unaware how Ellen and Charlotte often shared friends' letters with each other, and that she must go so far as to sign an agreement to this effect. 'Write him out his promise on a separate slip of paper, in a legible hand – and send it in your next.'[36]

That Charlotte should now accept demands meant to limit the friendship she cherished since girlhood both alarmed and dismayed Ellen. To show

Arthur he was in no position to instruct her the way he felt at liberty to do with Charlotte, she wrote back in the sweet, firm tone she used once with Patrick, to demand a reciprocal agreement. She addressed it to 'The Reverend, the Magister' in sarcastic acknowledgement of his assumption of authority over them both. On a separate sheet to her letter to Charlotte, she wrote:

> My dear Mr Nicholls, 'As you seem to hold in great horror the *arden-tia verba* [burning words] of feminine epistles, I pledge myself to the destruction of Charlotte's 'epistles' henceforth if You pledge *yourself* to *no* censorship in the matter communicated. Yours very truly, E. Nussey.[37]

Charlotte did not pick up on her anger and replied gladly that Arthur thanked her for her promise and told her he said they were now free to 'write any dangerous stuff we please to each other. It is not "old friends" he mistrusts, but the chances of war – the accidental passing of letters into hands and under eyes for which they were never written.'[38]

Arthur's new censoriousness might have been provoked less by a mistrust of Ellen and more by a realisation that Charlotte being indiscreet risked both their reputations if she became known as the curate's gossiping wife. It was remiss of them both not to see how Ellen could receive this without injury. It must have been apparent to her they were not considering the implications of Arthur's demand as Charlotte tried to laugh it off:

> All this seems mighty amusing to me: it is a man's mode of viewing cor-respondence … They may be right in a sense. Strange chances do fall out certainly. As to my own notes I never thought of attaching importance to them or considering their fate – till Arthur seemed to reflect on both so seriously.[39]

Quickly, she changed the subject back to matchmaking and told her Arthur's clerical friends, the Sowden brothers, stayed overnight and the younger asked after her. Having none of it, Ellen said nothing in response. A pencil note added by her years later reads: 'Mr N continued his censor-ship, so the pledge was void.' He had no idea that Ellen had preserved more than 500 letters from Charlotte, many indiscreet and confessional, and had no intention of burning any of them. Their argument, laid to rest for the moment, would come to haunt both in the years to come.

✐

Charlotte spent the last months of 1854 looking ahead. She made plans for the start of the new year and as always concerned herself with the well-being of parishioners, friends and their families. She was occupied by visitors around the anniversaries of Branwell and Emily's deaths in late autumn and winter and was heartened her father and husband got along as though their early disagreements had never happened, as they canvassed together for the National Patriotic Fund to aid widows and veterans of the Crimea. 'Papa continues pretty well, I am happy to say,' she told Ellen, 'and my dear boy flourishes.'[40] She marvelled at Arthur's heartiness and stout good health, which must have seemed miraculous in a house where there had been so much infirmity and sickness. Every morning, in all weathers, Arthur took a walk before breakfast, running up the slope behind the parsonage then swinging his arms and beating his chest to rouse his circulation. By the time he got back to the schoolroom for morning scripture, he would be so overheated he opened all the windows, freezing the other teachers and children. They thought him spartan and hard but could not deny his conscientiousness and dedication.[41]

He believed activity, fresh air and exercise would encourage the same vigour in Charlotte and one day at the end of November interrupted her writing to invite her on a walk on the moors. As recent snows were thawing, the waterfall a few miles away would be flooded with melting ice water. Charlotte told Ellen the next day:

> I had often wanted to see it in its winter power, so we walked on. It was fine indeed: a perfect torrent raving over the rocks white and bountiful. It began to rain while we were watching it and we returned home under a streaming sky. However, I enjoyed the walk inexpressibly and would not have missed the spectacle on any account.[42]

They were soaked by the time they got home and even though Charlotte changed she developed the start of a cold later that night. As it worsened over the next week, Arthur insisted she put off the visit to Ellen. Before their marriage she would not have thought twice about going but with someone else making the decisions about her welfare it was impossible:

> If it just depended on me, I should come but these matters are not quite in my power now: another must be consulted and where his wish and judgment have a decided bias to a particular course I make no stir, but just adopt it. Arthur is sorry to disappoint both you and me, but it is his fixed

wish that a few weeks should be allowed yet to elapse before we meet. Probably he is confirmed in this desire by my having a cold at present.[43]

She proposed seeing Ellen in the new year and, thinking further ahead, James Kay-Shuttleworth, who dropped by in the autumn with ideas about clerical vacancies that might suit Arthur. Now separated from his wife, James had been living alone at Gawthorpe since Janet's doctor advised her to remain in the German spa town of Bad Homburg with Rosa Poplawska, and as far away from her husband as possible, for the good of her health. James read Charlotte some of the novel he had written about an idealised version of himself and proposed the same to Elizabeth. She had not seen Elizabeth since she came to stay the previous autumn and wondered whether she could come once the serialisation of *North and South* ended in the summer. 'I wish she'd write to me,' Elizabeth told Katie Winkworth. 'Should I, to her? Last time I wrote it was a sort of explanation of my way of looking at her Church (the Establishment) and religion; intended for her husband's benefit. She has never answered it.'[44]

At Christmas, Charlotte's wishes to Ellen speak of her unmistakable contentment:

> Arthur joins me in sincere good wishes for a happy Christmas & many of them to you and yours. He is well, thank God, and so am I, and he is 'my dear boy' certainly, dearer now than he was six months ago. In three days, we shall actually have been married that length of time!'[45]

Her cold started to subside over the new year but she did not fully recover. As it lessened, a new set of unfamiliar symptoms began to emerge. In the first weeks of January, her six months of uninterrupted stable health came to an end as something that felt like an unshakable indigestion took hold. She tried to explain it to Ellen:

> My health has been really very good ever since my return from Ireland till about ten days ago, when the stomach seemed quite suddenly to lose its tone – indigestion and continual faint sickness have been my portion ever since. Don't conjecture, dear Nell, for it is too soon yet, though I certainly never before felt as I have done lately. But keep the matter wholly to yourself.[46]

She could not put it into words just yet, as it may have seemed impossible, but she strongly suspected that against any expectations she might have had until now, she was pregnant.

CHAPTER 10

1855

Spring Flowers

Charlotte persevered through the first frozen weeks of 1855. She and Arthur paid a few days' visit to James at Gawthorpe, taking strolls in the damp grounds that exacerbated her cold, then, once home at the parsonage, hosted one of Arthur's cousins over from Ireland. She grew more tired as the weeks passed, found she could not stomach food and vomited every day until nausea and fatigue meant she had to confine herself to bed. By 20 January, she had become too feverish to write letters and dictated replies to Arthur who cancelled her rescheduled visit to Ellen. As letters for her continued to arrive, he and Patrick both had to pick up the responsibility of replying to them without consulting her. Arthur brought in the young local surgeon, Dr Amos Ingham, who told him her symptoms would settle down over the next few weeks.[1] Being dissatisfied, he sent for a second opinion of 'better advice than Haworth affords' from a Bradford doctor, William MacTurk. He agreed with Ingham: Charlotte was in the early stages of pregnancy and her body would adjust in time.[2] In response to his concerns, Patrick told James that Charlotte was still confined to bed 'where she still lies, oppress'd with nausea, sickness, irritation, and a slow feverish feeling and a consequent want of appetite and digestion.' Both doctors thought 'her sickness is symptomatic and that after a few weeks they hope her health will again return. Nevertheless, the trying circumstance gives much uneasiness in our little family circle.'[3]

To Arthur, it must have felt as though the entire household was being struck down, as by this point only he and Martha were still standing. Not only was Charlotte desperately sick, but Patrick was developing his recurrent bronchitis and their elderly housekeeper, Tabby, had grown so poorly since before Christmas that Martha arranged for her to move in with relatives a few streets away.

Becoming more alarmed, Ellen offered to come to Haworth to help but Patrick and Arthur advised her it would be too much for Charlotte and to hold off until she was better. On Valentine's Day, Arthur told her the cause of Charlotte's sickness was still undetermined – an indication perhaps that he did not trust the diagnoses or felt a confirmation of pregnancy should come from Charlotte herself – and that 'she is completely prostrated with weakness & sickness & frequent fever. All may turn out well in the end, & I hope it will.'[4] His wife was in no state for a visitor, he explained, suggesting he thought Ellen meant to be entertaining rather than helpful, and insisted if she saw Charlotte she would see for herself she was not capable of anything. Unhappy with this, Ellen appears to have tried Patrick, only to be told the same.

Unable to keep from vomiting any food and drink she was fed, Charlotte quickly became malnourished. Nineteen-year-old Tabitha Brown was brought in to assist with the household duties of cleaning and cooking while her older sister Martha nursed Charlotte. She remembered Charlotte had become so worn and thin that her hands were almost transparent if she held them up to the light:

> Her face was so drawn that she looked like a little old woman. It was pitiful to see her, for food would not stay with her. When her father came into the room she put forth all her strength and said 'See papa, I am a little better: don't you think I look better?' The poor old vicar could not agree.[5]

Without nourishment she failed. Her vomiting became severe enough to contain traces of blood. As she deteriorated and grew more incapable, the family pulled help from anyone who could offer it. Martha and Tabitha were joined by the family's laundress and seamstress, a local woman in her thirties named Hannah Dawson.[6] The Brown sisters tried to encourage Charlotte whenever she was awake by talking about the prospect of her baby. They remembered Charlotte saying, 'I dare say I shall be glad some day, but oh I'm so ill and tired.'[7] At times she mustered enough strength to write a few brief notes to friends. 'No kinder better husband than mine it seems to me can there be in the world,' she told one. 'I do not want now for kind companionship in health and the tenderest nursing in sickness.'[8]

Certain now of Arthur's devotion and 'mindful of my own mortality' she formalised her feelings in return and decided to make provision for him in a new will.[9] It reversed her marriage settlement that would have seen her estate pass to her father should he survive her. Now she entrusted everything to Arthur, leaving him her entire estate on the understanding that he would look after Patrick should she be unable. A further clause that made provision for any child of hers that might survive shows she had not entirely given up on a future in which she might bear a 'child or children'. Her father and Martha witnessed her shakily signing it in bed on Tuesday, 17 February.

A week later, she was able to write to Ellen and told her that her father was feeling better, but they were upset that Tabby had died and was already buried. She dictated a note to another friend a few days later:

> Let me speak the plain truth – my sufferings are very great – my nights indescribable – sickness with scarce a reprieve – I strain until what I vomit is mixed with blood. Medicine I have quite discontinued – If you *can* send me anything that will do good – *do*. As to my husband – my heart is knit to him – he is so tender, so good, helpful, patient.[10]

The recipient sent her more medicines regardless: none helped. At the start of March, Charlotte, gaunt from dehydration, scratched a note to Ellen in pencil that she was now so weak and hoarse from coughing she could barely speak above a whisper and had become as thin as one of Ellen's other friends who had suffered during pregnancy:

> I am reduced to greater weakness – the skeleton emaciation is the same … I cannot talk. Even to my dear patient constant Arthur I can say but few words at once. These last two days I have been somewhat better and have taken some beef tea, spoonsful of wine & water, a mouthful of light pudding at different times.[11]

She rallied for a couple of days before deterioration began, and she drifted back into the fog of apathetic bewilderment brought by severe urinary infections. She murmured a little while she was awake and tried to tell her father she was not suffering. On Saturday morning, 31 March, Ellen opened a letter Patrick had frantically written the day before:

> My Dear Madam,
> We are all in great trouble, and Mr Nicholls so much so that he is not so sufficiently strong and composed as to be able to write.
> I therefore devote a few moments to tell you that my Dear Daughter is very ill and apparently on the verge of the grave.

If she could speak, she would no doubt dictate to us whilst answering your kind letter, but we are left to ourselves to give what answer we can. The Doctors have no hope of her case, and fondly as we a long time, cherished hope, that hope is now gone, and we [have] only to look forward to the solemn event, with prayer to God, that he will give us grace and Strength sufficient unto our day.[12]

Ellen left for Haworth immediately. She got to the parsonage in the middle of the morning to be told she was too late. Charlotte had died in the early hours. At first, Patrick could not face her and sent a message, presumably through Martha, that she must stay for the funeral. Martha offered to take her upstairs to say goodbye to Charlotte's lifeless body but, distraught, Ellen protested that she could not bear it. Martha had gathered evergreens and early spring flowers from the moors, telling her they could both go in together and lay them on her as a last tribute. White anemones, bluebells and pink thrift should have started to appear in the deep lanes by then, with cornflowers and harebells emerging here and there across the distances of the heights:

> My first feeling was no I *cannot cannot* do it. Next, I was grateful to the maid for giving me the tender office. What made the task impossible at first was the rushing recollection of the flowers I spread in her honour at her wedding breakfast and *how* she admired the disposal of the gathering brought by Martha.[13]

Years later, Ellen told George Smith she was haunted by the moment, admitting 'her death chamber is in vivid remembrance. I last saw her in death.'[14] Ellen remembered the pitiful sight of her friend, wasted by undeserved agony and illness, littered in what few moorland flowers of little promise could be scavenged from the intemperate wilds around her. These flowers were symbols of the beauty of which Charlotte herself dreamed and worked to shape, her mind turned away from emptiness and disappointment towards goodness – towards redeeming absence and loss into imperishable prose. As time passed, these recollections mounted into a pyre of grief and fury that would burn in Ellen's memory for the rest of her life.

None of the household could have slept. After Dr Ingham told Patrick and Arthur the previous morning nothing could save Charlotte and it was simply a matter of hours before her life ebbed away, they alternately sat by her bedside or knelt to pray as Martha, Tabitha and Hannah nursed her into the night. Worn out in the early hours, Arthur went to rest in the next room, then, realising Charlotte was taking her last breaths, the women called him to come quickly. Unable to control his sobs any longer, he leant down and embraced her. Emotionlessly, Patrick stood up and walked out. Appalled, Martha led Tabitha and Hannah out so Arthur could be alone. Assuming Patrick's room was empty, they opened his door but stopped abruptly. He was on his knees sobbing, 'My poor Charlotte! My dear Charlotte!' Years later Tabitha reflected, 'I understood Mr Brontë better then: I never understood him before.'[15]

As was the custom of mourning at the time, all the window shutters were closed and the clocks stopped.[16] Undertakers brought a coffin and lifted Charlotte's body into it. Dr Ingham returned to certify her death, giving the assumed cause as three months of 'phthisis', progressive wasting, leading to a mistaken belief she too had died from tuberculosis. Her symptoms correspond more accurately with hyperemesis gravidarum, a pernicious form of morning sickness. The bells of St Michael and All Angels tolled for Mrs Nicholls, wife; for Currer Bell, writer; for Charlotte Brontë, daughter, sister, woman, sounding the unmistakable announcement of death over the rooftops to disperse across the moors.

She was buried four days later, on the morning of Wednesday, 4 April. Patrick and Arthur followed her coffin 70 yards to the church, where the family vault had been opened. Behind them walked Ellen and Margaret, Martha and Tabitha with their parents, then Nancy Garrs, the Brontë children's nurse from decades before. Villagers drew lots to send a representative from every household, making a cortege of more than 500 men and women, rich and poor, from all trades and none.[17] Those who could not get into the church to hear Rev. Sowden read the service packed the graveyard and the narrow lane to see that singularly lonely woman carried through the crowd to her final resting place. Afterwards, the mourners dispersed and left the little party of father, widower and friends to return to the parsonage for a funeral tea. Ellen stayed no longer than she could tolerate and left after an hour. She would never see Patrick or Arthur again.

Nearby in the stationery shop at the top of Main Street, whose windows were stacked with the Brontë novels, owner John Greenwood made haste to break the news of Charlotte's death to her famous friends. He had been on cordial terms with her family for over a decade, supplied them with writing paper and ink, and ordered books for them on request. He remembered Charlotte had been always kind to him, asked after his family and even introduced him to Elizabeth when she visited in 1853. Yet even though they were little more than acquaintances, he felt so shocked by her death he told Elizabeth and Harriet he had lost his best friend. From Ambleside, Harriet replied to his letter at once:

> I am deeply indebted to you for your kindness in informing me of my poor friend's departure. It is seldom that I use the word 'poor', which has now slipped from my pen; but she so loved life, her lot was so singular in surviving so many of her family, and I trust so happy at last in having formed new ties, that I did hope for longer life for her, though I often feared that it could hardly be.[18]

Delicately, she addressed the fact she and Charlotte had not spoken for years after Charlotte cut her off:

> If you would do me the kindness to furnish me with a few particulars of her later years, I should be most thankful. She had not written for so long that I do not know the name of her husband or anything concerning her for above two years. I have often inquired, but could never learn where she was living after her marriage; and knowing neither her name or place of abode, was helpless.[19]

Charlotte's death made Harriet think of the prospect of her own, which for decades she had been certain was imminent. 'You may possibly be aware that I am fast following her,' she told Greenwood theatrically, 'I am mortally ill, and my departure is only a question of hours or months.' In fact, she had another twenty-two years to live. Thinking out loud with this stranger, Harriet began to consider Charlotte's legacy and whether by association she would play any part in it. Had any of her letters to Charlotte been found among her papers, she wondered? If so, she wanted them back to add them to her own archive for her future executors. Greenwood replied that as he understood it, Arthur had burned, unread, all the letters Charlotte had saved from her friends.[20] Harriet's vanity was pricked, and she resolved to confront Arthur about it once a suitable time had passed. Returning to her camaraderie of shared doom with Charlotte, she remembered that despite the unignorable difficulties in Charlotte's nature, her virtues were not hard to find:

Will you have the goodness to offer my respects and assurances to Mr Brontë? To CB's husband I really dare not send any message – so deep is my sense of his bereavement in the loss of such a woman. Vast as was her genius, and infinitely as I admired it, I honoured yet more her integrity and unspoiled uprightness, simplicity, and sense. She was a noble woman, such as society ill can spare.[21]

Greenwood's letter to Elizabeth was redirected from Manchester to London where she was staying with relatives and arrived on the day of the funeral. She was thunderstruck:

I can not tell you how *very* sad your note has made me. My dear dear friend that I shall never see again on earth! I did not even know she was ill. I had heard nothing of her since the beginning of December when she wrote to a mutual friend saying that she was well and happy. I was meaning to write to her this very day to tell her of the appearance of a copy of my new book which I was sending to her. You may well say you have lost your best friend; strangers might know her by her great fame but we loved her dearly for her goodness, truth and kindness and those lovely qualities she carried with her where she is gone.

I want to know *every* particular. Has she been ill long? What was her illness? You would oblige me *extremely* if you would, at your earliest leisure, send me every detail. I am writing by this post to Mr Brontë. You do not name Mr Nicholls. Pray let me hear from you again, dear Sir. I loved her dearly, more than I think she knew. I shall never cease to be thankful that I knew her: or to mourn her loss.[22]

Still incredulous, she sent her condolences to Patrick straight away. He replied the next day to thank her. 'My Daughter is indeed dead and the solemn truth presses upon her worthy and affectionate Husband and me,' he wrote and added with magnanimous consideration, 'But others also have or shall have their sorrows and we feel our own the most.'[23] He told her Charlotte's death aborted her 'bright prospects of happiness' with Arthur, unaware Elizabeth knew Charlotte would have been married longer had he not obstructed it. 'But in the inscrutable providence of God, all our hopes, have ended in disappointment, and our joy in mourning.' She died peacefully, he told her, after three months of sickness. 'But our loss we trust is her gain.'[24] When he thanked George Smith for his sympathies a few weeks later, he told him they would never see her like again.

As Patrick wrote, reports of his daughter's death began reaching the public. The *Bradford Observer* broke the news the morning after her funeral, to be picked up and repeated by the national papers over the days and weeks to come:

> *Death of the Authoress of Jane Eyre.* Mrs Nicholls, formerly Miss Brontë, and who as 'Currer Bell' achieved lasting renown by the publication of *Jane Eyre*, died we regret to state on Saturday last at her father's house in Haworth. She was the last survivor of a family of six children. *Shirley* and *Villette* were also novels from her pen. All her writings are specially distinguished for great power of conception and vigorous portrayal of character.[25]

The next day, Good Friday, Elizabeth was surprised to see an article beginning 'Currer Bell is dead!' in London's *Daily News*. It read: 'The early death of the large family of whom she was the sole survivor prepared all who knew the circumstances to expect the loss of this gifted creature.' Its anonymous author assumed Charlotte had died of consumption, surmised then by some to be a hereditary condition. It described her public success and the acclaim for her novels but was infused with an unusual intimacy with her personal life. It summarised the conditions of the deplorable school that ultimately killed her elder sisters when they were children and stunted her growth, of her returning from further education in Brussels to her two sisters, brother and elderly father in 'those dreary wilds' of Haworth, 'a place where newspapers were never seen or where she never saw any and in a house where the servants knew nothing about books, manuscripts, proofs or the post.' After the deaths of her siblings, it said, her father:

> was too much absorbed in his studies to notice her occupations ... [and] rarely broke the silence and there was no one else to do it; in that forlorn house, planted on the very clay of the churchyard where the graves of her sisters were before her window; in such a living sepulchre her mind could not pray upon itself; and how it did suffer, we see in the more painful portions of her last novel *Villette*.[26]

The details had an unmistakable insinuation of authority. Elizabeth recognised all the anecdotes as those Charlotte herself shared when she used to talk about her life. The article confirmed this: 'Now and then uttered to her very few friends, things which may alas be told now without fear of hurting her sensitive nature; things which ought to be told in her honour.' Elizabeth realised its author must be someone who knew Charlotte personally. Furthermore, something about its style was familiar. She consulted friends to see if they agreed. 'I and most others believe it to have been written by Miss Martineau,' she concluded.[27] Elizabeth's intuition was rarely wrong. Harriet, it seemed, had wasted no time in capitalising on her ex-friend's death. She received word the same day as Elizabeth and while Elizabeth sent sympathies, Harriet wrote an article and sent it to the *Daily News*. She was on good terms with its editor, William Weir, and had published many articles with him over the previous three years, but she must have worked with unflinching industry to produce 2,000 words in the hours after Greenwood told her Charlotte was dead, to post it the same afternoon in order for it to be typeset the next day to make print on Friday morning. A day later, it was picked up by the *Leeds Mercury* for the north of England, exposing details of the hitherto private lives of the residents of Haworth parsonage.

Greenwood's letters to Harriet and Elizabeth have not survived, but we can reconstruct what he told Elizabeth from her replies. He wanted to tell her Charlotte was ill as soon as he heard but was afraid of being accused of meddling in his neighbours' business and it looked as though her father and husband failed to recognise the symptoms of a difficult pregnancy soon enough to prevent its fatal complications. Elizabeth's sense of stupefaction was evident. 'How I wish I had known!' she told him, 'If I had come, I could have induced her.' She acknowledged inducing premature labour would have made the family angry unless they understood it was 'absolutely necessary for her very life. Poor poor creature! I can not understand it at all.'[28] The *British Medical Journal* of the time describes a method: a course of castor oil and quinine administered three times a day for three days to a healthy woman before the thirty-seventh week of her pregnancy. As Greenwood did not know Charlotte was nursed by three women and attended daily by two doctors, who likely would have all known this method, he assumed she had been left to deteriorate in solitude, failed by Patrick and Arthur's incapability, and giving Elizabeth the misapprehension that she died of their neglect. It reinforced her growing animosity towards both. 'Dear dear Miss Brontë,' she wrote sadly.

Greenwood had not seen Charlotte for nearly a year after being aggrieved by her lack of response to a wedding gift he sent her. After he moved his shop higher up Main Street, a photographer took over his old premises and Greenwood arranged for him to take a photograph of Patrick. He told Elizabeth he had sent it to the parsonage while Charlotte and Arthur were on their honeymoon but never got a word of acknowledgement. Having assumed the role of official stockist of the Brontë novels he was surprised then resentful. Elizabeth tried to rationalise the lapse. 'It is so extremely unlike her, whom we both mourn so truly, not to welcome and meet even more than halfway any little kindness and attention that might be offered,' she assured him, 'So much so that I am inclined to think that it must have been the extreme and growing languor of ill health which made her perpetually delay thanking you for your picture of her father.'[29] She wondered if Patrick might have hung it up then bashfully taken it down again before Charlotte and Arthur came back from Ireland, out of 'a sort of shy feeling at having his portrait taken ... when he so often said that he would not.'[30] She ventured he should check with Arthur that they had received it in the first place, that way she could also determine how Arthur felt about photographs and whether he would ever allow Charlotte's portrait of to be copied as a memento 'for her friends. But I am sure it is too soon to name or propose it ...'[31]

She said she felt disinclined to trouble Arthur and Patrick directly or to visit them until a suitable mourning period had passed, so asked if he could keep her informed in the meantime. Her journalistic senses were tingling. She sensed she had found the ideal informant in Greenwood: close to the source, indiscreet and quite disloyal. 'I need hardly say how completely confidential I consider your most interesting letter. *Anything* else you can ever remember to tell me about her will be most valuable.'[32]

Greenwood and Harriet were not the only ones who felt opportunities had come with the death of Charlotte Brontë. While Elizabeth ruefully suspected it was only a matter of time before Thackeray reappeared and got in touch with the parsonage, Harriet's Lake District neighbour Matthew Arnold was thinking about how he too could capitalise on the situation. Only one week after the funeral he wrote to *Fraser's Magazine* to pitch an elegy: 'a thing in memory of poor Charlotte Brontë which I think may suit you when it is done, and which I should like to appear at no great distance of time from her death.'[33] There had been practically no contact between him and Charlotte after their dinner with Harriet five years earlier and since then, the disagreeable impression she left with him was demeaned further by *Villette*. Reading it, he told a friend, could only be made worse if one had met its author:

[It was] a hideous, undelightful, convulsed, constricted novel ... It is one of the most utterly disagreeable books I ever read and having seen *her* makes it more so. She is so entirely ... a fire without ailment, one of the most distressing barren sights one can witness. Religion or devotion or whatever it is to be called may be impossible for such people now: but they have at any rate not found a substitute for it and it was better for the world when they comforted themselves with it.[34]

He produced a poem of 190 lines entitled 'Haworth Churchyard' and had it published in the May issue. In it, he remembers Charlotte the way he knew her: as Harriet's comrade in art and fate. Having accepted Harriet's belief she was on the verge of death, he describes them both as doomed talents, intertwining their fates and borrowing the morbid imagery from her *Daily News* essay – including her erroneous assumption that Charlotte and her siblings were buried in the churchyard and not inside the church. When she saw it, Elizabeth took pleasure in pointing out the mistake to him. He replied that he was sorry she had told him and – with the intransigence that would become a common trait in perpetuators of Brontë myths – suggested it was not he but the family who were at fault for choosing 'the wrong, uncongenial spot' in which to be buried.[35]

'You can not think how your letter interests me. You may depend upon it that anything you wish me to keep secret shall not be revealed.' Elizabeth hoped to draw more information out of Greenwood, who must have been flattered such an eminent novelist had taken him into her confidence. Did he remember when he first heard Charlotte was Currer Bell? What did he know about her childhood and her first visit to London when she revealed her identity? He told her he got to know the family when he started selling stationery twelve years earlier:

> They used to buy a great deal of writing paper and I used to wonder whatever they did with so much. When I was out of stock I was always afraid of them coming, they seemed always so distressed that I had none.

They were so consistent he became afraid of disappointing them and sometimes walked 10 miles to get more:

> I did so like them to come when I had anything for them; they were so much different to anyone else, so gentle, and kind and so very quiet. They never talked much; but Charlotte would sometimes sit and inquire about my family so feelingly.[36]

The more questions Elizabeth asked, the more apparent it became he had been exaggerating his connection to the Brontës and over-estimated their interest in him. Despite describing Charlotte as his 'best friend' it was obvious she and her siblings were simply nicer to him than his other Haworth customers. 'Poor fellow,' Elizabeth concluded, puzzled by the hold they had over him, 'Is it not sad? And does it not altogether seem inexplicable and strange?' she wondered.[37] In reply to her question about the portrait of Charlotte hanging in the parsonage, Greenwood told her he heard George Smith had a duplicate. This gave Elizabeth the opportunity to open a dialogue with George and introduce a proposal of her own:

> I cannot tell you how I honoured and loved her. I did not know of her illness or I would have gone straight to her. It seems to me that her death was as sad as her life. Some time, it may be years hence, but if I live long enough, and no one is living whom such a publication would hurt, I will publish what I know of her, and make the world honour the woman as much as they have admired the writer.[38]

George admitted his friendship with Charlotte had lapsed and it had been some time since he last had any contact with her. Elizabeth said it was the same for her:

> I never wrote to her again after that October letter; and I do regret it now! I think it is from finding that you are suffering from a somewhat similar regret (that of not having cultivated her intimacy more assiduously) that makes me write so openly and so much at length to you.[39]

She was keen to emphasise how despite the gap, they had been close enough for Charlotte to divulge much about her own past and her father's family history. All of it, she suggested, deserved being committed to paper even if no publisher was interested, testing the water to see whether George would bite:

> It was from finding how much names and dates which she then gave me in speaking of her past life had passed out of my memory, that I determined that in our country-leisure this summer I would put down everything I remembered about this dear friend and noble woman, before its vividness has faded from my mind: but I *know* that Mr Brontë and I *fear* that Mr Nicholls would not like this made public, even though the more she

was known, the more people would honour her as a woman separate from her character of authoress. Still my children, who all loved her, would like to have what I could write about her; and the time may come when her wild sad life, and the beautiful character that grew out of it may be made public.[40]

Her intention stated, Elizabeth sketched out the general shape and tone such a memoir could take:

I thought that I would simply write down my own personal recollections of her, from the time we first met at Sir J.K. Shuttleworth's, telling what was right and fitting of what she told me of her past life, and here and there copying out characteristic extracts from her letters. I could describe the wild bleakness of Haworth and speaking of the love and honour in which she was held there. But ... you will see that this sort of record of her could not be made public at present without giving pain.[41]

During this exchange, she must have decided to secretly test the public response such a work might have. For only two days later, on 6 June, *Sharpe's London Magazine* ran an anonymous feature with the title 'A Few Words About Jane Eyre'. It described 'a lady' meeting Charlotte Brontë at the house of a mutual friend; of the austere parsonage in its bleak wild position in Haworth; and summarises the abbreviated form of autobiography Charlotte told at Briery Close. Save a few introductory and connecting lines, it is identical to two letters Elizabeth wrote once she got back. No payment receipt or acknowledgement of her authorship has ever been found, but it is unquestionably Elizabeth's work. Either unknown parties brought together letters to two different recipients and created a composite essay or, more probably, she submitted it herself. As an astute negotiator of contracts, Elizabeth would not have allowed her writing to be published without permission or without payment and would have fired off a complaint as soon as she saw it. As no complaint was ever made even to friends, it is reasonable to conclude that she compiled the texts and submitted it to be published anonymously, as with the rest of her work, and waited with curiosity for any reaction. To her surprise, she heard nothing from the Haworth vanguards, Patrick, Arthur and John Greenwood. She never expected that it would be Ellen, outraged at what she felt was a grotesque caricature of Charlotte, who would light the touch paper and begin the sequence of events that would change all their lives forever.

CHAPTER 11

1855

A Grave Duty

On the day *Sharpe's Magazine* was released, a copy found its way to Birstall and into the hands of Ellen Nussey. Attentive to any references to Charlotte in the press she read 'A Few Words About Jane Eyre' with horror and wrote to Arthur straight away. She told him it had 'much hurt and pained' her. 'You will be certain to see the article and I am sure both you and Mr Brontë will feel acutely the misrepresentations and the malignant spirit which characterises it.'[1]

Ellen, still stunned by Charlotte's loss, thought Arthur was ignoring everything the press published about her, however derogatory or sensational. This galvanised her volcanic grief to fury. 'Will you suffer the article to pass current without any refutations?' she demanded, 'The writer merits the contempt of silence but there will be readers and believers.' Scathingly, she asked if he could rouse himself to consider defending his wife and 'do justice to one who so highly deserved justice', suggesting Charlotte had been deprived of rewards in life, only to be robbed further in death by his failure. Charlotte was revered by 'those who best knew her', Ellen told him, and if he was not willing to defend her, 'Should not her aged father be defended from the approach the writer coarsely attempts to bring upon him?' By situating Arthur outside Charlotte's most intimate circle, of friends and father, Ellen betrayed the animosity she nurtured since Charlotte first told her about their relationship. Back then, she had worried Charlotte was demeaning herself out of desperation and suspected Arthur was a doltish opportunist obstructing access to her. Nothing was changing her opinion. She insisted he pursue the matter even if it meant bringing in someone else to defend his late wife where he could not. By a remarkable coincidence, having no idea who wrote the objectionable article, Ellen told him she had already thought of the perfect candidate:

I wish Mrs Gaskell, who is every way capable, would undertake a reply, and would give a sound castigation to the writer. Her personal acquaintance with Haworth, the Parsonage and its inmates fits her for the task, and if on other subjects she lacked information I would gladly supply her with facts sufficient to set aside much that is asserted if you yourself are not provided with all the information that is needed on the subject produced. Will you ask Mrs Gaskell to undertake this just and honourable defence? I think she would do it gladly. She valued dear Charlotte and such an act of friendship, performed with her ability and power could only add to the laurels she has already won.[2]

Arthur kept her waiting until the start of the following week to respond. Coolly, firmly and without conceding any ground, he told her they would never have seen the article had she not drawn it to their attention, implying her a participant in any injury they might feel. He had ordered a copy then read the article aloud to Patrick when it arrived. 'Remarks respecting Mr Brontë excited in him only amusement – indeed I have not seen him laugh as much for some months.'[3] He said they thought the many mistakes were not made from an unkind motive as he – Arthur assumed the author to be male – 'professes to be an admirer of Charlotte's works, pays a just tribute to her genius and in common with thousands deplores her untimely death. His design seems rather to be to gratify the curiosity of the multitude.' If it had been otherwise, Arthur insisted, they would not have dignified it with an answer. 'Charlotte herself would have acted thus; and her character stands too high to be injured by the statement in a magazine of small circulation and little influence.' He added that despite being physically well they were both 'lonely and desolate'.[4]

Unhappy but undeterred, Ellen wrote to Patrick that articles would continue to appear and multiply errors until he sanctioned someone to correct them. A few days later he contacted Elizabeth:

Having reason to [think] that some may venture to write her life who will be ill qualified for the undertaking, I can see no better plan under these circumstances than apply to some established Author to write a brief account of her life – and to make some remarks on her works. You seem to me to be the best qualified for doing what I wish should be done. If therefore you will be so kind as to publish a long or short account of her life and works, just as you may deem expedient and proper Mr Nicholls and I will give you such information as you may require.[5]

He told her she was the first person he had approached and that Arthur approved. Unnecessarily, he added, 'Could my Daughter speak from the tomb I feel certain she would laud my our choice.' His change of thought between describing it as 'my' then 'our' indicates an unsatisfactorily resolved ambivalence between them on the subject. Arthur later expressed his resignation to Ellen: 'My own feelings would be to take no steps in the matter but I do not think it right to offer any opposition to Mr Brontë's wishes.'[6]

Patrick, Arthur and Ellen had no idea how little persuasion Elizabeth would need. With Patrick's suggestion that Charlotte's spirit would endorse it, Elizabeth had a sense that forces beyond her own plans were at work. She forwarded the letter to George, assuring him it came 'most unexpectedly' and that she had 'taken some time to consider the request'. That her letter was dated the day after she received Patrick's indicates how little time she took. 'Of course, it becomes a more serious task than the one which as you know I was proposing to myself, to put down my personal recollections etc. with no intention of immediate publication, if indeed for publication at all.' She told him she would have to omit everything relating to Charlotte's 'home and the circumstances which must have had so much to do in forming her character. All these can be merely indicated during the lifetime of her father and to a certain degree in the lifetime of her husband.' Now that it was no longer an abstract, Elizabeth felt the weight of the responsibility but did not baulk. 'I am very anxious to perform this grave duty laid upon me well and fully. Of course, it strengthens my determination to go over to Haworth as now I must see Mr Brontë.' She did not mention what form the 'Life' would take but as she did not ask George to consider commissioning her to write a book, she may still have envisaged – as Patrick and Arthur had – producing an extended article in one of the national journals. Notwithstanding that, she still wanted his support 'by confiding to me any information respecting her which you may possess and not be unwilling to impart.'[7] Her thoughts went back to Charlotte's portrait and whether Patrick and Arthur would let her have it photographed. 'I'm so afraid of forgetting her face,' she told George, 'and that was such a beautiful likeness.'[8]

She must have contacted Patrick the same day or the next to ask if he could start her off with some information about the main events in Charlotte's life. He replied with the first of several long letters that began with autobiography and progressed to a family history. At this stage, his brevity suggests he was still under the impression Elizabeth was planning an essay, not a full-length book. His own father had been an orphan, he told her:

It was said that he was of an Ancient Family. Whether this was or was not so, I never gave myself the trouble to inquire since his lot in life, as well as mine, depended under Providence not on family descent but our own exertions.

He recounted his early life in County Down as the eldest of ten children brought up respectably by his parents' 'application and industry' on a few acres of rented farmland; that he set up a school at the age of 16 before making an extraordinary leap to England to study, aged 25, at St John's College, Cambridge before his ordination in 1806 and his first curacies in Essex and Shropshire. Over the next nine years, he took curacies in Dewsbury then Hartshead-cum-Clifton where he met Maria Branwell, whom he married at the end of December 1812. They remained in Hartshead, where their first two children, Maria and Elizabeth were born in 1814 and 1815, until they moved to Thornton, where Charlotte, Branwell, Emily and Anne were born in its vicarage. Patrick was appointed Haworth's perpetual curate and moved his family in 1820 and there, he told Elizabeth:

> my family afflictions began. After a happy union of nine years and only one year's residence my dear wife died and left me with the care of six small children. Soon after my wife's sister came and afforded me her assistance for twenty years.[9]

He wrote about how he sent his daughters to school. Maria and Elizabeth boarded at Cowan Bridge in Kirkby Lonsdale in the summer of 1824, to be joined by Charlotte and Emily in the autumn. Maria and Elizabeth caught consumption that winter and declined in the early months of 1825. Maria was brought home in February and died three months later, a few weeks before terminally ill Elizabeth was returned. Patrick removed Charlotte and Emily a fortnight before she perished. 'They died within six weeks of each other. Maria in the eleventh and Elizabeth in the tenth year of their age. Maria had a powerfully intellectual mind. Elizabeth had good solid sense.'

Charlotte, Emily and Anne continued their educations with Margaret Wooler and then Charlotte and Emily at a girls' finishing school in Brussels in their twenties. He never mentions that Branwell painted and wrote, or that he himself had published poetry and prose before his marriage:

> When my daughters were at home, they read their manuscripts to each other and gave their candid opinions to each of what was written – I never interfered with them at these times. I judged it best to throw them

upon their own responsibility. Besides a clergyman bordering on the age of 80 years was likely to be too cold and severe a critic of the efforts of buoyant and youthful genius. Hence it came to pass that I never saw their works till they appeared in print.

His only son was 'a young man of varied and brilliant talents but these he marred by living too freely which brought on a decline that shortened his days'. He added that the toll her siblings' deaths took on Charlotte was apparent to him now:

> During the illness and deaths of her brother and sisters Charlotte had a hard task to perform. She watched over them with a mother's kindness and care and spent sleepless nights and weary days without one word of complaint and only regretting that she was not able to do more for them in their seasons of distress. I never knew one less selfish than she was, or more disposed to suffer herself to save others from suffering.

He assured Elizabeth he would provide her with anything else she might need and suggested they meet once he was no longer 'labouring under so great a weight of sorrow'. He added that her co-operation had given him and Arthur a great deal of satisfaction: 'It has broken in like a ray of light on our gloomy solitude.'[10]

Reading his account, it became clear he was leaving out more than he was sharing. Little of it corresponded with Charlotte's narratives of deprivation and loneliness, or indicated the manipulations and volatility that caused her so much pain. When he told Elizabeth that Charlotte married with his full consent, Elizabeth knew it was not entirely true. She sent his letter to Harriet to ask what she thought. Harriet felt the same. That Patrick's 'facts' – a word she surrounded with inverted commas of dubiety – 'appear to her & me wholly irreconcilable with what "Currer" told us.'[11] She invited Elizabeth to Ambleside so they could compare their own letters from Charlotte and discuss what they remembered her telling them. This discrepancy between Charlotte and Patrick's perspectives was Elizabeth's first indication that telling the story of her life would be anything but straightforward.

By the start of July, Elizabeth's summer was already booked out with meetings, visits from friends, appointments and travel. Plymouth Grove was to be redecorated, making it 'abominable with paint, and smells so badly' that she let the children stay with a friend.[12] Between seeing her husband off to Switzerland then packing for several weeks with relatives in Scotland, she was preoccupied with Charlotte. She had no idea how to approach writing a biography, especially of someone so private:

> Until I can form some idea of the amount of information etc. to be obtained I cannot make any plan about her life. I am very much afraid of not doing it as it ought to be done; distinct and delicate and thoroughly well. But I will do my very best.[13]

Furthermore, a visit to Haworth was unavoidable and bound to be unpleasant. John Greenwood expected her to drop by his shop so he could ingratiate himself further – but she planned to avoid him – and the prospect of seeing Patrick again, deep in mourning, as well as meeting Arthur for the first time after hearing so many ambivalent reports, felt onerous. Cannily, she arranged to go to Ambleside afterwards so she could pick apart their statements with Harriet. She asked George to share his recollections and supply any other contacts that might help, then wrote to Sir James's sister, Hannah, knowing he was in London, for an interview with him but heard nothing until the autumn.[14]

She recruited Katie Winkworth for support and together they left Manchester early on Monday, 23 July for the train to Keighley. They got to Haworth at one in the afternoon in the 'broiling heat' as she described it. 'It was a most painful visit. Both Mr Brontë and Mr Nicholls cried sadly.'[15] Both approved her writing about Charlotte, even though Arthur still had reservations. Guided by Elizabeth, Patrick felt an unauthorised biography was inevitable and would repeat the scurrilous articles that had appeared since Charlotte's death. It would be better, he proposed, to anticipate that with their own informed account. Arthur was not convinced that telling Charlotte's life story was either inevitable or necessary and Elizabeth noted 'his feeling was against its being written but [he] yielded to Mr Brontë's impetuous wish.' Flattered at having secured the talents of a writer of Elizabeth's calibre, Patrick was insistent 'above all things that her life should be written and written by me' and refused to let any doubts sway her. Despite being secretly pleased he was encouraging something she already considered, she felt the weight of his expectations:

> I told Mr Brontë how much I felt the difficulty of the task I had undertaken yet how much I wish to do it well and make his daughter's most

unusual character (as taken separately from her genius) known to those who, from their deep interest and admiration of her writings would naturally, if her life was to be written, express to be informed as to the circumstances which made her what she was.[16]

While she saw Patrick underestimated both the interest in Charlotte and the consequences writing about her life might bring, she understood Arthur's cynicism. He suspected that, once engaged, the public's appetite for details might be so insatiable it would compromise them all and made it plain he was 'far more aware of the kind of particulars which people would look for and saw how they had snatched at every gossiping account of her'.

Returning to the brief account of Charlotte's life that Patrick sent her, Elizabeth asked him to elaborate on her childhood and schooling, conscious of how both informed *Jane Eyre*. While the dates he sent were useful, she explained, she needed to understand how a personality like hers had been formed. He replied that Charlotte's undemonstrative nature put him at a disadvantage since 'she was, from a child, prone to say little about herself and averse from making any display of what she knew.'[17]

Without his ability to recollect or even, it appeared, to have noticed the stages of Charlotte's intellectual development, Elizabeth must have wondered whether there was another record she could consult, such as a diary or letters. There was no trace of a diary and Arthur said he destroyed all of Charlotte's personal papers, including all letters she had received. He found drafts of her first and last unpublished novels, *The Professor*, written in the years before *Jane Eyre*, and *Emma*, started the autumn before she died. When Elizabeth asked see them, he refused, telling her they were uninteresting and unpublishable, as the former bore too much of a resemblance to *Villette* and there was too little of the latter. Friends may have kept some letters, he advised, and recommended she consider contacting the 'one person of all others to apply to': Ellen Nussey.[18]

They stayed later than planned until, pressed for time, Elizabeth asked Martha if she could quickly show them Charlotte's grave, assuming it would be too emotional for Arthur. Unexpectedly, he joined them then brought them back to the parsonage to fetch a dozen or so family letters Charlotte wrote in her twenties. Saying their goodbyes, Patrick's last words were, 'No quailing Mrs Gaskell! No drawing back!'[19] Before she left, she noticed hanging on the study wall was his own photograph, the ungratefully received gift of John Greenwood.[20]

The delay meant they missed their train back to Manchester, forcing them to stay the night at Skipton. The pressure of the sultry evening brought a darkness troubled by rolling peals of thunder. Torrential rain flooded the reservoir high up on the moors, bursting the banks of the stream that ran through Thornton, the place of Charlotte's birth, sweeping away everything in its path.[21]

The next day, Elizabeth and Arthur both wrote to Ellen. He explained his reversal was down to Patrick being swayed by more erroneous articles and had 'applied to Mrs Gaskell who has undertaken to write a life of Charlotte'.[22] He still had doubts and disagreed about how it should be done but said Elizabeth needed first-hand material to get started. 'For this reason, Mrs G is anxious to see any of her letters. Especially those of any early date. I think I understood you to say that you had some.'[23] He wanted her to send them so he could select what he considered appropriate. Ellen was affronted. Given his demand she burn everything, she must have suspected he would still carry this out if she co-operated. She left no record of her response but her actions speak for her. She never sent him a single letter and chose to negotiate with Elizabeth herself.

Writing hastily from the inn at Skipton, Elizabeth assured her she could trust her with Charlotte's letters and, hoping she would tell her more in person, asked to meet in the next few days when she might also catch Margaret Wooler and the Taylors.[24] Ellen happened to be with Margaret in Ilkley at that moment, and told Elizabeth she could have joined them but Margaret 'does not yield to my wishes' and had concerns. Coyly, she denied knowing about 'Mr Brontë's request' and chose not to divulge it had been her idea, just as Elizabeth never mentioned she had written the article she was being asked to correct. Ellen said she was glad Patrick asked her, as the idea 'is of the deepest interest to me'.[25]

She pledged to do everything in her power to 'aid the righteous work you have undertaken' but cautioned her not to set her expectations too high. She said she had kept almost every letter Charlotte sent her but had to destroy 'a small portion of the correspondence', a comment surely meant to provoke the question 'Why?' Scanning letters for revelations she felt she ought to conceal from the public, Ellen foresaw how a professional writer of Elizabeth's capabilities would likely draw more meaning than she herself had and resolved to protect Charlotte from her own indiscretions but felt no loyalty to Patrick or Arthur. She began to wonder whether amongst those she had preserved, there were any other details that gave away too much about herself and her own family. She took a pen and ink and started scoring out their names.

Having some time overnight to consider Elizabeth's questions about Charlotte's early life, Patrick wrote again, recalling a time when his children were small and used to play intricate games of make-believe from where their adult fiction sprung:

> As soon as they could read and write Charlotte and her brother and sisters used to invent and act little plays of their own in which the Duke of Wellington, my daughter Charlotte's hero, was sure to come off the conquering hero. When a dispute would not infrequently arise amongst them regarding the comparative merits of him, Bonaparte, Hannibal, and Caesar — when the argument got warm and rose to its height, as their mother was then dead, I had sometimes to come in as arbitrator and settle the dispute according to the best of my judgement. Generally, in the management of those concerns I frequently thought I discovered signs of rising talent which I had seldom or never before seen in any of their age. As they had few opportunities of being in learned and polished society in their retired country situation, they formed a little society amongst themselves with which they seemed contented and happy ... The above is a mere outline of the life of my happy little family till deaths came in fearfully rapid succession, till my daughter Charlotte was left alone.[26]

Alone now in a house that had been emptied into the tomb, Patrick must have seen the irony of being committed to live out his days with the suitor he rejected for his daughter. The hand of God had delivered him into a domestic arrangement with the man he had opposed for so long, to be his and not Charlotte's in sickness and in health. Without her for nearly four months her virtues were now unquestionable, and irreplaceable. Gone were her selfless sympathies and tireless efforts to cheer those who never consoled her. He was a broken man.

> She always distinguished herself and generally got the highest award. She was an excellent wife and daughter, a kind mistress, very charitable to the poor and liberal, according to her means, was generally beloved by all and most by those who knew her best.[27]

On her way back to Manchester, Elizabeth read the early letters Arthur gave her. While they had little biographical material, she was struck by Charlotte's erudition. She wrote to Ellen once she got home:

> I am sure you can be of more service to me than anyone else because you have been her dear friend for so many years and must have known her through all the progress of her character. From what I can judge from the letters Mr Nicholls has entrusted me with, her very earliest way of expressing herself must have been different to common.

She said she had a 'deep personal interest' in meeting Ellen quite apart 'from my difficult and terribly interesting task.'[28]

On the last Saturday of July, she took her daughters to Ambleside to stay with the Arnolds so she could go over to see Harriet and gather everything about Charlotte they could remember. Harriet showed Elizabeth all the letters she had received from her, including – in testimony to Harriet's transparency – those terminating their friendship. She could not remember the precise wording of her replies and speculated, as she had with John Greenwood, whether any survived. If so, she said, Arthur should have returned them as was the proper practise of executors after the recipient's death. She remembered Charlotte telling her that Wordsworth's son-in-law, Edward Quillinan, offered her a letter written by Branwell in 1837, asking for Wordsworth's opinion of his poetry. Charlotte declined and heard no more.[29]

In discussion, it became clear the stories Charlotte told them about her life and circumstances were the same set-pieces: the supposed uncivilised wilderness of Haworth; her father's destruction of her mother's clothes and her siblings' shoes; of her dying mother sobbing for her children; the hellish charity school; and her brother's death from 'his vices'. But contradictions and gaps were becoming apparent. Patrick's sober, spare accounts were missing these details and neither Elizabeth nor Harriet knew much about Charlotte's time studying in Brussels, even how long she stayed or which of her sisters went with her. She doubted Patrick's recollection that Charlotte and Emily had lived abroad for two years and referred her questions to George Smith, in the hope that during the production of *Villette* Charlotte may have given him or his mother 'any clue to her Brussels life – Madame Hezer's Rue D'Isabelle. I hear Mme Hezer has lost all her pupils since the publication of *Villette*,' she wrote, evidently wondering at the cause.[30]

She and her daughters left the Lake District the following Friday to travel to their holiday home in Silverdale near Morecambe Bay. They rented a folly resembling a church tower, standing unattached in a nearby farm's uncultivated land. Lindeth Tower was four storeys high with a kitchen on the ground floor, two bedrooms above, and Elizabeth's study at the top, where the farm labourers could see her writing.

She continued to try to arrange a meeting with Ellen and asked how she could persuade Margaret. Ellen told her Margaret would not accept by letter but would be unlikely to refuse her if she turned up unannounced, and offered to put her up for the night if it did not go to plan. 'I must be guided by your kind advice when I get to Birstall,' Elizabeth replied, 'especially as I agree with you that it would be better to take Miss Wooler by surprise.'

She wanted to extend her searches to find everyone who knew the Brontës, especially those who had employed Charlotte and her siblings or had known her in Belgium. She amassed lists of names from Ellen, Arthur and Patrick and canvassed her own wide circle to find anyone who could connect her. 'You once said you knew or had heard or had the means of hearing a good deal about Miss Brontë (Currer Bell),' she wrote to one, 'I want *every particular* I can collect, not necessarily for publication, but to trust to my honour and discretion, and to enable me to form a picture of our character, and a drama of her life in my own mind.'[31] She began trying to identify the originals of the families and towns in Charlotte's novels, telling another, 'You will think these vague, wild inquiries, but the answers are of consequence to me.'[32]

Charlotte had once been a governess in Leeds for the White family, Patrick told her, and Branwell and Anne both worked for the Robinsons in York. Mrs Lydia Robinson's name had already been mentioned to Elizabeth more solicitously in connection with Branwell and she knew she had been widowed, remarried, widowed again and was now Lady Scott.

Some investigations took her back where she started. Realising an old friend, Caroline Anne Davenport, knew Charlotte at the height of her celebrity, she asked for any particulars she could remember. Caroline replied she had only been an acquaintance, having dined with her once or twice when George was showing her off to literary London. She recommended Elizabeth speak to her cousin's husband, who assured everybody he met he was one of Charlotte's closest friends and saw her often, even after her marriage. Elizabeth knew his name already: Sir James Kay-Shuttleworth. She was due to spend a day back in Manchester so arranged two visits for the return journey to Silverdale: a morning with Ellen followed by a few nights at Gawthorpe with Sir James. As she knew Ellen was still in Ilkley with

Margaret, who could not be persuaded to see her, she had to ask Ellen to come home to Birstall to meet her there privately. Ellen leapt at the chance, and they met for the first time on the morning of Tuesday, 14 August.

Both having heard fond anecdotes of the other from Charlotte, Elizabeth and Ellen were primed to like each other at first sight. Finding Ellen just as Charlotte described her, Elizabeth thought her 'simple, affectionate, refined and sensible',[33] having no idea Ellen felt she had anointed her to this task after persuading Patrick to propose it. In advance, she had picked out over 300 of Charlotte's letters written over the entire span of their friendship, from their meeting in Margaret's school when they were 14, to those pathetic notes scrawled from her deathbed.

They talked past lunch and into the late afternoon, with Ellen answering Elizabeth's many questions so readily and unambiguously that Elizabeth only thought of more, especially about Charlotte's twenties. It was obvious how much for *Jane Eyre* was drawn from school and her time as a governess, from interactions with the flocks of curates and truculent neighbouring families for *Shirley*, but the people and experiences that informed *Villette* were still a mystery. Patrick's knowledge was as limited as it was with every other aspect of his daughter's life, Elizabeth noticed when she read his cursory replies. He had escorted Charlotte and Emily to Brussels in 1841 but only Emily stayed on with Charlotte afterwards, making the other key witnesses the friends who were there at the same time: Mary Taylor, impossible to be interviewed in person in New Zealand, and her sister Martha, who had been dead for thirteen years. Before Elizabeth had time to look at Ellen's letters closely, she searched those written after 1841 for any reference to Brussels. Instantly, she found a clue. 'From one of them I gather that the second year of Miss Brontë's residence at Madame Beck's she *received* £16 as English teacher.' She had not only been a student, it seemed, but had been promoted to teacher at the Pensionnat. '*Héger*, is that the name? Mr Brontë writes it, as I read, *Hezer*.'[34]

Ellen entrusted Elizabeth with her bundle of letters, and once she left Birstall for the 40-mile journey west to Gawthorpe Hall, Elizabeth began to read. In them, she heard Charlotte's voice developing and the woman herself growing 'more extraordinary and more incomprehensible, i.e. beyond the limits of my comprehension'.[35] Once at the hall, she found James in delicate health and his sister worn out from caring for him. He was weak and needed bed rest most of the afternoon and evening, resulting in Elizabeth having to stay over until he was well enough to talk the next morning. He brushed away his wife's absence as her preferring the milder climate of 'the south', but Elizabeth understood they had separated unhappily two years before and now Janet was living on the Continent with their three younger children and Rosa Poplawska. The two women had grown close enough in the years after Elizabeth saw them in Windermere to now sleep in the same bedroom in their house in Germany. While part of their household staff, Rosa had become protective of Janet from her husband's irascibility, eventually providing her with the loving companionship she lacked and the barrier to him she felt Janet needed. Their eldest son would remember this as resentfully as James and blamed his parents' estrangement on the intimacy offered by his governess, whom he dismissed as an upstart driven by social ambition and sexual jealousy to captivate his mother with her almost hypnotic influence.[36] While history has never divulged the precise nature of their relationship, its parallels with Jane Eyre's influence on Rochester may have been evident even to uninformed observers at the time. Unaware that Elizabeth knew all this about Janet as she was still corresponding with her, James told her she was holidaying in Eastbourne. He had nothing new to add about Charlotte, telling Elizabeth he only saw her once after she married.[37]

Back in Silverdale, Elizabeth read Charlotte's letters and copied out notable passages, becoming so absorbed over the next three weeks she only left the tower once: to ride 10 miles to Cowan Bridge just outside Kirkby Lonsdale, where the buildings that once housed the Clergy Daughters' School still stood. After looking around the grounds, she went the few miles to the school's current location, in the nearby village of Casterton. On seeing that the tidy, well-positioned school-house contained clean and healthy-looking children she asked the superintendent if she knew anything about the time when Charlotte attended it. The 'most prepossessing' woman refused to be drawn into a discussion about that and would only say how much had changed since then.[38]

When Susanna Winkworth came to Silverdale in the damp, blustery last week of August, she saw how committed Elizabeth was becoming to presenting the unmediated truth. Charlotte's own voice, still vivid in Elizabeth's memories now resonated from the bundles of letters, proving Elizabeth's early first impressions that her nobility was impossible to rationalise once considered against the scourging circumstances of her life. Susanna observed how this idea of reconciling the character with its situation was driving Elizabeth's enquiry, turning her project into a 'quest for materials' that had so far 'been most successful and I really think now she will make a capital thing of the 'Life' and show people how lives ought to be written'.[39]

By then, Elizabeth had received further messages from Arthur and Patrick. Arthur must have been responding to questions about the Brussels period, as he described Emily Brontë as a young woman who 'absolutely *repelled* people by her cold sullen manner'.[40] This contradicted how Elizabeth remembered Charlotte describing her in the highest terms of love and respect, so she sought to verify or challenge his statement through another witness. Coincidentally, she heard about a relation of Harriet's who knew someone who attended the Hégers' Pensionnat at the same time so wrote to ask a favour:

> Will you be so kind as to ask Miss Dixon what Emily was like personally? She must have been the most curious and the mysterious of the sisters. Her extraordinary morbid development of talent and repulsive manners and yet the worship she seemed to have obtained from Charlotte.[41]

As more people received Elizabeth's letters of enquiry, speculation about the extent of her biography and the private lives of the Brontës began to circulate. Village gossip reached Patrick that Elizabeth was asking vicars if it was true that Patrick had always been hated in Haworth and had been appointed against the church trustees' opposition. None of that could be truthfully said about him, he told her, but he had heard it about his predecessor, and perhaps people conflated them:

> The people here generally are poor, but whether rich or poor they have always been not only civil to me and mine but friendly when an opportunity offered of showing their disposition. My children generally and my Dear Daughter Charlotte in particular were both kind, liberal and affable with the inhabitants.[42]

Three weeks after she met Ellen, Elizabeth finished reading her batch of letters. 'I don't think even you, her most cherished friend, could wish the impression on me to be different from what it is,' she told her, 'that she was one to study the path of duty well, and having ascertained what it was right to do, to follow out her idea strictly.' The letters were too beautiful to be used merely as sources, as Arthur suggested and expected, or even to be paraphrased as she herself first planned. Now she tested a new idea, one partly intimated by Patrick's endorsement imagining Charlotte approving Elizabeth from the grave. Having been silenced in life by the men around her and now by death, Charlotte should be allowed to speak, she insisted to Ellen, 'I am sure the more fully she, Charlotte Brontë – the *friend*, the *daughter*, the *sister*, the *wife* – is known, and known where need be in her own words, the more highly will she be appreciated.'[43] To Elizabeth's relief Ellen needed no convincing.

In the first week of September, Elizabeth and Marianne took the train to Glasgow to stay with Elizabeth's maternal cousins. They went to the twenty-fifth annual conference of the British Association for the Advancement of Science, which Unitarians like the Gaskells were – in theory – interested. Presentations and seminars on all branches of science from archaeology to zoology ran over three days from Wednesday, 12 September at the city's Merchant's Hall.[44] Even so far from home, Elizabeth could not escape her task. At a dinner hosted by Glasgow's Lord Provost and a local landowner, Sir John Maxwell, at the end of the week, she happened to meet Richard Monckton Milnes who had been presenting on statistics, with one of the office bearers for the committee on Mathematical and Physical Sciences, a Dr William Scoresby. 'To my surprise he told me he had been the vicar of Bradford for some years,' she disclosed to Ellen. Until he left the curacy in 1847 he had known Patrick Brontë well and 'told me many curious anecdotes about the extraordinary character of the people around Haworth.'[45]

They stayed a week with Elizabeth's cousin and her husband in a house at the northern verge of the city centre where the townhouses gave way to fields, before taking a steamer from the crowded Broomielaw docks down the Clyde to Dunoon on the Cowal Peninsula in the Firth of Clyde. There they were hosted by Catherine Stevenson, her late father's second wife, and her daughter, whom Elizabeth had not seen in decades, resurrecting connections she thought were lost. As she worked to unearth Charlotte's past, her own seemed to be coming up with it.

The moment she got back from Scotland in the first days of October, she chased William Smith Williams and George Smith for the letters they promised to look out for her. Crossly, she reminded George he had kept her waiting for ten days, leaving her 'surprised and disappointed'. He snapped to attention and apologetically sent her a package of twenty addressed to him and his mother, 'some of them only fragments of dear Miss Brontë's. The remainder, he says, contain matter purely too personal a nature.'[46] She curtly thanked him but made it clear she was less impressed than Charlotte. He might be obsequious, she thought, ('more civil than satisfactory' as she commented to Ellen), and too vague and inaccessible to be entirely likeable. Where Charlotte tortured herself with worry over what she could have done to provoke any tardy response from him, Elizabeth concluded it was because he was inefficient and commanded he attend to her requests promptly.

George's letters were a start, she told Ellen, but she knew he had more and planned to drop in on him unexpectedly, just as Ellen recommended she do with Margaret and everyone else who had less than their own enthusiasm about Charlotte's biography. Elizabeth knew Williams and Smith must be withholding more material and was adamant they would be as transparent with her as she demanded. 'I am sure I have not got half of what Mr Williams and he together *might* give: and what they *shall* give, or I'll know the reason why.'[47]

She was back in Manchester only a matter of days before she arranged another meeting with Ellen. This time, under Ellen's persuasion, Margaret did agree to see her and Ellen made the introductions. Duly, Margaret took them to the building that once housed Roe Head school where she, Ellen, Mary and Charlotte first met, before Ellen whisked Elizabeth off on a tour of some of the Birstall locations she thought Charlotte had in mind for *Shirley*. Elizabeth told Ellen she felt Margaret gave her very little direct information, understandably for a first meeting, but felt comfortable enough to send Margaret direct questions. She evidently extracted a promise from her to look out her letters from Charlotte, for a few weeks later Elizabeth confirmed 'your valuable parcel of letters was received in safety, and I promise that the utmost care shall be taken of them and that they shall be returned to you before very long.' Reading these, Elizabeth found yet another version of Charlotte to the one who wrote to her family, to Ellen, George and to herself. 'I hardly know how it is, but I like them better than any other series of letters of hers that I have seen.'[48]

When Williams sent her his selection in December, she had the same experience again and commented how curious it was to see 'how much the spirit in which she wrote varies according to the correspondent'.[49] She was particularly struck by the remarkable differences in tone between Charlotte's letters to him and those to George at the same address, sometimes written on the same day. She detected notes of tension and reservation in the exchanges with George and noticed that by contrast she sounded 'heartily at her ease with him [Williams] which I don't think she does in those I've seen to Mr Smith'.[50] It was becoming clear Charlotte had been a woman who expressed herself from behind figurative masks, using multiple guises and varying voices that all reflected and synchronised with the nature and expectations of her recipients, accumulating to a sum total of traits that comprised the whole woman behind this artifice.

Elizabeth set Marianne and Meta the task of copying them out and recruited a family friend, the 22-year-old niece of Charles Darwin, Frances

'Snow' Wedgwood, to stay over and help. Once they finished transcribing each letter, Elizabeth and William checked them against the originals. At the start of November, Snow told her sister she was 'rather sick of writing' as the process took 'an immense time. I have been about two hours at them today & shall set to again as soon as I have despatched [my letter to] you.'[51] They often read aloud particularly interesting sections, 'some indeed which were too intimate for publication', and as they progressed, came to one describing the Gaskells themselves, written to George Smith's mother after Charlotte's first visit to Plymouth Grove. When Elizabeth read aloud Charlotte's description of her 'four little girls all more or less pretty & intelligent', William laughed and asked if 'less' was underlined.[52]

Elizabeth became impossibly busy as work continued through November. Alongside writing to strangers about their contact with Charlotte, she negotiated French translations of her novels while managing a household disrupted by a sick servant, to host unending visits from friends. Meanwhile, letters from Ellen came requesting updates on progress. Always alert to any mention of Charlotte in the press, Ellen saw a few lines in the gossip columns at the start of December: 'Mrs Gaskell of Manchester has undertaken to write a 'Life' of Charlotte Brontë (author of 'Jane Eyre'), having been requested to do so by both father and husband.'[53]

She cut it out and sent it to Elizabeth and Arthur to ask if either of them knew who leaked the information. As usual when Arthur dealt with Ellen, he was dismissive, and made sure to remind her she was disturbing them. 'Mr Brontë knew nothing of your paragraph in *The Mercury* until he saw it in print. It is, however, no secret that Mrs Gaskell has undertaken the biography.'[54] Ellen may have noticed how Arthur avoided denying responsibility, yet with nothing to gain from doing it he had no need to deny anything. 'I have no idea *who* put in that little paragraph,' Elizabeth told her. She suggested it might have been George before adding wryly that 'he seems too indifferent to have even taken that much trouble.'[55] If she herself was not responsible, it was fortuitous that someone made it known. Within weeks she started receiving offers from publishers.

Arthur told Ellen they had not heard from Elizabeth in a while but continued to have every confidence 'that she will do ample justice to Charlotte – but I am quite sensible that she has undertaken a very difficult task with only slender material'.[56] He and Patrick often discussed it and assumed Elizabeth would have to use her novelistic skills to extract anything from the thin seam of information they allowed her. Patrick told her:

We so frequently talk over and meditate on these things that we are forced at last to solve the difficulty by saying that you must draw largely on the resources of your own mind. My daughter had that to do in no small degree.[57]

With no idea that Elizabeth's interest in Charlotte was taking her so far beyond a sketch that she had now committed to travelling to every location Charlotte had ever visited and tracking down anyone who had known her, they could hardly imagine it was expanding beyond their expectation of a long-form article.

Judging both men by what little they had told her, Elizabeth discredited them as the most reliable sources. Their recollections were so scant and unenlightened, and their perspectives so narrow and biased she began to think even strangers might have taken fairer, more accurate perspectives than they. She wrote to servants from the family's early days, Martha Wright in Burnley and Nancy Garrs in Bradford and hunted down women who had attended Cowan Bridge (Patrick could only recall one particularly memorable name of Melanie Hane) and asked if anyone knew the whereabouts of the old teachers, especially the headmistress who had inspired the sadistic Miss Scatcherd. She told George she managed to find one she believed to be the original of the kindly Miss Temple, a woman named Ann Connor, married to a clergyman in one of James's estates in Leicestershire. 'She may give me some particulars of that terrible Cowan Bridge time and possibly some explanations which may modify that account of the school in *Jane Eyre* which took such a strong hold in the public mind.'[58]

As her daughters copied Charlotte's letters, Elizabeth confessed to Ellen she had not written a line of the book. 'I feel that I can do so much more by *seeing* people than by writing. Of course, this takes me a much longer time, but I think the result will be all the more satisfactory.'[59] She thought back to when Arthur refused to let her see Charlotte's unpublished manuscripts and especially the one that sounded like a raw version of *Villette* and wondered what he could be trying to hide. She looked ahead for dates in the new year when she could pounce on George and William Smith Williams in London and asked Ellen to come to Manchester as soon as possible. And she toyed with the idea that her research could go even further, out of England and across the Channel to Belgium, to Brussels and Monsieur and Madame Héger, who must surely – she suspected – hold the key to a period in Charlotte's life that no one wanted to discuss.

arlotte Brontë drawn by George Richmond during her London visit of July 1850. After an engraving of it
s included in Elizabeth Gaskell's *Life of Charlotte Bronte*, it became an iconic image of the nineteenth century.
ational Portrait Gallery)

A caricature by Branwell Brontë inside the cover of the family's copy of Goldsmith's *Geography*, circa 1833, may be of Charlotte. The overhanging forehead, deep-set eyes and weak mouth resemble descriptions of her. (The Brontë Society)

Anne, Emily and Charlotte Brontë by Branwell Brontë, circa 1834. Elizabeth Gaskell based her descriptions of Anne and Emily on this after Charlotte showed it to her in 1853. Branwell abandoned his incomplete and disproportionate self-portrait and disguised it with the central pillar. (National Portrait Gallery)

Haworth Parsonage photographed from the churchyard around 1856. It may be one of the daguerreotypes taken for Elizabeth Gaskell. (The Brontë Society)

Branwell Brontë sculpted by Joseph Leyland, 1846. The likeness was described as exact by those who knew Branwell. (The Brontë Society)

Arthur Bell Nicholls, photographed circa 1855. (The Brontë Society)

Patrick Brontë, photographed before 1860. This may be the image taken in 1854 for John Greenwood. (The Brontë Society)

Left: Martha Brown, photographed circa 1860. (The Brontë Society)

Below left: Ellen Nussey, photographed in the 1870s. (The Brontë Society)

Below: Margaret Wooler, photographed in old age. (The Brontë Society)

Right: Lady Janet
Kay-Shuttleworth, painted
by Francis Grant, circa 1840.
(National Trust)

Below: Harriet Martineau, painted
by Richard Evans in 1834.
(National Portrait Gallery)

Below right: George Smith, drawn
circa 1848. (The Brontë Society)

Left: Sir James Kay-Shuttleworth, photographed in 1862. (National Trust)

Below left: William Thackeray, photographed in 1863. (National Portrait Gallery)

Below: Rachel Felix, photographed in 1853. (Public Domain)

A carte de visite of Elizabeth Gaskell, taken by Alexander McGlashan around 1860. (The University of Manchester)

CHAPTER 12

1856

The Promised Land

Elizabeth wrote twenty pages of *The Life of Charlotte Brontë* through the first seven weeks of 1856. Beginning with present circumstances, with death not birth, she listed the names from mother to last-lived daughter inscribed on the memorial slabs over the Brontë vault, mapping a genealogy of the family's narrow span of decades and presented the question her first reading of *Jane Eyre* prompted, only partially answered by meeting Charlotte: what forces could have shaped such an uncommon individual. As she explained to George:

> Leaving all authorship on one side, her character as a woman was unusual to the point of being unique. I never heard or read of anyone who was for an instant, or in any respect, to be compared with her. And everything she did and every word she said and wrote bore the impress of this remarkable character.[1]

She considered the setting of Charlotte's life and death, of that low horizon of dark moors and the village Charlotte characterised as forlorn and hopelessly cut off from civilisation. Visiting both had confirmed and refuted that. Elizabeth opened the book by recounting her journey on the Leeds and Skipton railway, pulling the reader into neighbouring Keighley, a town embracing modernity, erasing its own past by widening roads and flattening the old-fashioned gabled houses to push into its fields the relentless factories that would tint the atmosphere 'dim and lightless with the smoke'. The long ascent over the hills to Haworth dropped to a valley, then climbed a steep road, before a turn led to the even steeper Main Street and the small church where Patrick preached near his family's memorial slabs. Elizabeth obtained a transcription of them from John Greenwood and noted the dates were different to Patrick's recollection. After the landscape came its people, contrasting that constitutionally isolated family within a populous village and its unique 'society amidst which her earliest years were passed, and from which both her own and her sisters' first impressions of human life must have been received'.[2]

Despite her dedication to local history and with now over 400 letters by Charlotte, Elizabeth still held doubts about her own capabilities:

> I never did write a biography, and I don't exactly know how to set about it; you see I have to be accurate and keep to facts; a most difficult thing for a writer of fiction. And then the style too! That is a bugbear. It must be grander and more correct, I am afraid.[3]

For Ellen, there could be no room for doubt. If Elizabeth met obstacles, Ellen proposed solutions. When Elizabeth complained of the lack of first-hand accounts describing Emily and Anne, Ellen wrote two essays about them, posted them to Elizabeth, then checked regularly if she had read them and how she planned to use them. She proposed coming to Manchester to discuss them in the first weeks of January – which Elizabeth had to decline – and tried to hurry Elizabeth along fearing Charlotte's place in the public memory was fleeting. Industrious as she was, Elizabeth could not write fast enough for her. By late February, she got Marianne to take over replying to Ellen's letters, assuring her she did not think interest in Charlotte would subside, as biographies – such as a recent one of Matthew Arnold's father – often appeared as much as a decade after their subject's death. And because 'interruptions will come and come unexpectedly' Elizabeth could not tell her when it would be finished but that there was no possibility of it being ready before the end of the year.[4]

Determining a release date was impossible but a publisher was certain. No contract has survived, yet it is clear Elizabeth always felt the book belonged with Charlotte's publisher rather than her own. Informal discussions with George had progressed by Holy Week when she accepted an offer for the US edition, leaving the formalities of British contracts and payments with George until the end of the year. Offers for overseas rights had been coming from as soon as the press first reported she was writing Charlotte's life, with three publishers sending her bids for a first refusal, starting at £10, then £35 and finally, the one she accepted, of £75 – nearly £6,500 at present value – all 'curiously different values to attach to the same thing,' she commented.[5] Appleton & Co of New York offered so far above her expectations she had to check it was legitimate and not a ruse by a pirate publisher to get her material.

Pressured by expectations and frustrated by the dead ends of her research, she was grateful for George's encouragement after he read what she had written:

> I was, and am, very anxious to do it *thoroughly* well as anything about her ought to be done. I don't mind how much I labour at it, only I am vexed to find on reading it over that my English is so bad. But it *shall* be good before I have done.[6]

With both the book and transcription of its raw material underway by the middle of March, Elizabeth considered how to close the last gap in her research: Charlotte's time in Brussels. She cancelled all unnecessary social activities and sought connections. Through friends she got the address of the Belgian ambassador, from whom she expected to 'get plenty of *grand* Brussels introductions' and contacted the head of the Belgian police, who turned out to be a fan of her work and offered to host her. 'So I mean to make him serviceable, as I find he holds a good position for ascertaining past facts in Brussels.'[7] Knowing no one in Belgium who could carry out interviews or research for her, she accepted the only realistic solution was to travel there herself. Mistakenly believing the Hégers closed their school after it was identified as the one full of eavesdroppers in *Villette* she knew she had to be discreet, even covert, and pursued opinions 'without stating my reason for wanting them'.[8]

Marianne planned her mother's route at the start of May and through the recommendation of a family friend found her lodgings in Brussels. As the trip meant a stop in London at the end of April, Elizabeth turned it into a holiday for her youngest two daughters, and with housekeeper Ann Hearn, took Flossy and Julia, leaving William, Marianne and Meta at home in Manchester. She wanted to show them London 'in the true country cousin sense of the expression – and every day is planned crammed full' with excursions to Windsor, Hampton Court and Kew Gardens and visits to relations and friends. Provisionally, she planned for Hearn to take the children home on Friday, 2 May before she sailed from Dover, but an offer from her friend Lady Coltman to host the girls and Hearn for a weekend concert in Kensington Gardens meant Elizabeth could extend their holiday and include 19-year-old Meta, to be brought from Manchester on Thursday, 1 May by Eliza Thornborrow, an occasional well-liked family servant she wanted for her companion to Brussels. The following week, when the younger girls were to go home, Elizabeth, Meta and Eliza would leave for Belgium.[9] Elizabeth asked Marianne to get her father to confirm he could send Meta and have Eliza agree she could come both to London and Belgium. 'Think and plan for me,' she asked, overwhelmed by the continually moving arrangements, 'I am utterly worn out and perplexed.'[10]

When George heard she was in London, he invited her to meet him and his mother but she told him it would have to wait until she got back as every hour was already allocated in a frantic hunt for the only people who could steer her once she got to Brussels: the Wheelwright sisters, who attended the Hégers' school alongside the Brontës. George may have remembered Charlotte visiting Laetitia Wheelwright in Kensington whenever she stayed with him and shortly Elizabeth sent a note of introduction, asking to call to 'ascertain all the particulars she can' and stressing she 'will feel extremely *obliged* to the Miss Wheelwrights if they will suggest any clues to information there'.[11]

She found Laetitia remembered Charlotte and Emily well and had kept up with Charlotte until the last weeks of her life but only learned of her death from the newspapers. She had met her in Brussels in the autumn of 1842 when she was 14 and Charlotte was 26. Her physician father had brought them from London that July, enrolling her and her four sisters as day pupils at the Pensionnat Héger in the second term of the year, after the Brontës' first as full-time boarders. She sketched out how she and her sisters first encountered them amongst the French-speaking Catholic girls, all more than a decade younger, taking to Charlotte more than the withdrawn and socially hostile Emily.

After the interview, Elizabeth apologetically asked Laetitia if she could repeat herself on paper:

> I distinctly recollect your account of Emily's appearance and manners but I forget what you said was the first impression made by Charlotte on any casual observer. I suppose she was *extremely* shy? I shall be very much obliged to you if you will answer all my questions. I can only regret that some of them are repetitions of those whose answers I have forgotten.[12]

Laetitia promised to forward her letters from Charlotte and told her, as she would subsequent biographers, that Charlotte had written to their admired professor, Constantin Héger, for about two years after she left but ended it abruptly.[13] She knew Charlotte became so invested she suspected delays in his replies were because her letters were being intercepted or destroyed before he got them, so asked Laetitia and other friends still in Brussels to deliver them personally. Laetitia thought it irrational and never entertained the notion that Charlotte might be correct.

Once Meta and Eliza arrived from Manchester, the party stayed overnight at the Victoria Hotel in Euston Square then left London on the evening of Tuesday, 6 May. The two-and-a-half-hour railway journey brought them to Dover at eleven at night where they boarded a steamship for the overnight sailing to Ostend. Elizabeth was already exhausted before she set off and wrote to Marianne in Manchester, 'I am in despair and can hardly keep from perpetually crying, which is partly being so overtired.'[14]

Landing on the Belgian coast at dawn, the women had time to breakfast in Ostend before the first train at seven fifteen, through the East Flanders cities of Bruges and Ghent, took them to Brussels three hours later.[15] Elizabeth had written ahead to book rooms in an English-speaking boarding house at 47 Avenue de la Toison d'Or, in what was considered the most fashionable and healthy quarter at the time. The tall, narrow establishment was run by an English couple who offered 'visitors and families all the advantages of an English and Continental house, combining society, comfort and a good table, upon moderate terms'.[16] As well as its obvious attractions to Englishwomen abroad, the boarding house had another appeal. Only twenty minutes' walk away were four flights of broad steps that led to a side street so sunken that the chimney pots of the houses were below the level of the top steps; this was the Rue d'Isabelle, on which stood the Pensionnat Héger, still open to students.

> Opposite to the lowest flight of steps, there is a large old mansion facing you, with a spacious walled garden behind – and to the right of it. In front of this garden, on the same side as the mansion, and with great boughs of trees sweeping over their lowly roofs, is a row of small, picturesque, old-fashioned cottages, not unlike, in degree and uniformity, to the alms houses so often seen in an English country town. The Rue d'Isabelle looks as though it had been untouched by the innovations of the builder for the last three centuries; and yet any one might drop a stone into it from the back windows of the grand modern hotels in the Rue Royale, built and furnished in the newest Parisian fashion.[17]

It is likely that Elizabeth approached the proprietors – 47-year-old Constantin Héger and his 52-year-old wife Zoë Claire Parent Héger – as she had everyone else, sending them a note of introduction and requesting to call at the first opportunity. In reply she received an invitation and found Monsieur Héger to be open, even interested in meeting her. But as soon as Madame heard she had come to ask questions about Charlotte Brontë, she refused to speak to her. This was not enough to arouse any suspicions, as others had done the same. For every person who was happy to be interviewed about Charlotte, there were as many who were not. Patrick was enthusiastic when Arthur was reluctant; Ellen was passionately committed where Margaret had needed persuasion. With those who had reservations, Elizabeth had shown she was sympathetic to their sense of propriety and discretion. As with all the others, she went with foreknowledge, having heard about them from Charlotte even before she read *Villette*, which Charlotte said was largely autobiographical. As a novelist herself, she suspected Charlotte could not have meant this literally, as autobiography rarely made good fiction, but once she found the school to be physically identical to the one in *Villette* she may have gradually realised Charlotte had been serious. Furthermore, Madame Héger's opposition would not be incompatible with Elizabeth's suspicion she was the original of *Villette*'s sinister Madame Beck, whose interferences threaten Lucy Snowe's love life. Evidently, something had caused an acrimony that still lasted.

On her last visit to Manchester, Charlotte had told her she feared *Villette* being sold in Belgium after George secured her £100 for the French translation. But she could not have known a pirate edition was already circulating there, that the Hégers had read it, and soon readers were making connections to the Pensionnat Héger and between the school's staff in the book – the charismatic Paul Emanuel and his jealous cousin Madame Beck – with the Hégers themselves. While curious tourists came to look at the school, boarders began to avoid it. Madame Héger blamed the book specifically for her school's eventual failure.

Elizabeth must have explained to Constantin she had come for his impressions of Charlotte and Emily Brontë and to hear what he could remember of teaching them. It is not known whether she conducted the interviews in French or English but as he was more proficient in English than she was in French we may assume they conversed in English. He told her the Brontës knew nothing of the language when they arrived, having learned it – Elizabeth explained – from books and hearing pronunciation from an English-speaking tutor. This kept them from integrating with the French-speaking student majority, but even if they had been more fluent at first, their differences in age, nationality, religion and sociability would still have marked them out. He took them for French language classes while other tutors took them for German, arithmetic, drawing, music and singing. In the first few weeks before he got to know Charlotte and Emily, he explained, he could not help but notice them in the school corridors and garden, where they walked together in silence.

> The two sisters clung together, and kept apart from the herd of happy, boisterous, well-befriended Belgian girls, who, in their turn, thought the new English pupils wild and scared-looking, with strange, odd, insular ideas about dress; for Emily had taken a fancy to the fashion, ugly and preposterous even during its reign, of gigot sleeves, and persisted in wearing them long after they were 'gone out'. Her petticoats, too, had not a curve or a wave in them, but hung down straight and long, clinging to her lank figure.[18]

He observed how they spoke exclusively to each other, only referring to anyone else when unavoidably necessary. Emily rarely spoke at all, even with Charlotte. 'They were too full of earnest thought, and of the exile's sick yearning, to be ready for careless conversation or merry game.' He taught them through the first semester, observing the considerable differences in their natures and talents that were undeniably superior to their peers. He considered Charlotte unselfish, accommodating a long-established imbalance of controlling will from Emily, who he thought egotistical and exacting. Her genius was greater than Charlotte's, he reasoned, and both he and Elizabeth knew Charlotte had felt the same. Emily was logical and pragmatic but tenacious enough to make her impossible to reason with. 'She should have been a man,' Héger told Elizabeth, 'a great navigator. Her powerful reason would have deduced new spheres of discovery from the knowledge of the old; and her strong imperious will would never have been daunted by opposition or difficulty; never have given way but with life.' Emily's imagination, he remembered, would have made her a notable historian who would have overwhelmed readers with her power to evoke people and places. Her rhetoric would have persuaded them to convert their opinions to the opposite.

Knowing both sisters should be ill-served by the standard methods provided to the other students he consulted his wife about how best to teach them. It was proposed he read the French classics with them then dissect their strengths and weaknesses together in a seminar. He asked Charlotte and Emily how they felt about the plan. Emily answered first that she did not like it and thought it risked damaging the fluency and originality of the texts. Charlotte agreed but said that as his pupil she was duty bound to comply with his wishes. He found a compromise by selecting an extract from a French text and comparing the exaggerations and nuances in its style, then asked them to write essays of similarly analytical argument on subjects of their own choosing, advising them, 'It is necessary before sitting down to write on a subject, to have thoughts and feelings about it. I cannot tell on what subject your heart and mind have been excited. I must leave that to you.'[19]

He told Elizabeth he kept their coursework because it had been so remarkable. She expressed an interest to see it. As with everyone she interviewed, she asked if Charlotte had ever written to him and whether he still had any of her letters. Every batch she had seen so far presented to her a different woman, remade to something more agreeable than Charlotte felt herself to be for each of her contacts. Héger told her he had only kept four. These were the most revealing yet. Written over a period of twenty-two months after she left his school in January 1844 and returned to England, they were unquestionably the confessions of a woman in love: impossibly, unrequitedly in love with a married man. At first, Charlotte had written every fortnight, sending at least ten letters until he stopped replying regularly in April 1844. He saved only one of that period from his wastepaper basket and tore up the rest. She persisted every few months, mentioning the following January that she still had not heard from him since the previous April, which seems to have prompted a reply that sustained her until the summer. He kept three from this period and the last from her, dated November 1845.

If they were in the same condition as when they were donated to the British Library sixty years later, they were already fragile. Elizabeth would have seen that three of the four had been used as scrap paper for the testing of different pen nibs and inks and to note the address of a local shoemaker, before they had been torn up into fragments then carefully sewn back together with white thread. Reading them, Elizabeth heard her friend's voice call out from ten years before, pleading in loneliness and hopelessness for contact from the first man to recognise her intelligence and talent:

All I know – is that I cannot – that I will not resign myself to the total loss of my master's friendship – I would rather undergo the greatest bodily pains than have my heart constantly lacerated by searing regrets. If my master withdraws his friendship from me entirely I shall be absolutely without hope – if he gives me a little friendship – a very little – I shall be content – happy, I would have a motive for living – for working. Monsieur, the poor do not need a great deal to live on – they ask only the crumbs of bread which fall from the rich men's table – but if they are refused these crumbs – they die of hunger – No more do I need a great deal of affection from those I love – I would not know what to do with a whole and complete friendship – I am not accustomed to it – but you showed a *little* interest in me in days gone by when I was your pupil in Brussels – and I cling to the preservation of this *little* interest – I cling to it as I would cling on to life.[20]

Héger explained he had replied at first, but Charlotte's letters were so frequent and her attention so unflattering, so increasingly unwanted that he requested she ration her letters to him and only write, if she must, once every six months. Charlotte's finest, more powerful feelings, whose opportunity for expression was a privilege to her, were only a nuisance to him and in time, he saw her letters as meaningless as blotting paper to be scribbled on, effaced then discarded, to be sewn back together it has been surmised, by his wife. Broken, Charlotte was forced to comply, and crawled on with increasing desperation and diminishing hope.

Your last letter has sustained me – has nourished me for six months – now I need another and you will give it me – not because you have any friendship for me – you cannot have much – but because you have a compassionate soul and because you would not condemn anyone to undergo long suffering in order to spare yourself a few moments of tedium … [S]o long as I think you are fairly pleased with me, so long as I still have the hope of hearing from you, I can be tranquil and not too sad, but when a dreary and prolonged silence seems to warn me that my master is becoming estranged from me – when day after day I await a letter and day after day disappointment flings me down again into overwhelming misery, when the sweet delight of seeing your writing and reading your counsel flees from me like an empty vision – then I am in a fever – I lose my appetite and my sleep – I pine away.[21]

Héger eventually asked her to redirect her letters to a different address, Laetitia told Elizabeth, to a boys' school where he also taught, so as not to arouse his wife's suspicions. Charlotte refused and never wrote again. For context, Héger told Elizabeth she should look for his replies. 'He is sure she would keep them,' she confided to Ellen, 'as they contained advice about her character, studies, mode of life. I doubt very much if Mr Nicholls has not destroyed them.'[22]

She allowed this possibility, that Arthur had already burned everything he found in Charlotte's possession but balanced it against what he had told her: that he still had some. There was a possibility they existed, assuming Charlotte generally kept the letters she received – many people ordinarily destroyed letters once they digested their contents – but Elizabeth knew this would require another visit to Haworth and another tricky negotiation with Arthur, who already felt infringed upon by the very nature of Elizabeth's task. When she reconsidered his reluctance to show her the manuscript of *The Professor*, she began to wonder at his reasons. Could it be Charlotte's unfiltered account of her love for Professor Héger? Had she reconsidered it once she accepted she would never hear from him again, then toned it down and reworked the same story a few years later as *Villette*?

Elizabeth was impressed by Héger's discretion about Charlotte's feelings for him. He had never spoken publicly about her or tried to publish her letters, but Elizabeth knew it must only be a matter of time before someone persuaded him to do so. Even if that happened, there could be no way to include them in her biography and still rationally explain Charlotte's interest in him. Additionally, if *The Professor* was a more explicit exploration of her love for him it would, if anyone should risk publishing it, destroy both Charlotte's posthumous reputation and Héger's professional career. It would confirm the suspicions of Charlotte's most hostile reviewers that characterised her as a woman of dubious sexual morals, and instigate speculation that Héger had been in an exploitative and adulterous relationship with one of his pupils.

Elizabeth took the train back to Ostend with Meta and Eliza to catch the night steamer across the channel. Even at this stage, she must have known the course of action she had to take next if she was to protect Charlotte and now Héger; somehow, she had to get the manuscript of *The Professor* and read it before anyone could publish it. And the only way to do that was to go back to Haworth and prise it out of Arthur's hands. There was, however, another possibility. As it had been considered by Smith Elder before they rejected it – which prompted Charlotte to send them *Jane Eyre* instead – at least one person in the company must have read it and should be able to tell her about its contents. Unless it had been passed on to one of their junior readers, that could only mean George Smith or William Smith Williams. As soon as she got to London, she asked to meet them.

The offices of Smith Elder at 65 Cornhill were in the back rooms of a shop that sold the books they had published – including all three of Charlotte's novels and their edition of Emily and Anne's. Here, Charlotte and Anne first materialised in July 1848 to reveal themselves to George as Currer and Acton Bell. Although Elizabeth had known of George professionally for some years through mutual friends and had been corresponding with him for just over a year, they had never met. She found him to be 'an agreeable, genial-mannered man with a keen eye to business' but was not as enamoured as Charlotte had been, even considering him 'rather too stout to be handsome'.[23]

She asked if he could take her to the Chapter Coffee House in Paternoster Row, the place Charlotte used as the starting point for two of the pivotal moments in her life: when she stayed there with her father and Emily on their way to Brussels in 1842, then six years later when she stayed there with Anne when they came to reveal their identities. Charlotte and Anne had romanticised it as the beating heart of literary London where poets and critics of earlier centuries socialised with their publishers and booksellers in search of ideas and commissions. They also knew of it from their father, who had stayed there as a young man just after he applied to take Holy Orders and was publishing occasional poems of his own. By the time they lodged there it was a shadow of its own past, a shabby run-down tavern cringing in the shadows of a gloomy side street. It closed in 1854 after the death of its then-owner and had its interior furnishings stripped before it was reopened as a pub. It turned out to be the final location of Elizabeth's investigation, as by the time she and George ventured there it had closed again. However, through the high, narrow windows Elizabeth could see some traces of the past Charlotte would have known: 'the small rooms were low and had heavy beams running across them; the walls were wainscotted breast high; the staircase was shallow, broad, and dark, taking up much space in the centre of the house.'[24] From where they stood on the pavement George could point out the window seat where he found Charlotte and Anne 'clinging together' the evening he came to collect them for their first trip to the opera.[25]

He brought Elizabeth home to dine with his family and meet the wife whom Charlotte never knew (Elizabeth thought her as 'very pretty' as one of Charlotte's characters in *Villette*), their 18-month-old daughter, and his mother, Elizabeth Murray Smith. She was '*exactly* like Mrs Bretton,' she told Ellen afterwards though did not want to flatter George with an agreement when he suggested it. William Smith Williams joined them for dinner, and sat with them 'grey-haired, silent and refined'. They talked about discovering *Jane Eyre* and how they received the manuscript of *The Professor* just over a month earlier in a brown paper parcel covered with the addresses of all those who had rejected it, 'not obliterated, but simply scored through, so that Messrs. Smith at once perceived the names of some of the houses in the trade to which the unlucky parcel had gone, without success'.[26] Williams remembered whole sections were so similar to *Villette* that it could not be published without being considered derivative. They still had all the manuscripts of Charlotte's other novels and may have shown them to Elizabeth on this visit before they parcelled them up and sent them to her so she could examine them more closely.[27]

George suggested she should persuade Patrick it was impossible to critique Charlotte's work without seeing everything else she had written including *The Professor* and – of greater interest to him – *Emma*. That was a manuscript of fifty pages no one had seen, and the last fiction Charlotte had written. George wondered whether it had any commercial potential and if Charlotte's happier state of mind after her marriage might have given it a different character to *Villette*. Furthermore, if Elizabeth was going to ask Patrick for Charlotte's unpublished novels, she might as well go further and ask for her letters to him too, George suggested. With an eye to the development of *The Life of Charlotte Brontë*, he remembered that while staying with him, he often saw her writing 'long, constant and minute' letters to her father recounting her activities and all her meetings with celebrated strangers, such as his favourite, Thackeray. As ever, George saw an opportunity to publicise his own authors by having them mentioned in the book almost as endorsements. In response, Elizabeth may have asked if he would carry out a reciprocal task. She wanted the book to include a picture of Charlotte but knew the only one they could copy was hanging in the parsonage. She had been told Arthur refused John Greenwood's offer to have it photographed and was too afraid to ask him directly. As the portrait had been a gift from George to Patrick, might he bring more weight to the request? George agreed. He would ask Patrick rather than Arthur, to send the portrait back to him to have it photographed professionally, telling him, disingenuously, it was only for himself.

A week or so after she got back to Plymouth Grove, Elizabeth received the results. They did not bode well for her obtaining the manuscripts. Patrick himself was agreeable but told George that Arthur was against it, so could not comply. 'Perhaps I have no right to complain,' George told

Elizabeth in resignation.[28] 'It seems as if Mr Brontë's own consent or opinion on these matters had very little weight with Mr Nicholls,' Elizabeth complained to Ellen once she had a chance to recount everything that had happened, certain Ellen would be sympathetic, as she saw him as a usurper of their claim to Charlotte. In truth, Arthur may simply have disbelieved George only wanted a copy for himself, suspecting that as soon as he parted with it, his wife's likeness would be reproduced without his permission and commercially exploited in whatever way George could sell it. In the short and long term, Arthur's instincts would be proven correct.

'I want to write you a long letter and tell you all my adventures,' Elizabeth told Ellen at the start of July, once she had caught up with the private and business correspondence that had accumulated at Plymouth Grove in her absence. 'Brussels, where Mme Héger, understanding that I was a friend of Miss Brontë's refused to see me; but I made M Héger's acquaintance and very much indeed I both like and respect him.'[29]

Ellen practically jumped when she saw Elizabeth's handwriting and wrote back that she had been desperate to know how the Hégers received her, an indication of how much she herself had heard about them from Charlotte. Elizabeth told her Constantin had been accommodating and sympathetic, but his wife had refused to co-operate. 'I feel pleasure in your account of Monsieur. He would do dear C[harlotte] justice, for he could understand her nature and the intensity of how it was never more manifested than during her sojourn at Brussels – and for some time subsequent ...,' Ellen commented.[30] Madame Héger's refusal only confirmed Charlotte's depiction of her as Madame Beck, she said, otherwise she would surely have taken the opportunity to challenge it. 'Did you obtain any of dear C's letters to Monsieur Héger?' she asked. Elizabeth must have told her she had and that Héger told her to look for his replies. Ellen needed no explanation as to why Charlotte would have received letters from Constantin for years after she left his school, indicating Charlotte had told her about them, but she doubted any evidence of Charlotte's love for him had been allowed to survive. Up until then, Ellen had been sure Charlotte planned to destroy all letters she received up to her marriage but with the emergence of some Arthur gave to Elizabeth, perhaps she had not after all, or some had survived – or perhaps Ellen had been mistaken; she told Elizabeth she could not be certain if Charlotte definitely *had* told her that or not.

Whatever the case, Ellen felt Arthur's lack of transparency was distasteful and he should 'have no reserve with you. His very affection should make him see it is wisest, best, and kindest to tell the whole truth to you in everything that regards her literary life or her domestic virtues.' Elizabeth told her going to Haworth was unavoidable now, even though, 'I am literally *afraid* of that.' Ellen said she wished she could convince Arthur herself that the more famous they could collectively make Charlotte 'the more highly will she shine and be the means of good to the readers of her Memoir'.[31]

There might be some room for leverage, she thought, as Arthur had told her he had a great deal of confidence in Elizabeth. If nothing else, Ellen assured her, Elizabeth's commitment would win over Patrick and he in turn would wear down Arthur into compliance with all his characteristic urgency and impatience. She hoped everything about Charlotte could be preserved reverentially, then added, without realising the irony, that she was sending Elizabeth the letters Charlotte had written from her deathbed. She had found them again not long before, absent-mindedly stuffed into one of her pockets.

CHAPTER 13

1856

Treason

Elizabeth knew going back to Haworth would require the kind of subterfuge and ingenuity needed for a heist. When she had taken Katie Winkworth the last time it was for company and to charm the two curates. This time she needed someone strident and authoritative whom Patrick and Arthur respected, prepared to browbeat them into giving her what she wanted. She knew the very man. She contacted Sir James to tell him her plan and went to Gawthorpe to meet him on Wednesday, 24 July.

To secure his help, she bargained that if he got the manuscripts and the portrait, she would allow him to be the first outside Smith Elder to read Charlotte's last unpublished novel, *The Professor*. She got Marianne to consult Ellen on their best method of attack; should she let Patrick and Arthur know they were coming, 'or take them unawares?'[1] In the past, Ellen always advised her to do just this, but when Elizabeth and James arrived at the parsonage unannounced, they found the household unprepared for guests. Martha was away, Arthur was alone and Patrick was in bed with rheumatism. To avoid inconveniencing them, Elizabeth and James had lunch in The Black Bull then went back in the afternoon once Patrick was able to come down to meet them for tea. She prepared James on what she needed him to do and being a man who was 'not prevented by the fear of giving pain from asking for whatever he thinks desirable', he did not hesitate to comment on the portrait of Charlotte hanging above the fireplace, 'as if he had known nothing of Mr Nicholls' reluctance'. He asked Patrick if he would permit them to have it photographed, to which Patrick meekly agreed, deferring to Arthur for permission. Before Arthur had a chance to object, James cut in. 'Oh! I know Mr Nicholls will grant it – and we will trust to Mrs Gaskell to send over a photographer from Manchester, for I dare say he would not like to part with the portrait.'[2]

With that, Elizabeth asked Arthur if he had found any more of Charlotte's letters, mindful of George's recommendation to fish for those she wrote to her father. Unexpectedly and contradicting what she had been told before, 'both he and Mr Brontë declared that all her letters were destroyed' and that nothing personal remained.[3] James instructed Arthur then to bring them all of Charlotte's surviving papers so they could examine them. Arthur complied and showed them the manuscripts of *The Professor* and *Emma* ('written in the finest pencil', Elizabeth noticed) then surprised them both with other material he had never mentioned before: a large package made up of bundles of loose papers crammed with miniscule handwriting and clusters of tiny hand-made books of different sizes, from half a page to some so small they were hardly larger than a postage stamp. 'All in this indescribably fine writing', Elizabeth saw, and describing the 'wildest and most incoherent things, as far as we have examined them, *all* purporting to be written, or addressed to some member of the Wellesley family'. These were the remains of Charlotte's childhood activities, the games of make-believe she played with her siblings of acting out improvised scenes of conflict and comedy then writing about them, ultimately producing an entire library of histories and biographies about soldiers and aristocrats who conquered imaginary tropical islands. Elizabeth thought they were extraordinary; the bizarre and feverish imaginings of a youth with enough creative ferocity to carry them to the edge of insanity. Uncomfortable yet thrilled, she watched how James firmly told Arthur they would borrow everything and 'coolly took actual possession of many things while Mr Nicholls was saying he could not possibly part with them'.[4]

Though not entirely comfortable, she went back to Manchester jubilant. The pile of juvenile writings was almost impossible to describe. They resembled doll-sized newspapers, with other larger pages written in a cramped imitation of type, like pages from printed books. Some of them read like the papers of William Blake, she thought, written when he was almost delirious with creative vision. Peering over the tiny script, her husband estimated they would print up to fifty volumes of ordinary-sized books. She knew she would have to incorporate this into her life of Charlotte and sent one of them to George to ask if he thought it would be possible to photograph a page from it 'as no words of mine could explain it'.[5]

While she scrutinised all of this and the pages of *Emma* over the days that followed, Elizabeth wondered what James made of *The Professor* after he took it back to Gawthorpe to read on his own. She had not shared with him the alarm she felt about its possible content and kept quiet about what

Héger had told her, having ruled out including anything about Charlotte's infatuation. She resolved there could not be so much as an indication of it and feared *The Professor* might divulge her secret. Its title alone suggested it related to Héger even more directly than *Villette* and if it reached the public, Héger might be forced to sell or publish Charlotte's letters to defend his own reputation. Elizabeth knew they were courting disaster and confided in George, 'I cannot tell you how I should deprecate anything leading to the publication of those letters of M. Héger.'[6] Before she had returned from Brussels, Héger sent her a letter; it was waiting for her at home. He enclosed some of the essays Charlotte and Emily had written for him and 'I also enclose a few extracts from the texts of the letters Mlle Charlotte wrote me.'[7] Choosing representative parts of both would take diplomacy and discretion, she concluded, and only shield readers from the full truth, which she felt was beyond their entitlement.

A week later she went to stay with a cousin in Evesham. There a letter came from James that turned her blood cold. He declared *The Professor* was wonderful and must be published. Not only that: he should edit it. It would add to Charlotte's standing as a novelist, he told her, so long as he rewrote 'certain coarse and objectionable phrases'.[8] Elizabeth was horrified. He explained he would delete the unsavoury sections, rewrite them then 'make the necessary alterations' by revising the entire book himself. He begged her to introduce him to George so he could pitch it. The bullish sense of prerogative that enabled him to get the papers now emboldened him to turn it into an opportunity for himself. Elizabeth saw how keen he was to represent himself as a closer friend of Charlotte's than he had been, and by using her work might also fulfil his long-held ambition to become an author. 'He over-rides all wishes, feelings and delicacy,' she complained sheepishly to George. 'I saw that in his way of carrying everything before him at Haworth, deaf to remonstrance and entreaty.'[9] She cautioned James to reconsider. Conscious of Charlotte's derision when he tried to lecture them about the dangers of women writing fiction and worried that he had no concern for the consequences of unleashing the novel, she asked him to let her read it before he did anything, by forwarding it to her husband so he could bring it to Evesham. To make matters worse, George would not dismiss the idea of publishing James's edition and imagined the immense sales, particularly if they could be buoyed by aristocratic promotion or associated scandal. After all, it was notoriety that helped sell thousands of copies of *Jane Eyre*.

Knowing she was losing ground, Elizabeth switched her objections from the ethical to the technical; James was not a professional editor, she warned

George, and they should remember how Charlotte's 'felicity of expression and deep insight' made her incompatible with equal talents, let alone lesser ones. She herself would never consider tampering with Charlotte's prose and was sure had Charlotte been alive she would have chosen William Smith Williams to edit her, as she described his skills in the highest terms. Unabashed, James ignored her and contacted Arthur to insist it be published under his direction, telling him – unknown to Elizabeth – that she had agreed they should edit it together with Arthur's permission.[10] Quickly, and determined to undermine him, Elizabeth wrote to Arthur too. She repeated her concerns about James's interference and emphasised that as the manuscript was the one Charlotte herself prepared it should be considered final and not needing revisions. Even so, she told Arthur, he must not let anyone coerce him into publishing it. She may have suspected he lacked feelings of agency and authority and, in order to thwart James, tried to foster both by reminding him that as Charlotte's executor only he could decide the fate of her writings. She would soon come to regret this.

She spent an anxious week at Evesham waiting for her husband to bring her the manuscript of *The Professor*, writing all day from breakfast and troubled by dreams about *The Life* if she managed to sleep at night. When William eventually came, she dropped all plans and gave herself over to reading it. To her immense relief, it was not what she expected. She told a friend it took the form of the autobiography of a male English professor teaching in a Belgian school, 'so on that ground there would be no objection to publishing it'.[11] Although she disagreed with James that it would add to Charlotte's reputation, finding it 'a very curious link in her literary history, of showing the *promise* of much that was afterwards realised', at least now she could give up her opposition to it.[12] In fact, after reading it she felt so neutral she declined to either recommend or disqualify it to George. He, on the other hand, jumped at the chance of an essentially new novel by Currer Bell and, as he often did once a clear path to an opportunity presented itself, started thinking in numbers. He asked her what he should pay Arthur for it, whether he should offer more or less than he paid Charlotte for her other novels and if she thought its sales could be boosted if he launched it at the same time as the biography. He may have asked Arthur for his expectations, as soon Arthur told him he thought it only fair he pay the same as he had for *Villette*, which he guessed to be 'about £220'.[13] George agreed and paid him promptly before Arthur could find out he had actually paid twice that for it.

A few days later, Elizabeth heard from Arthur. She had won a partial victory. He had resolved to not let James edit *The Professor* and had already told him. Nevertheless, after reading the novel aloud to Patrick they both decided it did need some improvements and now he felt *he* should edit it himself. Elizabeth gave up; she referred him to George and told them to continue negotiation between themselves.

As the autumn stole in, Elizabeth's industry became obsessive. She wrote *The Life of Charlotte Brontë* every day from breakfast until five in the evening with only short breaks for meals and walks. While in Evesham, she produced 120 pages and the same again by mid-August, amounting to the first 71,000 words, taking her up to the 1840s when Charlotte was in Brussels. She got back in touch with Laetitia Wheelwright about her memories of her schooldays. 'If you could give me any details about Charlotte and Emily's school life – their exact position in the school, their duties and occupations, if they had a bedroom to themselves, even the school hours – all these details would be invaluable.'[14]

The further she moved through Charlotte's life, the more questions she had, considering no detail too insignificant for examination. 'I suppose biographers always grow to fancy everything about their subject of importance, but I *really* think that such is the case about her,' she said, and taxed her correspondents with long digressive chains of questions that required prompt answers, growing sharp with those who did not comply.[15] 'If you knew the amount of writing I am getting through you would think I deserved a few replies,' she snapped at George when he did not respond quickly enough.[16]

Receiving new information and impressions extended the earlier sections of the book, forcing Elizabeth through continual rewrites to rebalance them. Owing to the non-chronological way she received details she covered her pages with 'many erasures, insertions at the back of leaves etc.'[17] and described the process to a friend:

> Among the mass of minute writing I found quantities of fragments – very short but very graphic – written when she was about 12, giving glimpses of her life at the time, all of which I had to decipher and interweave with what I had already written – in fact I had to rewrite about 40 pages.[18]

Progress stalled to wearyingly circuitous amendments as the material facts of Charlotte's life shifted in a continual flux, pulling Elizabeth towards Charlotte's death.

'The remainder will consist so very much of letters,' she resolved, 'involving merely copying.' Mindful that her original proposal to Arthur, the one essential in securing his co-operation, was she would only use Charlotte's private letters for research and not quote directly from them, she began to test George to see if he objected to her doing the opposite, weaving in substantial extracts that her daughters copied into the manuscript. She explained that regardless of how Arthur had 'a strong objection to letters being printed at all and wished to have all her letters (to Miss Nussey and everyone else) burned' they were too evocative not to be preserved or reproduced in print. 'Her language, where it can be used, is so powerful and living that it would be a shame not to express everything that can be in her own words. And yet I don't want to alarm Mr Nicholls' prejudices.'[19] Essentially, she sought a promise from George that he would support her against the complaints she expected from Arthur once he saw how extensively she had quoted his wife. And by making a case for the improvement of the book – which was ultimately George's product and financial investment – she appealed directly to his business sense, privileging their shared aim in the certainty it would over-ride any qualms he might have.

Aside from the discussions with Elizabeth about whether *The Professor* should be published, Arthur and Patrick had heard nothing from her since she visited in July and continually speculated on how her work was progressing. From the outset, Arthur had been alert to the dubious potential consequences for himself that a biography of his wife could bring. Yet Elizabeth only had to consider how gleeful he had been about being depicted in a book before, as the Rev. Macarthey in *Shirley*, to suspect it was objectivity he feared, not exposure. His reservations may have prompted Patrick to deliberate on how he too would be presented and he sent her, as an example of the discredit an unsympathetic stance might take her, a shilling booklet published that spring called *Jottings on Currer, Ellis and Acton Bell*, which he described as 'a strange compound of truth and error'.[20] It was a hash of extracts from Charlotte's biographical prefaces about her sisters, with some of their poems, and paraphrases from the scurrilous articles published since Charlotte's death, relying much on the one written by Harriet Martineau as soon as she heard Charlotte was dead. It said Patrick married his wife in Penzance against their friends' wishes and then moved her directly to Haworth – neither of which was true – but he was mainly unsettled by its characterisation of him as a 'somewhat extraordinary and eccentrick personage'[*sic*]. This was unjust, he told Elizabeth, as he saw himself more like a character from her own pen, such as Margaret Hale's kindly and beloved curate father in *North and South*. He was just like him, he tried to convince Elizabeth, a non-conforming individualist, 'peaceable, feeling, sometimes thoughtful and generally well-meaning'. Elizabeth's response has not survived. She might reasonably have concluded this only proved Patrick had little self-awareness, and underestimated not only her own powers of observation but his daughter's.

It became clear both men were counting on her discreet and courteous protection from the public and for Elizabeth to elevate them together in the same vein of tribute they expected for Charlotte. All that stood in their way were the contents of Charlotte's letters and everything she had told her about both men. At this point, no one outside the Gaskell household had seen enough of Charlotte's letters to understand how far her perspective would contradict those of her father and her husband. Exposing it would preserve the truth of the woman, as Elizabeth saw it, even if it surprised them with a different side to her than they had known.

This brought an impossible choice. Elizabeth could be guided by how Charlotte's survivors wanted her to be represented and thereby diminish her for the sake of their pride, or she could present Charlotte's own words and allow her unmediated voice to be heard for the first time. By doing the latter she would betray the living. By doing the former she would betray the dead. She started to think about what constituted as libel and may have considered that at least the living had recourse to it. Without defenders, the dead were left to the vagaries of how their survivors chose to represent them.

Exhausted as she was, she told George she might have a draft by Christmas. By the second week of September, she had come to the events of ten years earlier, 1846, the year Charlotte turned 30 and a time of significant domestic and professional upheaval for her, when she and her sisters were first published. Elizabeth contacted the publishers who had rejected them to ask if they had kept any of their letters and planned how she would treat their hostile reviewers. She asked George and William Smith Williams for their correspondence from that period and whether they thought any of Charlotte's critics would be willing to speak to her. She was planning a 'tirade' against one in particular, she said, who she felt had 'no right to make such offensive conjectures' and thought it might be prudent to cut some expressions that could be considered coarse from *The Professor* to allow her to strengthen her challenge.[21] 'For I would not, if I could help it, have another syllable that could be called coarse to be associated with her name.'[22]

Needing more information about the Brontë household at that time, Elizabeth turned to Ellen for the particulars. She remembered what Charlotte herself had told her about Branwell's 'vices', the euphemism Charlotte used when describing her brother's descent into drug misuse and alcoholism and the destructive effect it had on the household, and how after his death she found his pockets filled with letters from the married woman who rejected him. The parallel with her own situation and Constantin Héger could not have been lost on her, only making his death more bitter by the confirmation of how far they had grown apart from childhood intimacy, that neither had spoken to the other about their comparable experiences.

As Elizabeth started to uncover the details and causes of Branwell's collapse, she wondered if she was probing too far into the family's secrets. Additionally, by then Arthur had agreed with George to publish *The Professor* as soon as was possible leading Elizabeth to doubt whether any of this could be done decently or truthfully without invading the privacies of strangers and injuring their feelings. By the end of the month, the exertion and strain of writing *The Life of Charlotte Brontë* brought her to the verge of collapse. She fainted and her family called a doctor. He prescribed a break. He told her she should get some rest by the sea and forbade her to read or write anything for a fortnight. 'The doctor said I was to have my mind at ease,' she told George, 'How could I?'[23]

'Do you mind the law of libel?' she ventured once she was feeling better. 'I have three people I want to libel: Lady Scott (that bad woman who corrupted Branwell Brontë), Mr Newby and Lady Eastlake, the first and last not to be named, the mean publisher to be gibbeted.'[24]

Elizabeth returned to work with renewed vigour, 'getting on so beautifully, feeling or fancying the interest growing with every page'. But soon a new blow came. With an end in sight and discussions of a publication date already under way, she impressed her vision for *The Life* on one of the reviewers at the *Athenaeum*, Henry Chorley. He asked her if she had secured permission to weave so many quotations from Charlotte's letters into her text. She assured him she had as all the letters were personally and willingly donated by their recipients, with some such as Ellen, looking forward to seeing their extracts in the book. What he had to tell her came as a shock. Permission could only be granted by the deceased's inheritors, not whoever possessed their letters and described a successful legal challenge raised by Byron's executors after his letters were published without approval.[25] Panicking she turned to George, 'Now I did *not* know all this.'

If Arthur had the legal right to prohibit her quoting anything Charlotte had written, it meant he had the power to block the book from being published. The question was whether he was aware of that. Elizabeth found him an unpredictable man at the best of times and was certain he would refuse her if she needed permission now. She wondered if she should feign innocence. 'If I did not ask him, but went on as I am doing, I *think* he would sigh and submit.'[26] George ruled that out, knowing they needed a legally sound agreement to protect them both. Their challenge would be gaining Arthur's approval without alerting him to its implications.

Over the next few days, he and Elizabeth had to collude to work out a way forward. If they approached Arthur and he refused, Elizabeth would be faced with rewrites so substantial it would move publication further away and impact George's potential sales. As always, his business ingenuity came to the rescue. All they needed from Arthur was a signature. He proposed sending him an officious-sounding contract, worded to bewilder him into signing away the permissions he and Elizabeth needed. 'I think on the whole [that is] the best mode of dealing with Mr Nicholls,' she told him in relief.[27] The form George created was not preserved, but Arthur's response indicates George suggested this was normal in publishing to safeguard against any unwarranted legal claims. But Arthur was not the fool they took him to be. He wrote back:

> I must decline signing the document you have sent not because I have, or ever had, the slightest intention of making any pecuniary claim on Mrs Gaskell on account of the work on which she is engaged; but simply because if I did so I should be thereby precluded from making any further use of the MS referred to.[28]

He assured George he had no intention of obstructing Elizabeth in any way from writing the 'tribute' as Patrick first suggested, and in fact was happy to co-operate. But he drew the line at surrendering his wife's copyright, telling George that while he did not approve of the project, he acquiesced in Patrick's favour and endorsed Elizabeth as its author:

> I would rather she did it than anyone else, as I knew her kindly feelings toward my wife – I have accordingly from time to time forwarded her some MS, but never with any idea of giving over the exclusive right to them. This is all that I have had to do with the matter.[29]

George realised they were in trouble. He appears to have insisted that Elizabeth had incorporated so many quotations from Charlotte's letters in good faith that it would be impossible to remove them without jeopardising the entire book. Arthur was immovable. He replied, 'I never authorized her to publish a single line of my wife's MS & correspondence; such a thing was never mentioned – in fact until the receipt of your note I was not even aware that it was contemplated.'[30] George applied more pressure and may even have implied Arthur could be held financially responsible for the failure or cancellation of the book, perhaps by suggesting he had disingenuously led Elizabeth to believe she was at liberty to quote from the letters, as would be a standard with literary biographies. Cornered, Arthur felt he had to surrender:

> I have signed the enclosed document as it seems to be taken for granted that I am to do so, tho' why it should, I know not, as I never entered into any arrangement with Mrs Gaskell to convey to her the copyright of any of my wife's MS for the purposes of the Memoir or any other. I trust I shall not be required to do anything more in a matter, which from beginning to end has been a source of pain and annoyance to me; as I have been dragged into sanctioning a proceeding utterly repugnant to my feelings. Indeed nothing but an unwillingness to thwart Mr Brontë's wishes could have induced me to acquiesce in a project, which in my eyes is little short of desecration.[31]

Victoriously, George passed the signed contract to Elizabeth. 'I am so glad that it was you, and not I, that had "the fierce correspondence" with Mr Nicholls,' she told him gratefully, 'I should have been daunted at once.'[32]

Her relief was mixed with chagrin as she knew her incursions with Arthur were not yet over. She still needed a copy of Charlotte's portrait but no longer as a personal memento, now she wanted it for the book. Even though Arthur was fiercely protective of it and preferred it to remain private, she decided she could enhance the book by including an engraving, along with a view of the parsonage and churchyard. She sourced a photographer named John Stewart, whom she described to George as a 'first-rate amateur', who specialised in landscapes, and asked George for the specifications needed for a photograph to be engraved. Stewart took Elizabeth's lead and did not write ahead to arrange a visit to the parsonage but simply turned up at the door. He was told Arthur was out and he must wait until he came back before he did anything. 'I am very sorry you had to wait so long,' Elizabeth said, 'I am very sorry you will have to go again.'[33] Under Arthur's supervision Stewart took three daguerreotypes of George Richmond's portrait of Charlotte, giving 'a solemn promise' the images would be returned to him once Elizabeth had chosen the one she wanted. Once developed, Stewart chose the best and posted it to her. She contacted him as soon as it arrived to say it had been so damaged in the post it was impossible to use. 'But we all think from what we can see that it is most beautiful and correct and pleasing. It is very like her; and a very good copy of the drawing.' He told her to send it back to him because Arthur was demanding he return to him all three copies, seeking to keep any distribution of Charlotte's likeness under his control. 'And this although he knows it is to be engraved and consequently numerous copies circulated!' she told George as an example of Arthur's peevish irrationality. Stewart went back with the three photographs for Arthur, and to take views of the parsonage and the churchyard from the neighbouring field and a distant view of the village from the other side of the valley. On his third visit, he took more photographs of the portrait, which this time reached Elizabeth safely. She told George she would send one to him to be engraved, then asked an intriguing question, 'Will you let me know what Mr Richmond says about the photo copyright? I don't fancy he will make any difficulty.'[34] This indicates George was seeking permission from the artist George Richmond to reproduce his portrait. The issue of the intellectual ownership was apparently still in their minds, and one wonders whether they made Arthur aware they only needed his co-operation rather than his permission as the right to give it lay elsewhere.

Elizabeth was grateful. She wrote to Stewart, 'Thank you over and over again, and do let me have the pleasure of doing something for you some time.' Now that she mentioned it there was a favour she could do him, he responded, could she pull strings to introduce him to William Thackeray? Elizabeth wrote to George, 'Oh if once I have finished this biography, catch me writing another! I shall be heaved overboard at last.'[35]

CHAPTER 14

1857
The Life of Charlotte Brontë

In the week before Christmas 1856, Elizabeth submitted as much as she had written. She had completed the first volume covering the period of Charlotte's life up to 1846, and most of the second volume up to 1853, and asked George to read it all with an eye to keeping them both within the law as much as possible, as long as he understood she had no desire to make any significant changes. As he read it over, his concerns grew and he wrote with a list of objections. He told her she could not 'indicate so clearly' the society hostess who had an affair with Branwell Brontë and needed to make her less of a villainess, singling out the phrase, 'He died! She lives still – in Mayfair.'[1] He asked her to rephrase parts about Emily and Anne's publisher exploiting their inexperience by charging them to print their books then neglecting to pay their royalties afterwards. Lastly, and unexpectedly, he preferred she deleted everything about himself and his mother.

Elizabeth spent Boxing Day drafting her protestations. She said she did not agree she had identified Branwell's mistress, calling her 'Lady [–] in Mayfair' to obscure her among the number of other titled women there, 'though we will hope not so many as bad as she is'.[2] He had been a talented but directionless young man used and discarded by a self-indulgent social climber whose subsequent marriage brought her wealth and a title and the inequity of their fates, she implied, could only be the product of a class hierarchy that allowed the powerful to protect themselves, regardless of their abilities or qualities, while others of remarkable talent suffered and failed. She was making the same argument about Charlotte.

She deliberated on whether to remove details about T.C. Newby's treatment of Emily and Anne but counterargued it might warn other writers from doing business with them, but she knew it was one of her less contentious slanders and was willing to drop it. Understandably, George wanted her to consider his professional standing and avoid making him an enemy of his peers.

What disturbed him most, however, was the prominence she had given himself and his family in Charlotte's life, magnifying their significance beyond truth. As he saw it, they only saw her once a year and found her an unsettling guest whom nothing could make comfortable. As her biographer, Elizabeth had a duty to prioritise Charlotte's perspective above others and knew how much she appreciated their hospitality. Showing this, she argued, allowed her to present Charlotte's gentler side that contradicted caricatures of her as a scornful harridan. Above all, Elizabeth argued, she wanted to show Charlotte as a more relatable woman than the press had portrayed her and how, with George and his mother, she took a particularly feminine 'pleasure in protection – chaperonage – whatever you like to call it'.[3] Her implication, cannily, was that without the material George objected to, she had nothing new to present to his potential customers.

She had quoted Charlotte's first impressions of George as 'a young, tall, gentlemanly man' and William Smith Williams as 'a pale mild stooping man of fifty' and George thought even these were much too personal to be included.[4] Elizabeth wrote she meant to delete them and other remarks 'that related to anyone's appearance, style of living' whom the public were not already interested in. In a last attempt to prevent cuts, she told him there was so little of this kind of description in Charlotte's letters it might be considered rare, but she knew it was better to acquiesce than insist, feeling piqued enough to point out that if he objected to being written about, he should have done so when Charlotte herself mentioned him in her Biographical Notice, 'However, *that* goes out and voila, fini!'[5]

Nevertheless, she knew writing about him would be unavoidable when it came to *Villette*, but certainly could not mention how they were estranged by Charlotte's jealousy. She presented a diplomatic resolution:

> I do not promise, for I'm quoting much from memory, that there shall be no more references to you or to your mother but they are of this incidental kind, bringing out something of *her* character and not in anyways referring to your private employments, habits or circumstances, far less to your appearance.[6]

Compromised, yet refusing to be thwarted, Elizabeth knew telling large truths might require sacrificing lesser ones if she was to successfully convey her message about Charlotte's life: that even first-rate talents and virtues were not enough to qualify some for personal success, or for women to be considered equally to men. Without knowing it, she was fulfilling a prediction Mary Taylor made when Ellen shared doubts about how to describe Charlotte's life without making enemies of those who had treated her badly. Assuming she meant Charlotte's male relations, Mary replied:

> If for the sake of those who behaved ill to her, the truth cannot be spoken, still people should not tell lies. The fact reached me even here that Mr Brontë did not choose his daughter should marry ... I can never think without gloomy anger of Charlotte's sacrifices to the selfish old man. How well we know that, had she left him entirely and succeeded in gaining wealth, and name, and influence, she would have had all the world lauding her to the skies for any trivial act of generosity that would have cost her nothing. But how on earth is all this to be set straight?[7]

Before she emigrated at the start of 1845, Mary had tried to persuade Charlotte to break away from her father and Haworth, having hoped her time in Brussels would give her an appetite for a larger life free from domestic chains, as it had with her. 'If Charlotte had left home and made a favour of returning, she would have got thanks instead of tyranny,' she told Ellen. In January 1856, Mary received Elizabeth's letter of introduction, sent the previous August, asking for her memories of Charlotte and for any correspondence she could share. Fearing Charlotte's letters might be lost or stolen, Mary destroyed all but one, and sent that with a reminiscence beginning when she first met Charlotte at Margaret Wooler's school and repeating what she told Ellen about her principal characteristic:

> [Charlotte] thought much of her duty and had loftier and clearer notions of it than most people and held fast to them with more success. It was done, it seems to me, with much more difficulty than people have of stronger nerves and better fortunes. All her life was but labour and pain; and she never threw down the burden for the sake of present pleasure. I don't know what use you can make of all I have said.[8]

Mary was impressed by Elizabeth's assiduousness but could not understand why she would accept the challenge of trying to untangle the truth about Charlotte's family circumstances. 'Mrs Gaskell seems far too able a woman to put her head into such a wasp nest, as she would raise about her by speaking the truth of living people. How she will get through with it I can't imagine.'[9] That said, Mary knew that disturbing the balance might be right, necessary and just for Charlotte and for every other woman in her situation:

> I wish I could set the world right on so many points, but above all respecting Charlotte. It would do said world good to know her and be forced to revere her in spite of their contempt for poverty and helplessness. No one ever gave up more than she did and with full consciousness of what she sacrificed. I don't think myself that woman are justified in sacrificing themselves for others, but since the world generally expects it of them, they should at least acknowledge it.[10]

As different as women like Mary, Ellen and Elizabeth were from each other – Elizabeth the charming, subversive and shrewd professional; Ellen, whose sentiment and love for Charlotte were fusing into an evangelical zeal to preserve like pressed flowers the after-images of the Brontës; and Mary the drily witty pragmatist and independent businesswoman abroad – this was the one perspective upon which they all agreed. Charlotte's comfortless life – of sacrifices and duty to her father, her brother, to her employers, to the many who knew they could exploit an emotionally damaged woman who only sought meaningful connection – deserved a compensation of glory denied to her in life. Elizabeth's biography might be the best medium to redress that imbalance and restore the seething, passionate voice that silenced itself for the sake of others.

By now, Elizabeth felt that everyone who had wilfully wronged Charlotte deserved every public shame and libel she planned for them. '*No one* can know all she had to go through,' she told a friend, 'The merciful judgement of all connected with that terrible life lies with God; And we may all be thankful that it does.'[11] If she showed Charlotte as a heroine of service, sacrifice and duty, even when the desire to fulfil an immeasurable talent demanded expression, her biography would become an act of revenge, executed by her on behalf of Charlotte and in tribute to her. As she had written in *North and South*, 'Loyalty and obedience to wisdom and justice are fine; but it is still finer to defy arbitrary power, unjustly and cruelly used – not on behalf of ourselves, but on behalf of others more helpless.'[12]

Elizabeth continued to argue with George as 1857 approached, dismissing as an insult his offer of payment far below what she would expect for a novel, let alone a work requiring so much travel, labour and research, 'to say nothing of the anxiety' this one cost her. 'I have put these points before you in order that you may judge whether I am unreasonable or not in expecting some advance on your present offer,' she told him. Chastened, he changed the figure in his proposal from £600 to £800 (or £68,000 at present value). 'The sum you propose *fully* satisfies me and I hope you won't have reason to repent of it,' she told him, before adding '*Do* let me abuse Mr Newby as much as I dare *within the law*.'[13] She insisted she knew what she was doing and urged him to support her. 'I ask you this as you were a friend of Miss Brontë's and must be as anxious as I am to place her where she ought to be. I don't *promise* to alter what you do not like. I only promise to consider it.' Determined to make that the last word on the matter she told him to send what he had to the presses and print up proof pages that she could start correcting immediately. Foreign publishers wanted the rights, she told him, and printers vied for the honour of producing it.

As the book moved towards being printed and read in a matter of months, she prepared herself for divided opinions, informing George she planned to ignore reviews and leave the country. 'I look forward also with a feeling of dread to the expression of opinion, both public and private which will cut me in two ways.'[14] Certain Arthur and Patrick were likely to be offended by what she had written about them, she decided to show them nothing. Originally, she had promised she would not allow anyone other than her husband and the staff of Smith Elder to read the book before them. Now, she reasoned in another of her moral contortions, if she herself read it aloud to someone, rather than them read it themselves, she was not entirely breaking that promise. She invited Ellen to stay in January and pre-empted the parsonage's response to the book by telling George to give Arthur a goodwill payment of £100 as a donation to the village's fund to buy a water pump.

Packets of proof sheets with their corresponding manuscript pages arrived before Elizabeth had written the end. By then, she had reached the period when she knew Charlotte and using her own letters and notes could write with the certainty of an eyewitness. She was still asking questions of George about Charlotte's last eighteen months as he negotiated the book's distribution on the Continent, selling the French and German rights to Hachette and arranging for Appleton's in America to receive proofs once her husband corrected them.

Ellen went to Manchester on Monday, 12 January to stay for the week, primarily to listen to Elizabeth read her *The Life of Charlotte Brontë*. Unexpectedly, Elizabeth was unwell but when Katie Winkworth – never one to miss an opportunity to meet anyone connected to the Brontës – dropped by to be introduced to Ellen on the Saturday she found she was better, heartened by Ellen's enthusiasm. Katie was curious to see Ellen, having heard so much about her, and found her likeable, observing she had been 'pretty once, not a sparkling beauty at all, but a quiet one, tolerably regular features, large eyes, soft complexion, and thick wavy brown hair'. When asked what she thought of *The Life*, Ellen found it 'excessively interesting and seems to approve it altogether'.[15]

The other reason Ellen had come to Manchester was to take back her many bundles of letters. It was clear Elizabeth had used them to give large parts of the book the authority and substance of an autobiography. Whichever approach she expected her to take, she was relieved Elizabeth held true to her only stipulation: that regardless of what Charlotte's letters revealed about the Brontës she and her own family must not be identified. To ensure that, she had blackened out every mention of her mother and siblings in Charlotte's letters before she gave them to Elizabeth and, with a shrewdness her amiability concealed, demanded she avoid using her first name. At first Elizabeth tried to talk her round as she was naming everyone else in Charlotte's life from Margaret Wooler to Martha Brown and said the narration would suffer if she had to use a blank line where her confidante's name should be. Ellen remained firm and Elizabeth settled for using only the letter 'E' to identify her.

Once she heard a gratuity was going to Arthur, Ellen – an unmarried, unemployed woman living on savings and dividends from private annuities – wondered if her own contribution merited some compensation too. She received it eventually: a free copy of the book. It was sent to everyone who assisted Elizabeth 'with lending me letters or giving me drawings, information etc.'. Ellen said nothing about how far this fell short of her expectations, but over time her ire would build that she was disrespected by Elizabeth, nor appropriately thanked for her consultation or her donation of material, until she was telling anyone who would listen that *The Life of Charlotte Brontë* could not have happened without her.[16]

Now the book was finished, Ellen thought it would interest Elizabeth to see her recent letter from Mary, where she warned of the complications Elizabeth would face. Half amused, half concerned, Elizabeth paraphrased it to George. 'Does Mrs Gaskell know what a hornets' nest she is pulling about her ears?'[17] Despite Elizabeth's misgivings, Ellen's response was enough to assure her of success. She was astonished by the book and felt Elizabeth's descriptions of Charlotte, Branwell, Emily and Anne restored them back to life:

I was gratified to hear her say how completely the life at the Parsonage appeared to her reproduced, much of this was owing to the remarkable extracts from letters; but she said several times how exactly and accurately I had written about the life and characters.[18]

That aside, she assured George, she did not want to know what critics thought, as 'I am just the reverse of Miss Brontë: I never want to see or hear of any reviews; when I have done with a book, I want to shake off the recollection thereof forever.'[19] As her husband finished correcting the first set of proofs, she asked George to chase the printer to send the rest and approved suggestions for the page layouts.

At the end of the first week of February, she finally wrote the book's conclusion, the scene of Charlotte's funeral, bringing the narrative back to its beginning and returning Charlotte to a state of non-being; dead at the beginning and end of her own story. She told Laetitia Wheelwright on Saturday, 7 February to expect a gift copy once it appeared. 'I have today finished my *Life* of Miss Brontë; and next week we set out for Rome.' She enclosed the letters Laetitia had loaned her with thanks and began doing the same with everyone else's letters, dispatching them with notes of gratitude and the date the book was due to be published. George arranged for the manuscript to go to their printer and set the publication date as 25 March, in time for the second anniversary of Charlotte's death and two weeks before Easter.

Lastly, she sent him three daguerreotypes taken by John Stewart: of Richmond's portrait of Charlotte; of the parsonage and the churchyard taken from the field facing them; and of Haworth from the other side of the valley. Regretfully, the two landscapes were unusable after all Stewart's trouble. However, she told George, 'They give an idea of wildness and desolation; but not of height and steepness and of the sweeping line of moors beyond.'[20] She sketched out an elaboration of the first landscape and presumably had Meta, who had taken drawing lessons from Ruskin, draw it proficiently. Under her mother's direction to give a suggestion of steepness, Meta lifted the line of the horizon so that it rose behind the squat cottage she made of the parsonage into a swell of mountains reminiscent of the romantic Scottish pastoral engravings Charlotte loved, then narrowed the neighbouring houses to heighten the gothic austerity of the irregularly slabbed churchyard. After he received it, George appears to have asked if it was exaggerated, for she replied with an assurance that no indeed, 'the gravestones in the Haworth Church Yard are FLAT, not many headstones; and not a tuft of grass between.'[21] She told him both this and Richmond's portrait would look well engraved and printed on tinted paper with white highlights. He instructed illustrations as she suggested, from one of England's finest and most prolific steel engravers, James Armytage, and arranged for them to be inserted as the frontispiece illustrations for volumes one and two.[22] Just as the Haworth scene moved from photograph to sketch, to drawing to engraving, the likeness of Charlotte passed through the same process of alteration and interpretation, leaving its original form behind to become another's idea of it.

'As I have five minutes, I just write to thank you for all your kindness and obligingness,' Elizabeth told George as she made the final preparations to leave England on Friday, 13 February.[23] She wished him good luck with the launch of *The Life* and told him her husband would answer any enquiries. Two days later, she set off with Katie Winkworth, Marianne and Meta for Rome via Paris and Marseilles. They would be away for fifteen weeks, returning at the end of May, by which time and against all expectations the book would have sold through its entire first edition. Even as they sailed across the English Channel from Dover, the first whispers emerged in the *Bradford Observer*: 'Mrs Gaskell's *Life of Charlotte Brontë* is now nearly ready and reports speak highly of its great interest and admirable execution.'[24]

She left George a long list of people to receive copies, including Ellen, Patrick and Arthur, Margaret Wooler and all others who had either loaned letters or granted interviews. The book was published in the Victorian equivalent of a blaze of publicity orchestrated by George with large advertisements in the high circulation newspapers:

MRS GASKELL'S MEMOIRS OF CURRER BELL
Now ready in 2 vols, post 8vo, with a portrait of Miss Brontë
and a View of Haworth Church and Parsonage.
Price 24s, cloth.
'THE LIFE OF CHARLOTTE BRONTË'
Author of *Jane Eyre*, *Shirley*, *Villette* etc.
By Mrs Gaskell, Author of *Mary Barton*, *Ruth*, *North and South*.
London: Smith, Elder and Co, 65 Cornhill.[25]

Ironically, this was the first time Charlotte Brontë's name had appeared on the title page of any book, and in keeping with its revelatory nature, it was also the first time for Elizabeth. Having only ever published anonymously she now faced her public as 'E.C. Gaskell, author of *Mary Barton* etc.'. Unsurprisingly, the first reaction came from Patrick. Four days after he received it, he told George he read it:

> with a high degree of melancholy interest and consider them amongst the ablest, most interesting and best works of the kind. Mrs Gaskell ... has done herself great credit by this biographical work which I doubt not will place her higher in literary fame even than she stood before.[26]

A few days later, he wrote to thank Elizabeth personally, too late to reach her before she left. She had always been his first choice of biographer, he wrote, and if she had declined he would have had to propose it to lesser writers 'with a tenacity of purpose, usual with me' to make a biography of his daughter happen even if he had to write it himself, admitting that would have made a 'short though inadequate memoir'. Its completion and execution were beyond what he could have expected, he wrote, and the experience of reading it:

> afforded me more satisfaction than I have felt during many years of our life ... You have not only given a picture of my Dear Daughter Charlotte but of my Dear wife and all my Dear Children, and Such a picture too, as is full of truth and life. The Picture of my brilliant and unhappy Son and his diabolical Seducer are Masterpieces. Indeed all the Pictures in the work have vigorous, truthful and delicate touches in them which could have been executed only by a Skilful female hand.[27]

He had noticed 'a few trifling mistakes' that might be corrected in the next edition but said otherwise he and Arthur sent their kind and respectful thanks. In his wife's absence, William Gaskell replied to ask which errors he meant. Patrick told him the principal one was that he had limited his daughters' diet by depriving them of meat:

> Thinking their constitutions to be delicate the advice I repeatedly gave them was that they should wear flannel, eat as much wholesome animal food as they could digest, take air and exercise in moderation and not devote too much time and attention to study and composition. I should wish this to be mentioned in the second edition.

As an afterthought, he mentioned at the bottom of the page: 'PS the Eccentric Movements ascribed to me ... have no foundation [in] fact.'[28] He was referring to the statements Elizabeth collected about how in anger he rolled up a hearthrug and burned it in the fire and sawed the backs off chairs to stop his children slouching. Initially, he thought these were more amusing than insulting but as the weeks passed, disquiet grew at the parsonage.

Overwhelmed at first by Elizabeth's recreation of his lost family, Patrick did not notice how much it subdued Arthur. For him, reading it was indescribably painful. The woman who had almost been the mother of his children had indeed been restored but at the permanent expense of his own dignity and privacy. The public could now enjoy intimate details of his first and only love affair, of how he abandoned his home and job after Charlotte rejected him, before she overcame doubts and eventually married him against her father's stern resistance. Now every face in every service he conducted, the eyes of every child in the schools, everyone in his parish in fact, would be lit with scrutiny, alert to the kind of details about him they did not even know about their own relations.

He read descriptions of himself as a 'grave, reserved, conscientious man' who had loved Charlotte long before he made it known to her. 'How deep his affection was I scarcely dare to tell, even if I could in words,' Elizabeth had written, 'he was not a man to be attracted by any kind of literary fame. I imagine that this, by itself, would rather repel him when he saw it in the possession of a woman.'[29] His and Patrick's expectations that Elizabeth might find herself short of material were confounded by the conspicuous amount given by other people. She had included an explanation of her chief challenge, that it would be impossible to:

> show what a noble, true, and tender woman Charlotte Brontë really was, without mingling up with her life too much of the personal history of her nearest and most intimate friends. After much consideration of this point, I came to the resolution of writing truly, if I wrote at all; of withholding nothing.[30]

As noble as this sounded, he could see it was only partially true. Page after page quoted letters to 'Dear E', whom he and Patrick knew must be Ellen, allowing them, and every stranger who picked up a copy, to read for the first time Charlotte's private thoughts shared in confidence. Until then, he and Patrick had no idea how she had collaborated with Elizabeth, divulging every detail she remembered about their lives, while so concealing herself even her name was protected. Arthur realised how he had been duped by Elizabeth and George into signing away his permission so they could go against his wishes and print the hundreds of letters Ellen provided. Bitterly, he confronted George that his privacy had been sacrificed for Smith Elder's commercial gain and that *The Life* contained 'some things which ought never to have been published. It was not without reason that I instinctively shrank from the proposal of a biography but I suppose it matters not, provided the curiosity of the public be gratified.'[31]

If George replied to console or commiserate, his letter has not been preserved. Despite finding fewer factual errors than he expected, Arthur said Charlotte was depicted truthfully and supposed Elizabeth had 'done justice to her subject'. His telling choice of the word 'justice' recalls precisely the same use Ellen made of it when she demanded he engage Elizabeth to write about Charlotte in the first place. Elizabeth's skills aside, he explained, she had unfortunately delivered exactly what he feared she would, in the form of an indecent exposure of his own and Patrick's private behaviour and feelings.

He did not tell George it confirmed another doubt he harboured for far longer. Ever since he met Ellen and heard how she enjoyed gossiping with Charlotte about their mutual friends, he thought her too indiscreet to be loyal and worried Charlotte's trust was misplaced. He created a ruction when he tried to warn Charlotte after their marriage that she should be careful of the secrets she told Ellen, or at least get her to promise to destroy the evidence, ultimately anticipating this very moment. Now his suspicions that Ellen would one day deliver his wife's intimacies into the wrong hands had been justified.

Twenty miles away in Birstall, Ellen blanched when she saw her letters from Charlotte in print for the first time. But she was unrepentant. From her position of security, as an informant in the shadows, she insisted Elizabeth had done an admirable job in reporting the terrible truth. And surely men of the cloth more than anyone else should not fear that. She felt the book brought Charlotte the crowning vindication she deserved after a lifetime of servitude to a malignant father and an inadequate husband. Both had exploited Charlotte's inexhaustible charity and sympathy, Ellen felt, and if they had to answer for that as a result of a truthful tribute to her, they should castigate themselves for their actions, not her or Elizabeth for their exposure. 'What indeed have the pure and the upright to shrink from?' she practically smiled when she reflected on Arthur's mortification, 'they will have to face the great searcher of hearts before all the world in the great day of account, then why fear the little world of the present time?'[32]

Indeed, she congratulated herself, the judgement of the present world was nothing compared to the wrath to come.

CHAPTER 15

1857

That Unlucky Book

Acclaim for *The Life of Charlotte Brontë* was immediate. But even reviewers impressed by Elizabeth's writing were appalled by her material. *The Spectator* said it was 'one of the profoundest tragedies of modern life'; the reviewer of the *Daily News* thought 'a sadder book than this it has never been our lot to read. It is the desolate record of a brilliant but desolate career.'[1] Astutely, the *Literary Examiner* read between the lines and suspected facts had been left out to spare Patrick Brontë's feelings, leaving much 'to be inferred rather than absolutely learnt'. Charlotte's great sorrows, they concluded, were not caused by encounters with a hostile world, but by his deficiencies as a father and her inheritance of 'the family taint of mental sickness' which made the sisters 'less agreeable than they might otherwise have been'. Many were unsettled by the tone of intimacy created by so many confidential letters. Without Elizabeth's tact and skilful handling, they cautioned, it could have been slanderous and set a dangerous new precedent for intruding into the lives of private individuals, turning anonymous people into household names the press was now at liberty to discuss.[2]

As libraries and bookshops distributed copies across the country, complaints from such individuals began. The first, regarding Elizabeth's comments about the founder of the Clergy Daughters' School, the Rev. William Carus Wilson, was published in *The Standard*. His son, a vicar also called William, was incredulous she should have taken Charlotte's school memories seriously and disputed them all. 'I have seen letters from teachers and pupils who were there with her denying all that she stated regarding that invaluable institution,' he claimed. 'Miss Brontë left the school at the age of 9, Mrs Gaskell tells us, so what judgement could she form?'[3]

He argued that given Elizabeth's depiction of Patrick as 'a very austere and peculiar man, denying his children animal food, and they all being naturally very delicate … is it fair to trace all her sufferings in after life to the very short time she was at the establishment?' Her book was more than an unwarranted attack on a man like Carus Wilson, his son wrote – who lived 'solely for the good of others … opposite to the character Mrs Gaskell sketched of him' – it was an attack on the integrity of the church itself. Being the wife of a vicar who preached against the trinity, Wilson wrote, Elizabeth had a religious bias and was trying to make a larger political strike against Evangelicals.[4]

He was not alone in receiving the book in religious terms. Many, however, thought the opposite, that far from being a slight on Christian principles *The Life* was a template for them. Sir James, who in his wife's extended absence may have thought women could use a manual on being dutiful and self-sacrificing to men, saw the biography as a Protestant can-onisation that elevated Charlotte to a 'Christian heroine who could bear her cross with the firmness of a martyr saint'.[5] When William Gaskell repeated this to Ellen, she found it perfectly encapsulated her own increasingly reverential feelings for Charlotte who, in her mind, was departing from a woman of flesh and blood, from one who could be sharp, intransigent but compassionate, into a spirit more permeable, holy and imperishable, and adaptable to all who encountered her as a suffering romantic maiden in the pages of Elizabeth's book.

Just as Elizabeth had intended, all those who condemned Charlotte while she was alive now found themselves chastened. Charles Kingsley wrote to say he was ashamed to have written Charlotte off as a vulgar irrelevance:

> How I misjudged her! And how thankful I am that I never put a word of my misconceptions into print, or recorded my misjudgements of one who is a whole heaven above me. Well, you have done your work, and given us the picture of a valiant woman made perfect by sufferings.

His wife was particularly captivated by it, he told Elizabeth, and was 'more intensely interested in the book than almost any which he has ever read'.[6]

In May, William Wilson published another letter about Elizabeth's descriptions of the Clergy Daughters' School and offered extracts from a testimony by an associate of his father. This was Anna Andrews Hill, who had been head teacher and superintendent of Cowan Bridge for its first two years but had become untraceable for Elizabeth after she emigrated. Years before, Hill had been tipped off by a British friend that *Jane Eyre* depicted herself and Carus Wilson as the villainous Miss Scatcherd and Mr

Brocklehurst and was so incensed by Elizabeth's article 'A Few Words About Jane Eyre', published in an American journal the summer after Charlotte's death that she complained to the editor. She took issue with any assertion the school was the original Lowood and that the abuse inflicted upon Helen Burns by Miss Scatcherd reflected her brutalisation of Maria Brontë. The claims were only calculated to excite controversy, she said, and were unreliable. She remembered Charlotte and her sisters well and distinctly recalled Patrick enrolling them:

> Charlotte Brontë was only 10 years old when she left; she was a very bright, clever, and happy little girl, a general favourite; to the best of my recollection she was never under disgrace, however slight; punishment she certainly did not experience while she was at Cowan Bridge. In size, Charlotte was remarkably diminutive; and if, as has been recently asserted, 'she never grew an inch after leaving the Clergy School', she must have been a literal dwarf, and could not have obtained a situation as teacher in a school at Brussels, or anywhere else; the idea is absurd.[7]

Hill asserted Charlotte was delusional to create such a portrait and claim it was based on her own life:

> The talented Charlotte Brontë had no injurious motives in caricaturing an Institution which has been so great a blessing to the daughters of her own Church ... misled by a vivid imagination, and by the dim recollection of events that occurred thirty years previously, when she was a child, she published, in an unguarded moment, and unmindful of the consequences misstatements.[8]

Wilson quoted it in his defence of his father as proof of Elizabeth's bias, saying she must have seen it too. Until then, Arthur had been silent but this was the provocation he needed. Writing to the *Leeds Mercury* on 20 May, he suggested it was telling Wilson defended his father by being disingenuous as any suggestion the school was run on selflessness was false because it was publicly funded. He dismissed Hill's statements as she had 'strong reason to disparage the testimony of the avenging sister of Helen Burns (Maria Brontë), who was so cruelly treated by that *amiable* lady' and pointed out Elizabeth Gaskell had not relied solely on Charlotte's memories but considered those of other pupils she traced. Furthermore, Arthur argued, the identification of it with Lowood was made years before by members of the public who knew it from its reputation or their own experience. 'Yet the lady who was superintendent in 1824 was discreetly silent for more than seven years, in fact until the author was laid in her grave. So were Mr WW Carus Wilson and the reviewer.'[9]

This exposed Wilson's motivation. His father's school still existed and still relied on charitable donations. He wrote back the same day Arthur's letter was printed to protest that his father had challenged *Jane Eyre* when it first appeared and concluded it was best for readers to decide who was the more credible between Charlotte and the Rev. Carus Wilson:

> It is only natural that Mr N should seek to defend his wife's assertions, but considering that to add force to her fiction she casts odium on an invaluable institution and a public benefactor to mankind … I think Mr N should be the first to share in that regret.[10]

Even if Charlotte felt her recollection of the school was accurate, Wilson wrote, there were many more pupils who had defended it to him, insisting 'how happy they were there, how all loved my father, how entirely false the character Mrs Gaskell has sketched of him, and how good the food was, better (some have said) than they got at their own homes'.

Arthur shot back that he too had received letters about the school. He transcribed one for the newspaper to print:

> On first reading *Jane Eyre* several years ago, I recognised immediately the picture there drawn, and was far from considering it in anyway exaggerated; in fact I thought at the time, and still think the matter rather understated than otherwise. I suffered so severely from the treatment that I was never in the school room during the last three months I was there, until about a week before I left, and was considered to be far gone in consumption.[11]

The writer described how her mother was so horrified she refused to let her return. She had not known Charlotte, she said, and was not motivated to defend her beyond confirming her experiences had been similar to, if not worse than, hers.

Oblivious, in the shimmering heat of Italy, Elizabeth and Katie were guiding Marianne and Meta through the glories of Verona and Milan, Lake Como and Genoa in 'delicious quiet and *dolce far niente*',[12] while in Manchester, William was being inundated with dozens of angry letters about his wife and her book. Among them were complaints from represent-atives of Lady Lydia Scott, who until her second marriage was Mrs Lydia Robinson and had, until twelve years ago, employed Branwell and Anne as her children's tutor and governess at Thorp Green Hall, 10 miles from York. The siblings left a few months apart after Branwell's affair with Lydia became known to her husband and he was suspended then sacked. Branwell told friends he and Lydia were in love and expected to resume their relation-ship once her husband died. Six months later, Charlotte told Ellen he was suffering from drunkenness. After another six months, he was told Lydia's husband was finally dead but seeing Branwell again would be impossible as she would be disinherited and lose her claim to her husband's fortune. He told his friend Joseph Leyland he was stunned by a letter from her doctor that their affair had wrecked her marriage and killed her husband. At the time, Charlotte told Ellen that Branwell thought Lydia had lost her sanity from guilt and remorse. Distraught and furious, Branwell descended into emotional chaos and physical disintegration. He started extorting drinking money from his father and threatening suicide when he refused; he argued with increasing violence with them all and gave the household no peace. Martha Brown remembered him 'in a state of frenzy, walking round the table, clenching a knife in his hand, and wildly raving at the irrevocable decrees of damned fate'.[13]

He must have told conflicting versions of his own defence for Charlotte to tell Ellen at the time, 'I do not know how much to believe of what he says.'[14] Yet she and her father came to accept his justifications of being seduced then discarded by Lydia Robinson and blamed her for his down-fall. This at least was the account she gave Elizabeth that ended up in *The Life*. But a case against Lydia also came from another source. When George raised concerns, Elizabeth told him everything was corroborated by one of Lydia's cousins:

To think of her going about calling and dining out etc. etc. (her own relations have been obliged to drop her acquaintance) while those poor Brontës suffered so – for bad as Branwell was, he was not ruined forever till she got hold of him and he was not the first, nor the last. However, it is a horrid story and I should not have told it but to show the life of prolonged suffering those Brontë girls had to endure and what doubtless familiarised them to a certain degree with coarse expressions such as have been complained of in *Wuthering Heights* and *The Tenant of Wildfell Hall* ... You see *why* I wanted to contrast the two lives don't you?[15]

Lydia left no account of her side, but it seems likely she did have a sexual relationship with Branwell that he could not accept she declined to pursue. She remarried a few months after he died and by the time *The Life* was published had been widowed again. Elizabeth warned George in advance she intended to defame Lydia, ensuring without naming her there were enough details to identify her. Lydia asked her friend, James Stephen – later the grandfather of Virginia Woolf – to contact William Gaskell in Elizabeth's absence to demand the evidence: 'To every word of Mrs Gaskell's accusations, she [Lydia] solemnly and unequivocally opposed the most absolute and unqualified contradiction that it was in the power of words to convey.'[16] Stephen wrote to Smith Elder challenging four specific claims:

> The charge that she seduced the Tutor of her son into the habitual commission of adultery; that she pressed him to run off with her from her husband's house; that she 'made love to him in the presence of her own Daughters', and then bribed him to silence; and that at last she broke this man's heart by her own heartless inhumanity to him; this charge so shocking and so strange has been published by Messrs Smith & Elder in a book engaging a great popularity and a rapid circulation. They of course gave implicit credit to Mrs Gaskell for a diligent and impartial investigation of the Story and published it with a full conviction of its truth.[17]

Regardless of truth, these inferences, Stephen wrote, were utterly ruinous to Lydia's character and would prohibit her social and familial acceptance in the future. George replied they would investigate and recall any unsold copies. He did not mention that sales had been so sensational the first print run sold out within the first fortnight and there were few copies of the second edition left to withdraw. He contacted William, who went to Haworth to ask Patrick where the information about Branwell and Lydia Robinson had come from and whether he could provide any evidence of a relationship between them, such as letters from her. Patrick told him he remembered Branwell exchanged letters with Mrs Robinson constantly but as he himself never saw them could not verify they truly were from her. Not a page remained, he explained, as all were burned after Branwell's death by Charlotte, Emily and Anne.[18] William knew that without any written evidence to implicate Lydia all of it would be dismissed as hearsay. As to the lady's conduct, Patrick told him, everyone including her own children knew what she was like and even her gardener thought her a whore. William reported all this to George, who must have had his head in his hands by this point. He knew he had to act quickly to defuse the conflict before it proceeded to court and dragged them all under. 'Much gossip, it was found, existed,' he concluded diplomatically, 'but it was gossip of the kind which is apt to dissolve into mere vapour when tested in a court of law.'[19]

Faced with the possibility Lydia would sue himself and the Gaskells for slander, and destroy the reputations of everyone involved, George advised William to get his lawyers to publish a retraction. Left with no choice, William made a public apology on his wife's behalf, withdrawing:

> every statement contained in that work which impute show with lady referred to but not named therein any breach of her conjugal or of her maternal or of her social duties ... which imputes the lady in question a guilty intercourse with a late Branwell Brontë.

Additional evidence had shown it all to be untrustworthy, he concluded.[20]

George suspended the sale of the book and recalled any remaining copies from circulation. But he refused to be outdone. Ingeniously, he realised a way to overshadow the negative publicity and recoup his losses. He had held back on releasing *The Professor* until an opportune time presented itself, and now that moment had come. As William's apology was being reported by the newspapers, George rushed *The Professor* into print, distributed it with extraordinary swiftness and took out adverts announcing in large bold type that the long-awaited final novel by Currer Bell was out now. Anyone who wanted the latest on Charlotte Brontë could buy it from Smith Elder.

An uncaptured copy of *The Life of Charlotte Brontë* sailed from England and made its way to Mary Taylor in Wellington. To her surprise she had to agree Elizabeth had triumphed despite the challenge of risking 'a true description of those around [her]'. She had presented 'a true picture of a melancholy life' that did not ignore the deleterious influences of Patrick, Branwell and Arthur. 'Though not so gloomy as the truth, it is perhaps as much so as people will accept without calling it exaggerated and feeling the desire to doubt and contradict it.' She had already seen it described as an account of poverty and self-suppression, with none realising it a 'strange or wrong state of things that a woman of first-rate talents, industry and integrity should live all her life in a walking nightmare of "poverty and self-suppression". I doubt whether any of them will.'[21]

Two days later, Elizabeth and her girls arrived back from Italy. Alongside tirades about Cowan Bridge in the newspapers and the legal threats from Lydia, 100 angry letters were waiting for her, from the litigious to the absurd. Carus Wilson's son was furious, as was Harriet Martineau, Elizabeth was disappointed to learn, that she had exposed her argument with Charlotte. Haworth locals objected to being characterised as uneducated bores in ways that justified her descriptions, and two different people demanded she correct the setting of an event they both claimed happened in their houses. Threats of litigation were flying, George faced reputational ruin, and William was utterly exasperated. 'I am in the hornet's nest with a vengeance,' Elizabeth told Ellen in horror. 'I have much to tell you on this subject; but I am warned not to *write* and must keep it till we meet.'[22] She told her she had wept so much from fury since she got back that 'I am almost merry in my bitterness' and insisted she had written nothing false:

> I believe *now* I hit as near the truth as any one *could* do. And I weighed every line with all my power and heart so that every line should go to its great purpose of making *her* known and valued as one who had gone through such a terrible life with a brave and faithful heart. But I think you know and knew all this. One comfort is too that God knows the truth.[23]

All the same, she knew she must be apologetic to appease George. Many of the complaints alleged she had not been thorough enough to interrogate gossips and, by repeating them, made him look credulous and Smith Elder disreputable. 'I am at home, once more, and ready to do anything you may wish towards preparing the third edition,' she told him. She accepted the parts about Lydia Robinson must be cut, and offered new material as compensation, including Mary Taylor's recollections, received after the first edition came out. She also had more on the people of Haworth, about Harriet Martineau, and would revise the Cowan Bridge sections, which she promised to check with her lawyer. 'I hate the whole affair, and everything connected with it,' she told George bitterly, 'I am very sorry indeed you have had so much annoyance. I will make it up to you, as far as I can, by taking all possible pains with the third edition.'[24]

Around her, the fires of controversy showed no signs of abating. Soon after her return, the *Halifax Guardian* reprinted Arthur's side of the Cowan Bridge argument for a wider readership under the heading 'A Vindication of Charlotte Brontë'. Rather than bringing a conclusion it drew more accusations of partiality and further complaints that now veered into personal insults. Embarrassingly for Patrick and Arthur, it became even more personal than before. Letters castigating Arthur appeared from a woman named Sarah Baldwin, the daughter and wife of two vicars he and Patrick knew. She said she and her four sisters all attended the school in both locations and were 'unanimous in their testimony to the general excellence of the institution and its management and we feel it difficult to repress our indignation at the unjustifiable attack made upon it and its founder'.[25] She stayed at both sites for a total of seven years, she explained, with two at Cowan Bridge and five at Casterton, giving her a sense of authority over how both had been managed. She admitted she caught a fever at Cowan Bridge but retained 'vivid recollections of the motherly care and attention I received'.

Making a public correction of the dead was distasteful, she went on, unless their errors were so grave they threatened the integrity of an institution deserving reverence, and none had 'a stronger claim to sympathies and support of the Christian Church'.[26] While Mrs Baldwin was clear she had not known Charlotte at school – she boarded seven years after her – she did not mention she was personally acquainted with the Brontës. But in his seething reply, Arthur wasted no time in pointing it out. He told readers she was 'indulging in characteristic scolding' with no insight other than that of association and had no way of defending the school against Charlotte's recollection. Irked by this personal betrayal in public, Arthur was incensed, calling Mrs Baldwin 'a stranger to that delicacy of feeling which causes a lady to shrink from having her name paraded before the public'. Given the cause of their discussion was a memoir of his wife, he handed Mrs Baldwin an opportunity to score and she shot back, 'I cheerfully leave it to your readers, and to those who have considered Mr Nicholls's letter, to decide where the lack of delicacy of feeling exists.'[27] She took the opportunity to criticise him in kind, saying his argument was weak enough to be considered a sneer:

> Mr Nicholls's letter is written in a style so coarse and unusual among educated people, that it is quite undeserving of notice, and would have been allowed to pass at once into oblivion but for one or two misstatements it contains.

He should think twice before lecturing anyone on logic, she reprimanded, given the deficiencies of his own. She asked if he could seriously suggest she had no right to defend Cowan Bridge because she had not attended it at the same time as Charlotte. 'If so, let me ask, what is the extent of his acquaintance with the subject?' As he had not been a pupil there at all, he had, by his own argument, no qualification to contradict her 'with such boldness, and in so peculiar a style'.[28]

Elizabeth shot a letter to George that she was now receiving furious letters from William Wilson, threatening to sue and printing a pamphlet to denounce her. She could admit surrender on the Lydia Robinson matter, but she was ready to defend what she had written about Cowan Bridge. On that matter she found an unexpected comrade: Patrick. He was staunch that Charlotte's depictions of the school in *Jane Eyre* were acceptable as fiction, and Elizabeth's exposure of the inspiration was justifiable and merited no blame. 'I hope therefore that Mrs Gaskell, having strong proofs on her side, will make *no concessions* ... whether they cajole or threaten. There ought to be *no more concessions*.'[29]

The only difficulty was that those who had come forward were mostly poor and vulnerable to legal threat, Elizabeth explained. Many former pupils had ended up as governesses or the wives of impoverished men and told her they should be willing to go public only if it was absolutely unavoidable. Elizabeth worried that dragging them into the melee could bring them more financial trouble than her. She sent their testimonies with her copies of the school inspections to her solicitor for advice. He was satisfied Elizabeth had been honest but told her to choose between continuing this debate indefinitely or having a peaceful life.

In the newspapers, William Wilson congratulated Sarah Baldwin for her riposte to Arthur. 'Your readers will, I am sure, agree with me that she is *quite* able to take care of herself.'[30] He said all his friends were astonished by Arthur's rudeness in his last letter but assured them Arthur could be disregarded now because Elizabeth had admitted her errors to him and was 'most willing to rectify the injury she has done to my father and his institutions'. This was news to the parsonage. 'I scarcely know what to think,' Patrick told George, 'especially when I reflect on what has already been done.'[31] He could see Elizabeth was being coerced by public pressure and in spite of the many influential friends and supporters she had, he appears to have been the only one to say so to George. 'I sometimes fear the probable consequences, should any false steps be contemplated, though I would willingly hope there will not. I trust you will interfere with your advice and authority and adjust and properly regulate the whole concern.'[32] Patrick hoped that as publisher, George would remain steadfast in rejecting calls for *The Life* to be altered. But as the arguments became more venal, George doubted it was worth it.

'If Mrs Baldwin takes such a strong exception to my last letter,' Arthur told the editor of the *Halifax Guardian*, she should expect nothing less after charging him with 'distortion and exaggeration of facts and wilful misrepresentation.'[33] She could not see the fallacy in her own logic, he explained, to insist that if her experience was favourable after Charlotte's time, it must always have been so. He wrote that he had a letter of support from a pupil who was there in the years between Charlotte and her, who remembered the food being so scant and badly cooked that children refused it or were made ill by it. Those who refused to eat were left to starve for so long they resorted to stealing bread and were punished when caught. 'My sole desire in this controversy has been to defend the dead from aspersions cast on her by interested individuals,' he concluded. Neither he nor Charlotte had written about the present incarnation of the school or its management, he said. In fact, 'the only disparaging remarks I have ever heard made respecting it were by Mrs Baldwin's own father, on the occasion of the removal of one of his daughters.'[34]

The editor stepped in and appealed to Patrick for support. He said they received more complaints about this than was reasonable to print, and now another former pupil joined Arthur, Wilson and Mrs Baldwin in sending letters three to six pages long without showing progress to a resolution. Patrick refused to be drawn in but thought it best to drop the story. Three days later, they published an editorial to draw a line under the affair. They repeated the points Arthur had wearily made from the start: 'There were certain hardships and irregularities at Cowan Bridge School when Miss Brontë was there, which were remedied as soon as they became known.'

Sarah Baldwin was incensed. She wrote back, subverting the refusal to publish any more letters by paying for it to be printed as an advert. 'I will now take the liberty of setting these matters in their true light and then, as far as I am concerned, terminate this controversy.'[35] She insisted those former pupils endorsing Charlotte's perspective were 'cruelly playing upon Mr Nicholls' credulity'. She knew the pupil Arthur recommended as a witness to the indigestible food and chose to name her publicly: Elizabeth Gauntlett Smith, one of the daughters of the vicar of Olney. Her recollections, Mrs Baldwin reported, were less black and white than Arthur represented, since she remembered the catering being improved after she complained and called her years there 'amongst the happiest of my life'.[36] As someone who attended the school soon after Charlotte, Smith could either validate or repudiate its resemblance to Lowood. But the passage of time had made her moderate. As to be expected with fiction, Mrs Smith explained, Lowood was a combination of reality and invention that conveyed a generalised impression of Cowan Bridge but could not reasonably be regarded as reportage. 'This letter needs no comment,' Mrs Baldwin concluded triumphantly.[37]

Returning to Arthur's words about her father, she denied he had ever criticised the school, levelling the same criticism at Arthur she made of Charlotte, that his faults lay with his imagination rather than his memory. Unwisely, Arthur chose to reply to her privately, earning a fiery reply that called his rebukes 'grossly abusive' and him a disgrace to the clergy. 'Your mind seems to be fully made up to believe nothing but evil.'[38] Refusing to allow her the final word, he wrote again to the *Halifax Guardian* to make his the last they published on the matter. He summarised that Smith conceded the school's food was so inedible it forced children to steal, which he pointed out Mrs Baldwin could not deny, and insisted he was not mistaken that on a visit to the parsonage her father had criticised both the school and Rev. Carus Wilson's management. 'And now sir, I have done with this subject. I have discharged a painful but necessary duty. Henceforth, Charlotte Brontë's assailants may growl and snarl over her grave undisturbed by me.'[39]

Certain of Carus Wilson's negligence and culpability, Elizabeth remembered how after decades Charlotte could still weep bitterly for her two eldest sisters who never lived past girlhood, dying at 10 and 11 after contracting tuberculosis at his school, she refused to be threatened by his son trying to protect the business. She was adamant she did not need to invent any of the hardships she described. 'I can stand it all patiently,' she insisted, recalling Charlotte's miseries and futile attempts at hopefulness, '*You do not know what she had to bear; and what she had to hear.*'[40]

Despite his solidarity with Elizabeth, Patrick was bothered by comments she had made about himself in the book. Though he was magnanimous to the point of generosity when he first read it, after weeks of conversation with Arthur while he was arguing in the newspapers Patrick reconsidered whether he should let it stand unchallenged as it gradually dawned on him the gravest slanders had been made about him as a parent. He wrote to William Gaskell and George while Elizabeth was still abroad. 'I wish that Mrs Gaskell had been a little more cautious in the able and interesting memoir,' he complained, 'With respect to myself I wish to say but little. Somethings in reference to me Mrs Gaskell has stated fairly. Other things never had any foundation but in the imagination or evil intentions or ignorance of her informants.'[41] He was becoming troubled by her inferences that it was his inattention to his children's needs that helped ruin their constitutions, making them vulnerable to the illnesses that killed them. He protested he had never deprived his children of meat, as claimed, or any other wholesome food, while they were developing, nor encouraged them to wear inadequate clothing. Referring to anecdotes about him burning a rug, sawing up the chairs and cutting up his wife's dress, he made an emphatic denial: 'I never was subject to those explosions of passion ascribed to me and never perpetuated those excentric [*sic*] and ridiculous movements, which I am ashamed to mention.'[42]

Both William and George referred him back to Elizabeth, telling him to wait until she returned from Italy to discuss it with her personally. A few weeks later, Patrick wrote to Plymouth Grove again and received a reply from Marianne that her mother was home but too unwell to write. He suspected he was being fobbed off.

At the start of July, he made his discontent known to three visitors who dropped by the parsonage, Frank Leyland, William Dearden and William Brooksbank. Having all been acquainted with his son, the men had heard about Branwell's relationship with Lydia while it was happening and saw his subsequent decline. They remembered how his last months were dominated by his obsession over the end of the affair. As they heard it, presumably from Branwell, the Rev. Edmund Robinson had been impotent and a drunk, locking Lydia into a physically violent marriage that caught Branwell in the crossfire when he joined their household as their sons' tutor. Once Branwell started to defend Lydia from his alcoholic rages, her gratitude developed into emotional and then physical intimacy.[43] Patrick protested miserably that his son had been no worse than anyone else's, so had been left amazed by how much Elizabeth had made of it:

I do not see what the public has to do with it.[44] I did not know I had an enemy in the world; much less one who would traduce me before my death. Everything in that book which relates to my conduct to my family is either false or distorted. I never did commit such acts as were there ascribed to me.[45]

The men said they were disappointed he had heard nothing from Elizabeth, given the amount of press the book was generating. It was typical in a way, Patrick told them, because people had always regarded him as cold and a man without feelings, 'an abstraction'. Without any supporters he was fated 'to be dragged before the public; to be represented as an unkind father and charged with acts which I never committed'.[46] Up until that point, Patrick insisted that he had no idea where Elizabeth could have got her information about him. Now he seemed to have an inkling: he wondered aloud if she had been talking to his former servants.

Before they left, Leyland appears to have made it known he had other business. He showed him a notebook of poems written by Branwell that he had inherited from his late brother, Joe, a sculptor who received it from Branwell in exchange for a Romanesque plaster medallion he made of Branwell's profile. Leyland inferred he would be interested in selling Patrick his own son's notebook for the right price. Patrick shut him down and dismissed the idea.

Among the hundred letters waiting for Elizabeth when she got home was one from Arthur that listed the passages about Patrick he wished her to delete from *The Life*. Related to it was another, from George, prompted by Patrick's complaint that Elizabeth's descriptions of his behaviour were unfounded. He asked where she got her information. Wearily, she explained everything being complained about had come from eyewitnesses and conversations with Charlotte. Stories about Patrick forbidding meat, sawing up chairs, burning their shoes and a rug were 'all told to me on the authority of uneducated Haworth people', meaning past servants, 'and the cutting up of the silk gown, an anecdote so strongly resembling the others in character as to be confirmatory to a certain degree told me by Charlotte Brontë herself'. Indeed, Charlotte had also told it to her other friends over the years; Ellen and Margaret mentioned it in their interviews, 'both of whom believe it, I *think* to this day'.[47] Furthermore, Charlotte described his destructiveness to strangers, telling one in a letter Elizabeth had not seen that gathering up her mother and aunt's books and magazines, 'one black day my father burnt them because they contained foolish love stories.'[48]

It was Martha Wright who told Elizabeth that Patrick gave his children a spartan diet and sawed up chairs in a temper during one of his wife's pregnancies. As that happened before she joined the household, she must have heard it from the sisters who came with them from Thornton to Haworth, where she joined a year later to provide palliative care. Nancy Garrs was a 12-year-old Bradford nursemaid when she was hired after Charlotte's birth, joined by her sister Sarah as cook once Branwell and Emily were born. While Martha Wright was only with them for the summer of 1821 – Nancy left after Mrs Brontë's death and Sarah stayed on for another four years – she remembered them all, particularly the six children:[49]

> I used to think them spiritless, they were so different to any children I had
> ever seen. In part, I set it down to a fancy Mr Brontë had of not letting

them have flesh-meat to eat. It was from no wish for saving, for there was plenty and even waste in the house, with young servants and no mistress to see after them; but he thought that children should be brought up simply and hardily: so they had nothing but potatoes for dinner.[50]

When they saw this in *The Life*, the Garrs sisters protested that being called wasteful threatened their livelihoods. Patrick wrote them a reference refuting it, and took support from Nancy, who denied they were ever short of meat. Presumably, she did not mention she corroborated the story of Patrick destroying his wife's dress – and would tell it to Leyland years later – or that when Mrs Brontë's sister took over running the house, she thought them too wasteful to pour out their own quota of beer.[51] Additionally, Ellen, Margaret and Mary all remembered Charlotte being so undernourished when she joined Roe Head school that Margaret herself had to wean her on to meat.

In transmission from person to person, memories were evidently complicated. 'However, I submit,' Elizabeth concluded.[52] Accepting that some truths must be sacrificed if she was to silence her detractors, she assured Patrick she had accepted everything in good faith but would remove all the objectionable passages from the new edition at his request. She appears to have been blunt enough to tell him the information he disliked most had come from the lips of his daughter. Patrick replied with equal firmness, 'My dear little daughter must have been misinformed.'[53] He had no objection to being portrayed as an eccentric, and did not deny he was, 'only don't set me on in my fury to burning hearthrugs, sawing the backs off chairs and tearing my wife's silk gowns'. Anyway, he explained, had he been a more moderate man, 'I should in all probability never have had such children as mine.'[54] This, he did not realise, was her point.

Through the last changeable weeks of July into warm early August, Elizabeth drafted a redacted third edition. Once she had collated the lists of everyone's objections, she marked the offending sections she planned to cut or revise, diplomatically worded by her solicitor. By then she was so exhausted by the hostility and accusations of having fabricated evidence she told George he could have anyone edit it and cut anything they liked. Sarcastically, she suggested he add a disclaimer apologising in advance to anyone likely to be offended by *anything* she had written and promising to delete it all without question.

She confided all this to Harriet, showing her the most extreme letters she had received in praise and blame. Harriet had been too slow to get a first edition of *The Life*, but everyone in Ambleside had read it. 'Weeks before I saw it, my relations, friends & neighbours were talking about the extraordinary representations of me, my ways, position, & experiences, that appeared in CB's letters. The matter was notorious.'[55] She read the second edition with some admiration but was mystified by Elizabeth's cryptic account of her falling out with Charlotte and wanted to explain her side.

She began to suspect Elizabeth's sympathies had misled her into accepting too much at face value from Charlotte. Both had similar conversations with her, but scepticism inclined her to dispute Elizabeth's conclusions, such as that Branwell's affair killed him and triggered the declines and deaths of his sisters. She suspected the affair had been magnified as it passed from Branwell to Charlotte and then to Elizabeth, altering beyond its original, and probably, transactional nature. 'C.B. never gave the least hint of the affair to me,' she told Katie, 'she simply said her brother died of his vices.'[56] She doubted any evidence would ever be found, even if the letters in Branwell's pockets had not been burned by his sisters, suspecting they showed 'something very unlike what [Elizabeth] concludes from Charlotte Brontë's account.' Her hunch was correct. Interviewed many years later, Martha Brown remembered they had not been broken-hearted letters from Lydia Robinson, as Elizabeth described in *The Life*, but injunctions from her family doctor telling Branwell to leave her alone.[57]

At one time Harriet would not have hesitated to defend Charlotte's integrity – 'before any of her double-dealing became known to me' – but since her contradictions became public she concluded Charlotte had been disingenuous with everyone from her employers to friends, dramatising her own life so that when Elizabeth repeated her anecdotes in *The Life*, the blame for inventing them fell on to her. The alleged inaccuracies others objected to were not Elizabeth's contrivances or misunderstandings, she explained, but Charlotte's own distortions and Elizabeth's only mistake had been one of trust.

Reading about herself in Charlotte's letters she began to wonder if Charlotte had been a pathological liar. Sorrowfully, she told a friend:

I have long ceased to consider Charlotte Brontë truthful. As to intent, people's minds are so composite that one can't undertake to say how far people are at the moment 'conscious' of the untruths they speak: but that C.B. made no point of saying what was true, I am now sure. On all hands, her want of sincerity & good faith is coming out.[58]

That said, she could summon no sympathy for Patrick either, who she still considered a pompous and heartless monster, which 'I infer from his conduct to his children, and especially to C.B. I don't think he had the slightest affection for her, or feelings for any of them. He made a mere convenience of her.'[59]

To neutralise the controversy, Harriet advised, Elizabeth should promise to repair only the mistakes made through false information but insist on her right to form and express her own impressions.[60] It was important to appear contrite, she told her, even if she was not, telling another friend, 'I should like to have had some sign of humiliation and self-blame from Mrs G.' She considered her confidential situation with her as like being hidden behind a curtain together. 'If Miss Martineau advises me strongly to do anything,' Elizabeth wrote, 'I have such reliance on her strong sense and warm heart that I believe I should do it.'[61] When Elizabeth showed her Patrick's letter calling for corrections Harriet was shocked. 'The old monster!' she told Katie Winkworth, 'Anything so appalling as one sentence in it I am sure I never saw come from a human hand. Beautiful as the book is in many ways, I do mourn that Mrs G ever came in the way of that awful family.'[62]

Just when Elizabeth thought peace might settle, William Dearden took it upon himself to write to the *Bradford Observer* on Patrick's behalf. *The Life* had 'tarred and feathered' a venerable man 'on the verge of the grave', he claimed, because Elizabeth had trusted a single witness to Patrick's eccentricities, Martha Wright, rather than interview those Dearden saw as more loyal: Martha Brown and the Garrs sisters.[63] Martha told him sharply she had indeed been interviewed but would 'have no hand whatever in picking any faults against Mrs Gaskell' as her job required her to mind her own business, which she intended to keep doing.[64]

Scenting blood, Dearden pursued further charges a week later. Nancy Garrs was insistent the Brontë children had 'as much as they chose to eat' he said, and never witnessed Patrick burning children's shoes in her kitchen. They both assured him it was all 'a tissue of malignant falsehoods'.[65] He repeated what Patrick said when he visited, that he never knew he had enemies until he read what Elizabeth had written. 'She has injured the reputation of a good and amiable man' who deserved vindication. The national papers quoted him and repeated Patrick's comments that 'Everything in that book which relates to my conduct to my family is either false or distorted.'[66]

Harriet leapt to Elizabeth's defence and wrote to call Dearden (and by association, Patrick) a liar:

> I have seen two letters from Mr Brontë to Mrs Gaskell, one written soon after the appearance of the Memoir and the other five weeks after the date of his alleged complaints, in both of which the most entire confidence in and gratitude towards Mrs Gaskell are warmly expressed. It is impossible that the writer of those letters could have, in the interval between them, represented Mrs Gaskell as an enemy.[67]

Only those who had acted as Elizabeth's sources should have their integrity questioned, she continued. 'When I find that, in my own case, scarcely one of Miss Brontë's statements about me is altogether true, I cannot be surprised at her biographer having been misled.'[68] Reading this, Dearden turned to Leyland:

> If this be true, you and I did not hear on the 8th of July Mr Brontë complain of Mrs Gaskell's treatment of him in the memoir of his daughter! We did not hear him state that he had made his complaints known to Mrs G and received no answer! What motive could you or I have in misrepresenting facts?[69]

When Dearden sent Elizabeth a clipping of his letter she returned it with a disgusted note, telling him as she never read anything about herself 'from want of time and inclination' it would be of more use to him than herself.[70]

Despairing that his indiscretion was now national news, Patrick apologised to Elizabeth. 'With this article I had nothing whatsoever to do – I knew nothing of it until I saw it in print and was much displeased when I saw it there.'[71] He had been aggravated by commentators but held back from answering them because he was certain 'you were a friend to my daughter Charlotte and no enemy to me, and feeling confident that whatever you found to be mistakes you would willingly correct.'[72] To her credit, Elizabeth was sympathetic rather than annoyed. 'He really has been so steady in his way to me all along, that I would rather let them all go on attacking me than drag him into any squabble either with me or the public, or anyone.'[73] Patrick thanked her for her understanding, and in the grand rhetorical way in which he often wrote and spoke, told her that as receiving acclaim mixed with criticism was her lot in life, as with Charlotte, 'Then drink the mixed cup with thankfulness to the great physician of Souls.'[74]

Agitating for more controversy, Dearden took Brooksbank back to see Patrick on Saturday, 29 August. Leyland was not with them this time, Dearden remarked, because Patrick treated him so coldly in July, and this was an egregious way to behave towards someone who had once given him a gift, namely the medallion of Branwell. 'A present?' replied Patrick. 'Why he charged us £6 6s for it, when I always understood that we had a claim to it.'[75] Dearden did not know this. Patrick explained John Brown brought him it from Leyland, telling him he had to purchase it. As Patrick had not enough money at hand, he clubbed together with Charlotte and paid him. Decades later, Leyland himself was caught out when he put the same story of benevolence to Arthur. Trying to curry favour, he again described the medallion as his gift to the Brontë family, but Arthur knew the truth. 'I was not aware you had given the portrait to Mr Brontë,' he dismissed him, 'I know that my late wife gave £5 for it.'[76]

Dearden evaded this and turned the subject back to *The Life* to glean any sense of betrayal he could report. A few days later, Patrick repeated in writing what he told him in person: they should stop going to the newspapers about him and his family. 'I wish nothing more should be written about Mrs Gaskell in regard to the Memoir ... she has already encountered very severe trials.'[77] He clarified that, 'I never thought otherwise of Mrs Gaskell than that she was a friend of my daughter and no enemy to me. In alluding to enemies, I meant false informants, and hostile critics.'

Dearden ignored him and sent the *Bradford Observer* a riposte to Harriet's letter. 'I repudiate the charge alleged against me by that lady, of having misrepresented Mr Brontë – the onus of that charge, lies ... on other shoulders than mine.' Unlike Elizabeth, he went on, he had exercised great care in collecting facts about the Brontës and merely wished to address the 'gross wrong' done to Patrick by Elizabeth. Softening his original allegation after his latest conversation, Dearden insisted Patrick 'has not designated the whole of Mrs Gaskell's memoir the work of an enemy but has taken exception only to that portion of it in which he is misrepresented'.[78]

With extraordinary indiscretion, he quoted part of Patrick's latest letter, 'which I received from him yesterday morning', saying he never considered Elizabeth his enemy, omitting the appeal for no more to be written on the subject, and invited Brooksbank and Leyland to join his attack on Harriet.[79] In time, his motivations to inveigle a role as Patrick's spokesman became clear. A month later, he suggested he or Leyland should pitch another book to a publisher in reply to *The Life*, exonerating Branwell. In no uncertain terms, Patrick said he would never approve it, reflecting that despite his son's brilliance, 'his appetite was stronger than his reason, and thus all his fair prospects were blighted, his life shortened and great sorrow brought upon his sisters and me.'[80] He said he and Arthur would never assist anyone in writing Branwell's life or disclose his manuscripts to them. While Dearden and Leyland accepted this, they never abandoned the idea and thirty years later, Leyland published his own biography, about having been the brother of a man who was once friends with Branwell Brontë.[81]

In Manchester, Elizabeth persevered with the abridgements. She itemised the list of omissions requested by Arthur about Patrick, removed her descriptions of the Garrs as wasteful, and – at the request of Martha Brown – that of a village girl being 'seduced', and approved a list of legal bypasses made by her solicitor to her descriptions of Cowan Bridge. She hesitated over Patrick's ritual of firing a pistol, expecting him to deny that too. To her surprise, Arthur had not mentioned it but she told George it was better to take preventative action. 'I am willing to do anything for a quiet life, so if you can, please take it out.'[82]

Suspecting her use as an advisor was spent now a final edition was in the pipeline, Ellen tried to stay instrumental by offering unsolicited recommendations. She suggested Elizabeth write a preface and include an index to allow people to look up references to themselves. Elizabeth told George there was no way she would consider this, as she had already received complaints from everyone 'whose name has been named, I think; or whose grandmother's great uncle once removed has been alluded to'.[83] She joked she might incorporate the complaints themselves but ruled out a preface to avoid becoming a character in her own book. It was an objection only she seems to have had.

Proofs were ready at the start of August. She and her husband read, checked and returned them to George by the middle of the month. She sent the revisions about Lydia Robinson and Carus Wilson to a friend connected to both and told George that he should not stop the printing unless he got an objection in the next few days, writing in relief, 'Oh! I don't care what the people say of me. I am a great deal better than they give me credit for.'[84]

The redacted third edition was printed, bound and ready for distribution by 22 August. Ignoring the threats of litigation that necessitated it, George promoted it as an enhancement of the banned first edition, a 'New and Revised Edition with Emendations and Additions', placing adverts in the national papers every week throughout September. Alongside it and determined to capitalise on what was certain to be another wave of enthusiasm, he issued a cheap single-volume reprint of *Jane Eyre*, which instantly found as many new readers as the original ten years before. As soon as it appeared, one journalist noticed it already in the hands of every passenger in his railway carriage.[85] The appetite for material about Charlotte Brontë had become insatiable.

'You must be aware that many strange notions as to the kind of person Charlotte really was will be done away with by a knowledge of the true facts of her life,' Mary told Ellen, wary of how reverential she was becoming, magnifying Charlotte beyond all they had left: shifting anecdotes, disputed memories, and the jewellery and dresses the physical woman had vacated. Going by Ellen's unjust account of how Elizabeth won her confidence then pulled away when she was no longer useful, Mary thought Elizabeth sounded insincere and inconsistent but she cheered her fearless blame of Patrick, Branwell and Arthur as obstacles Charlotte should not have faced and hoped she would hold her nerve against the backlash. Now she considered the prospect of a 'mutilated' revision of *The Life* a travesty. 'Libellous or not, the first edition was all true,' she insisted.[86] The truth, however, as judicious Mary knew, was rarely straightforward and often problematic for all concerned.

When the new edition reached Ambleside, Harriet read it and became incandescent. Not only had Elizabeth elaborated on her quarrels with Charlotte to include what she told Elizabeth she had written to Charlotte to placate her, but she now included a new letter showing Charlotte telling George to decline Harriet's work in progress. 'From my house,' Harriet raged, 'she was writing to a stranger prepossessing him against [it].'[87] She saw no similarity between this and her own public condemnation of *Villette* and decided Charlotte's proclaimed worship of truth was hypocrisy.

Dearden wasted no time in telling Patrick that Harriet was calling Charlotte a liar. Patrick countered, telling Harriet that Charlotte had been an honest woman who 'if she had been disposed for malevolent misrepresentation would have placed you amongst the last she would have misrepresented.' Imagining she would be flattered, he told her Charlotte was fond enough of her to defend her against her enemies but he accepted Harriet might have been inconsiderate, insisting 'it was wrong since you must be aware that whatever you may write the world will read.'[88]

Harriet returned the shot as soon as she received it. While Charlotte may have had some personal affection for her, she told him firmly:

> it is not the less true that, as I have publicly and privately said, there is
> scarcely a statement concerning myself in her letters which is altogether

true; and I may add that some of them are more like hallucination than sober statement.[89]

She told Katie Winkworth about this 'vicious letter from Mr Brontë', after Dearden characterised her as making:

> an attack on his daughter. The misapprehension is entire; & off he goes into vehement insult, ending with 'yours most respectfully'. I have sent him a short answer, as kind as I could possibly make it, consistently with truth … It is a pity Mr Nicholls cannot keep him quiet.[90]

Far from keeping him quiet, Arthur took up arms again and looked for the part in the new edition that had enraged her. He told Harriet her recollection of her last exchange with Charlotte was wrong, as he checked it against her original letter, found among Charlotte's papers, and would not hesitate in exposing her as the untruthful one. 'I shall adopt the same means that you have, to inform the public that the individual who accuses my wife of *inaccuracies* has herself been guilty of a much graver offence.'[91]

It stopped her in her tracks. 'I am sure there could be very little difference between the original and my recollection of it,' she replied, startled at the prospect of being publicly held to account.[92] She explained she had no choice but to provide her side of the argument as well as she remembered it because:

> you informed Mrs Gaskell when she began the Memoir that you had destroyed all CB's papers. And Mr Greenwood wrote, in reply to an inquiry from myself, that my letters to CB had been burnt, his information having been doubtless obtained from yourself.[93]

She told him she had defended *The Life* against Dearden's accusations of fabrication:

> And now my plea for justice on Mr B's behalf is answered by insults from himself & threats from you! I shall expect the note you refer to, either the original, with its red ink marks, or a certified copy, with corresponding marks. This is the first step. We shall then see what next.[94]

Arthur was adamant he never told anyone he destroyed Charlotte's papers and scolded her for getting involved, saying her 'interference was wholly gratuitous' and extended the public argument he or Patrick could have settled.[95]

Agitated but convinced Greenwood told her Arthur destroyed all Charlotte's letters, Harriet asked Elizabeth if she had remembered it correctly; had Arthur told *her* the same? Elizabeth recalled it perfectly. She said he had, on more than one occasion, because she asked him more than once. She asked John Greenwood too and he told her the same, that Arthur had burnt every letter he found in his wife's possession. And furthermore, she explained, when she started work on the book, Arthur never showed her any letters from Harriet, but could paraphrase the one she quoted.

'What most astonishes me is the real or apparent prejudice you have,' Patrick cut in to Harriet:

if I may judge from some things you have written or said against her [Charlotte]. As I well knew her character for veracity and candour, and had many proofs of her affection and veneration for you, I entreat you on the grounds of mere justice to do justice to her in all you may think, say or write. And could she speak from the tomb she would ask for no more. Beware of the designs of prejudiced or reckless informants. That God may restore you to health and strength.[96]

Refusing to be swayed by emotive rhetoric, Harriet slashed back at him. 'I assure you, no person has excited any prejudice in my mind against your daughter: nor could I allow my judgment to be warped by any such influence.' She would not allow him to tell her she could not object to being defined by someone else's life story, she persisted, and he had no entitlement to expect anything else:

You see, I doubt not, that when you & Mr Nicholls procured the publication of a Memoir in which living persons are described, those persons must be expected to dissent from any account of themselves which was inaccurate. It is not only their right but their duty to do so, as no misrepresentation could be set right hereafter.[97]

Turning to Arthur, certain now he was the dishonest one, she told him, 'Before me lie two letters: yours received yesterday, in which you declare that you never told Mrs Gaskell that you had destroyed all CB's papers: & one from Mrs Gaskell.' Elizabeth and Greenwood maintained, correctly, that Arthur *had* told them he destroyed Charlotte's papers, yet now – Harriet put it to him – he would like her to believe otherwise. 'The three statements will lie by together. It is no concern of mine to discover where the mistake lies, as long as it is not my own.'[98] As Greenwood had described himself to her and Elizabeth as Charlotte's only friend in Haworth, they assumed his information had come from the parsonage. If it had, Arthur replied meekly, it was from gossiping with the servants – the excuse Patrick used for the leak about his peculiar behaviour – since, as Arthur put it, a shopkeeper could never have been considered Charlotte's friend, only the recipient of her money and advice. Repulsed by his snobbery, Harriet was steely and determined to win a submission now. She put it to him he had been disingenuous all this time in keeping 'craftily' quiet about the existence of letters his wife had preserved. They would have expanded the biography and given it the balance it needed. Set now to trounce his threat to publicly expose her, she told him he had also intentionally or accidentally transgressed a legal obligation to her. By law, she explained, he should have returned anything in her handwriting he found in Charlotte's possession at her death. Had he done so they could have avoided 'all the trouble we have respectively had in regard to the passage in my letter about *Villette*'.[99]

Apologetically, Arthur sent back all her letters, with the assurance he had never read them and the wish that he and Harriet could part on peaceful terms. She agreed, was courteous in response, but privately thought him pathetic, 'a man of narrow experience, who vents his irritation, when he has got into a difficulty, in bluster, which contrasts curiously enough with the anxiety to justify himself.'[100] In the end, she felt sorry for him and, 'I told him, as kindly as I could. As for Mr Brontë, I now not only believe him heartless as, on the whole, I did before but entirely distrust his sincerity.'

Her argument with him left her in no doubt that Patrick *had* told Dearden he considered Elizabeth his enemy, then in chagrin denied it to her, before he blamed Dearden when he was challenged, leaving Dearden baffled in the way Elizabeth had been when she was blamed for all the inaccuracies in *The Life*. Harriet needed to rebuke both men bluntly as she realised being nice to them 'only makes them more insolent'. It sounded to her as though no one had ever stood up to them or refused them anything:

> I fancy these gentlemen (who are not gentlemen however) have never before been opposed or called to account. In their own parish they reign by fear: & I hope it may be good for them to find they can get wrong.[101]

They were monstrous, she said, for having instigated a biography that 'misrepresents living persons, & then to complain of their simple dissent as an assault on the dead'.

The men's evasions, emotional appeals and distortions, and the vicious-
ness of her battle with them made her reconsider what she had been
thinking about Charlotte being unaccountably dishonest. 'Poor CB was
lost upon them,' she reflected in angry regret. 'Her father is shockingly
heartless: and Mr Nicholls now utterly forfeits our interest and esteem by
his insolent and mean tone … which nobody would have resented more
than [Charlotte] herself.'[102]

Perhaps, after all, the truth about Charlotte Brontë was just as Elizabeth
suspected from the moment she had met her seven years earlier: that after a
lifetime of emotional starvation and grief, one of the most talented women
of her generation was harried and manipulated by the men around her
into their serf, that her wish for concord, balance and stability had been
exploited into defeated compromise by all those who needed none and,
broken in spirit, she crawled, she knelt, then she tremulously stood until
the hammer blows of tragedy rained upon her again.

Harriet wondered how Charlotte ever stood a chance.

Part Three

Remaining

(1857–1896)

CHAPTER 16

1857
Fugitive Pieces

In the winter of 1857, an article about a walking tour of West Riding appeared in the pages of an English ladies' magazine. Drawn by some indefinable instinct, the author found themselves in the midst of a vision:

> Amongst high wavy woodlands that catch every fleeting cloud and passing gale, there stands a grey church in a desolate churchyard thronged with gravestones blackened by the rain. The windows of the steep-roofed, stone-built parsonage look down upon this dreary prospect. Beyond lie heathery hills; below, a land defiled with smoke, scorched with flame and animated by the grim genius of trade ... Yet in this rugged mine there glowed a jewel of rare and ardent lustre. Amongst this hard-handed, rough-hearted people there dwelt the wonder of our day. She passes before us, a Dantesque shadow, hopeless and steadfast, with soft abundant tresses and blazing eyes; and we long to draw nearer, and track her steps upon this lower world ... [Her] name has been on every lip, and whose soul we seem to know so well by the traces it has left of its presence in the realms created by its magic. We long to learn the earthly career of this matchless spirit ... Charlotte Brontë was one of six motherless children.[1]

Hoping for an encounter with the ghost that in the common imagination now haunted the paved and grassy provinces of churchyard and moorland, the visitor came from the same public titillated by *Jane Eyre* and intrigued by the mystery of Currer Bell. Now they wept over the heroine of *The Life of Charlotte Brontë*, who through Elizabeth's narration, had loved and suffered and died in ways that seemed emblematic of greater truths of life and suffering and death. Any curiosity they once felt in uncovering the 'real' Currer Bell was satisfied now in the story of a woman's work achieved against an onslaught of tragedy. Currer Bell, once a convenient myth made to hide the female reality, was extinct. Now that essence shifted into the form of a creature of air and light, a wraith on the moors with 'blazing eyes'. Charlotte Brontë, legend, was born.

When the third edition of *The Life of Charlotte Brontë* was released just six months after the first it was met with muted approval, like an act of atonement. As it was published overseas, new waves of incendiary reactions hit England. Elizabeth received a letter from a man 'who says I alluded to his mother in the character of Miss Scatcherd. Now as I don't know who his mother was, I can't possibly say; but as he sends me three sheets of angry abuse.'[2] Messages came from those who had been disgruntled, now satisfied with her repairs. Lydia Robinson's lawyers dropped their threats to sue. William Wilson now felt she had adequately lessened the blame on his father by incorporating a caveat that Charlotte's was only one perspective on the man and his school, and now Elizabeth was certain there could have been no other way to tell the truth about Charlotte and those around her, she told Patrick and Arthur she had done as much as she could and was putting any further requests for changes into the hands of her solicitor. 'I don't think there ever was such an apple of discord at that unlucky book,' she commented to George, determined now to put it all behind her.[3]

Seemingly, the only reviewers left unmoved were at *The Christian Remembrancer*. The periodical had taken every opportunity to attack Charlotte while she was alive and was interested enough in revisiting their curiosity to publish a fifty-eight-page review of *The Life* in October. It was '*the* book of the season, the one book that all the world has read and talked about', it declared breathlessly.[4] Even after redactions of the most scandalous material, their reviewer stated, damage to Elizabeth's reputation had been done. Having once called Charlotte an alien (insisting 'reserve *did* alienate her') they had to concede a new opinion forced by the details of her life. 'We do not blame ourselves for what has been said in our pages of the author of *Jane Eyre*. We could not do otherwise,' they began, 'But such revelations as this book gives us are a lesson to weigh words.' That concession made, they returned to their high-nosed sarcasm for what they deemed undeserved sympathy for an unpleasant person: 'it wounds our tenderest feelings to know her sensitiveness to such attacks; and when she sheds tears over *The Times* critique − of all things in the world to weep over! − our heart bleeds indeed ...'[5] From some, it seemed, Charlotte would never excite either sympathy or admiration regardless of the proofs for both.

With a mine of biographical information now, journalists turned from the literary evaluations of the Brontës' novels to reportage, travelling to Yorkshire to describe Keighley and the approach over the hills to Haworth, performing deliberately or unconsciously a re-enactment of the opening pages of *The Life*, as though by doing so they could enter into the very text. The village, the church and Patrick himself – now his address was known – began to attract visitors from across Britain and even traveling Americans who wished to experience elements of the most famous book of the season. Most were disappointed. Haworth bore little resemblance to Elizabeth's descriptions, or the frontispiece engraving. One visitor commented, 'We had supposed Haworth to be a scattered and straggling hamlet with a desolate vicarage and a dilapidated church surrounded and shut out from the world by a wilderness of barren heath,' but instead discovered 'a large and flourishing village … quaint, compact and progressive.'[6]

One American visitor was Henry Jarvis Raymond, a founding editor of *The New York Times*. Keighley locals were unimpressed when he told them he had come because of the Brontës, with one scoffing she would not walk 'ten steps to see where they lived, nor could she understand how a stranger from America should feel any interest'.[7] Once in Haworth, Raymond found people were less diffident, incorporating practised Brontë anecdotes into their hospitality. At The Black Bull, where he stayed overnight, the staff and regulars all offered stories about meeting Charlotte and Emily on the moors and lamented the loss of Branwell as one of the pub's legendary characters. None remembered Anne. They told him Patrick and Arthur were too retiring to see most tourists but might be charmed by a visitor from New York, and the next day he saw them for half an hour. He told Patrick *The Life* had prepared him for a bleaker village than he found. Arthur and Patrick smiled at each other, and Patrick said, 'Well, I think Mrs Gaskell tried to make us all appear as bad as she could.'[8] Similarly when the Rev. Thomas Akroyd of Liverpool visited he asked Patrick how literally readers should take Elizabeth's account:

> Mrs Gaskell is a novelist you know, and we must allow her a little romance, eh? It is quite in her line. But the book is substantially true, sir, for all that. There are some queer things in it, to be sure – there are some about myself for instance – but the book is substantially true.[9]

Misrepresentations aside, in some instances Elizabeth's descriptions were precise. At the top of Haworth's Main Street visitors now found postcards for sale in the apothecary beside jars and bottles and powders, showing the church, the parsonage and a likeness of Patrick visitors could identify solely from Elizabeth's description of him.[10]

The village was readily adapting to a swelling tide of visitors, whom only Patrick and Arthur were reluctant to entertain. Anticipating a trade for souvenirs, John Greenwood stacked up his shop windows with copies of the Brontës' novels and told customers he handled and sold the very paper they had been written on. He directed anyone looking for lunch across the street to The Black Bull, where the publican hired girls who once ran errands for the family and regaled them about Branwell's uncommon talents; they in turn forwarded those who wanted to see the Brontë grave to the new sexton, John Brown's shifty younger brother, William, who had taken over when John died five months after Charlotte. Building on his brother's business of charging half a crown to point out Charlotte during services, William Brown led visitors to their grave, indicated the sisters' pew and, as the mood dictated, produced streams of either the 'most delightful gossip about them all in general and of *her* in particular', or pathetic tears, as an approach to offer his own merchandise: more postcards of Patrick, the parsonage, the church, and Charlotte's portrait by Richmond kept secreted in his pockets like a greasy pack of gambler's playing cards.[11]

A mythical version of Charlotte Brontë fled into the hearts and imaginations of a public who embraced her, reimagined her, reshaped her to mirror their own wounds and failures, to respond emotionally to her story and develop a sense of protective exclusivity of the details of her life. Elizabeth continued to receive letters about her from all over the world but now they sought relics, any scraps of Charlotte's handwriting she could spare. She always refused, insisting her letters from Charlotte were too precious to give away.'[12] Some asked questions about their friendship, others seemed to be unaware of it and assumed enough of an expertise from reading press clippings and Charlotte's novels to feel confident enough to set Elizabeth straight. In all, a deepening sense of proprietary ownership was growing wherever *The Life* was read. She told George:

> I have had curious proofs of the great interest felt in her. A letter from a young Russian lady born and bred in a district on the south east of Moscow; odd Australasian islands; Americans by the dozen, all full of her. And these latter Yankees coolly describing her character at four or five sheets to me as I had never heard of her and giving *me* an abstract of the events of her life![13]

As Charlotte in death became an exemplar of duty and suffering, radiant with creativity and energised by the elements of the wilderness around her, her posthumous fame made reluctant celebrities of those who had known her. Those strangers to Haworth who jostled the villagers to join the congregation at St Michael's did so to scrutinise Arthur's features for cracks in his composure and glimpses of his grief; they read Patrick's mannerisms and old-fashioned rhetorical flourishes as proof of his eccentricity. Even the elderly retiring Margaret Wooler, who had allowed Elizabeth to name her in the biography, found her own friends now took pleasure in introducing her to women 'delighted to meet with one who had personally known our dear Charlotte Brontë and would not soon have wearied of a conversation in which she was the topic'.[14] Most felt it important Margaret knew how much they loved *The Life of Charlotte Brontë*, calling it the most interesting book they had ever read. Its themes of deprivation and domestic exploitation were appealing to those without voices, who recognised much of their own lives and pain in Charlotte's. To Margaret's bemusement, they treated her deferentially, as an eminent spinster, a grand old dame, the venerable 'Miss Wooler' – just as Elizabeth had written her.

Ironically, Ellen was also treated exactly as Elizabeth had written her – and just as she had insisted – as an invisible woman. Her request for anonymity proved unalterable and having not been named or written about to any great degree in *The Life* she remained unknown and unacknowledged until she was so pained she resorted to protesting she had been Elizabeth's ultimate source, *the* Brontë confidante, the soulmate called 'E' in the sensational story. As the years passed and it became clear she would never hear from the parsonage again, Ellen both denied she had collaborated with Elizabeth and complained she had not been credited enough. 'All that I desired and suggested when Mrs Gaskell was asked to undertake the memoirs,' she claimed, 'was a *lengthy article* in the leading Periodicals – sufficient to set the Public right as to real facts, and the prominent characteristic features in the sisters.'[15] After ruminating on it for years, she insisted Elizabeth got her:

> woeful details, not from the letters, but by searching for them among a class of people who are always proud to have something to talk about people who have become noticeable, & are written about. It is perfectly shocking that the memories of three pure & high-minded women should have been defiled by the gross details of their erring brother. Such lives as theirs were, ought to have come to light in their own sublime worthiness & purity.[16]

Her dissatisfaction with the success of *The Life* and its disproportionate failure to bring her any public acknowledgement or material gain continued for the rest of her life. In 1871, she published a tribute to Charlotte in an American magazine in the hope she might attract a publisher interested in her side of the Brontë story, which with growing certainty she felt should be whitewashed of all its unsavoury aspects, to elevate them beyond the contamination of ordinary human foibles. After all, she insisted, Charlotte had been a woman above *any* criticism, in every area of her life. 'Why question her faith,' she wrote, 'when daily she was …' and searching for the most appropriate tribute to her friend, now dead sixteen years, a phrase recurred from the depth of her memory. It had originally come to her through the letters of others, as an epithet reported by William Gaskell who heard it from Sir James Kay-Shuttleworth, a tribute that gained power through repetition as it echoed from one person to another now fitted Ellen's sentiments so precisely she thought they were her own words. All things considered, she declared, her friend Charlotte Brontë had been 'a Christian heroine, who bore her cross with the firmness of a martyr saint'.[17]

In the years that followed the publication of *The Life of Charlotte Brontë*, Elizabeth shook off the turmoil and turned back to fiction, serialising her short stories in journals and magazines, with some of her great novels still to come: *Sylvia's Lovers*, *Cousin Phyllis*, and *Wives and Daughters*. She visited Patrick one last time at the end of 1860, by which time he was practically bedridden:

> He is touchingly softened by illness; but still talks in his pompous way, and mingles moral remarks and somewhat stale sentiments with his conversation on ordinary subjects. Mr Nicholls seems to keep him rather *in terrorem*. *He* is more unpopular in the village than ever; and seems to have even a greater aversion than formerly to any strangers visiting his wife's grave; or indeed to any reverence paid to her memory, even by those who knew and loved her for her own sake.[18]

As public devotion to Charlotte intensified, fans contacted Patrick in his deep and permanent silence to offer condolences and ask for any mementos he could spare. Flattered, he took the letters his daughter sent whenever she was away from home, and with a pair of scissors cut off her signatures to send them out as autographs. With long precise slices he halved her letters then chopped them into eighths, reducing them to fragments small enough to be divided amongst all who asked, stitching to each a note: 'I herewith send you a scrap of my Daughter Charlotte's handwriting.'[19]

'Dear Papa. I left S
having settled all'[20]

'ed your first
your last today
undertaker's bill'

'Here lie the rem
daughter of the Rev
Yorkshire ...'[21]

It would take more than 160 years to put some of the pieces back together. From different continents, scraps no larger than the ones Héger made when he tore up his letters from Charlotte, were reconstructed despite missing at least three pieces, to show Charlotte was writing from Scarborough in the desperate days after Anne's death to assure her father she had arranged the funeral and headstone to spare him the sorrow of burying another of his children. And this was the material Patrick thought too unworthy to preserve and too insignificant to have shown Elizabeth when she needed it to tell the truth about his daughter's life. For strangers who had never known Charlotte Brontë these became collector's items, these incoherent but representative fragments her father made of her endeavours to console, reason or make sense of the life he had given her, disassembled and strewn across the planet.

CHAPTER 17

1896
Resurgam

'The Haworth of the present day has made a step onwards, like many other places,' Ellen observed as the sun set on the nineteenth century. By 1896, the village had a railway station connecting it along the valley to Keighley and thereby to the rest of Britain. In her day – fifty, sixty years earlier – she had to take a horse and cart or walk there and back, as Charlotte and her sisters had done. This was not the only change to Haworth. A building at the top of Main Street she remembered being a butcher, then the Mechanics' Institute that distributed the Brontës' novels, was now a homely little Brontë museum run by enthusiasts. Around the walls hung copies of Charlotte's portrait, photos of Patrick, and the parsonage and church as they once looked. Upstairs, low glass cases contained objects Ellen had once seen and handled herself or had even given to the sisters. There lay Patrick's clay pipe, some dim photographs of Branwell's paintings of his sisters, and Charlotte's discarded shoes, mittens and lace collars to be stared at by the curious. In the summer of 1896, Ellen, now 79 years old, was only one of 10,000 visitors who paid 3 shillings for an entrance ticket.[1]

The old church was demolished a decade after Patrick died in 1861 when his successor – not Arthur, as Arthur expected – decided it was too expensive to renovate and should not be preserved as a monument to the Brontës but to God. Given notice to move out, Arthur packed up the family's most personal effects and sold the rest of the house contents over a couple of days. Villagers who thought the Brontës were snobs, the wealthy who thought they were paupers, the tourists, the curious, the relic hunters and those in search of a bargain came to pick over the dressing tables, oil lamps, chairs and crockery used by the family. These objects, distributed across the world in the generations that followed, have been making the long journey back to the house ever since.

Once Patrick's successor took over, he commissioned a series of modernisations to bring his family comforts the Brontës had never known. Plumbing was introduced. The old scullery was demolished and replaced with a two-storey extension that ran an L-shape along the side of the house. This new wing required smashing through the walls of what had been the Brontë family's kitchen and the bedroom above it, occupied at different times by Branwell and Charlotte. Windows that looked on to the moors were bricked up and the wall running between the garden and the church lane was knocked down and rebuilt to accommodate the expanded size of the house. Around it, the overcrowded churchyard was perforated with young trees to drain it and decompose its human remains. By the time Ellen came back, the trees resembled a thicket, rippling in the summer winds off the moor.

Tourists had been coming to look at the parsonage since 1849, from the publication of *Shirley*, but *The Life of Charlotte Brontë*, with its atmospheric picture of it, cowering in the shadow of mountains that do not exist, and its tragedy of the lives contained there, cut down before they could blossom, identified its location and positioned it in the public consciousness as the setting for one of the most romantic stories of the age. The thousands who crowded the museum and then the church all stopped to peer at the house, a private residence whose tenant shut out the public and refused all who asked to see inside. They all came to see what remained of the past, to recognise and witness for themselves some tangible element of the story of fleeting lives transformed into permanence by Elizabeth Gaskell's prose.

Looking over the wall from the churchyard, Ellen remembered how the garden had once been a hemmed-in slope of sparse grass, thorns and currant bushes Emily and Anne hoped would fruit but perished in unrelenting winds. In the decades since, a lawn and beds with shrubs and flowers had civilised it into 'a perfect arcadia of floral culture and beauty'.

And then the house. 'The Parsonage is quite another habitation from the Parsonage of former days,' she observed sadly. The changes had been drastic enough to double its size and almost dwarf the original boxlike house the extension embraced. 'At first the alteration ... strikes one with heartache and regret,' she wrote, 'for it is quite impossible even in imagination to people those beautiful rooms with their former inhabitants.'[2]

Where men could demolish and replace, they could not entirely affect the landscape. While the parsonage was changed beyond her memories of the lost long ago, the hills behind the house were still there, still rising to heaven under the ever-changing shadows and lights of passing clouds. 'The

Brontës did not live in their house except for its uses of eating, drinking and resting,' Ellen consoled herself:

> *They lived* in the free expansive hill moorland – its purple heather, its dells and glens and brooks, the broad sky view, the whistling winds, the snowy expanse, the starry heavens – and in the charm of that solitude and seclusion, which sees things from a distance without the disturbing atmosphere which lesser minds are apt to create. It was not the seclusion of a solitary person which becomes in time awfully oppressive – it was seclusion shared and enjoyed by intelligent companionship and intense family affection.[3]

When Ellen turned her back on the parsonage she did so for the last time. She would never see it again and died within the year. In her farewell there was fondness and tribute, for not only the house, not only its ghosts, but for the whole age, to her own youth, to her own long life crushed under the weight of untold obligations attended off-stage as a handmaiden in the lives of others, which unlike Charlotte Brontë had never found its champion.

There she stood before what would in thirty years be opened as a museum, with all around her poised to be drowned out by the irrepressible tide of the coming century, inviting us – historians, tourists, pilgrims, the devoted, the curious and the bored – to take her place.

Epilogue

Patrick Brontë and Arthur Nicholls continued to live together and serve as vicar and curate until Patrick's death at the age of 84 in the summer of 1861. Turned out shortly afterwards by the church trustees, Arthur returned to Ireland where he married Mary Anna Bell, who met Charlotte on their honeymoon in 1854. He refused all interviews until he was in his eighties, living as a gentleman farmer near Cuba Court where he remained until his death in 1906. Martha Brown went with him as his housekeeper for a short while but returned to Haworth where she spent the rest of her life. They remained in touch until she died in 1880, aged 51.

Ellen Nussey never reconciled with Patrick or Arthur and dwindled into a poverty that made her vulnerable to frauds and con men seeking to deprive her of her cache of valuable Brontë letters. She died at home in Gomersal, near Bradford, in 1897.

George Smith died in London in 1901 after the complications of an operation.

Elizabeth Gaskell continued to publish short fiction and two more novels, *Sylvia's Lovers* and *Cousin Phyllis*, before she died suddenly in Hampshire, aged 55 in 1865, falling forwards into Meta's arms in the middle of a conversation. The unfinished novel she was serialising at that point, *Wives and Daughters*, was published the following year.

Elizabeth and Charlotte's homes, Plymouth Grove and The Brontë Parsonage, are now open to the public. *The Life of Charlotte Brontë* has never been out of print since 1857.

A Chronology of Charlotte Brontë and Elizabeth Gaskell

1810	
29 September	Birth of Elizabeth Cleghorn Stevenson, to William Stevenson (b.1772) and Elizabeth Holland (b.1771), in Chelsea, London.
1811	
29 October	Elizabeth's mother dies. Elizabeth is sent to live with her aunt in Knutsford, Cheshire.
1816	
21 April	Birth of Charlotte Brontë, third daughter of Rev. Patrick Brontë (b.1777) and Maria Branwell (b.1783) at Thornton, Yorkshire.
1817	
26 June	Birth of Patrick Branwell Brontë at Thornton.
1818	
30 July	Birth of Emily Jane Brontë at Thornton.
1820	
17 January	Birth of Anne Brontë at Thornton.
April	The Brontës move to Haworth, Yorkshire.
1821	
15 September	Charlotte's mother dies. Her maternal aunt Elizabeth Branwell (b. 1776) joins the Brontë household.
1824	
10 August	Charlotte joins her elder sisters Maria (b.1814) and Elizabeth Brontë (b. 1815) at Rev. Carus Wilson's school for clergymen's daughters at Cowan Bridge, followed by Emily on 25 November.

1825	
14 February	Patrick Brontë removes Maria from Cowan Bridge; she dies of tuberculosis on 6 May.
31 May–1 June	Elizabeth, Charlotte and Emily removed from school.
15 June	Elizabeth Brontë dies of tuberculosis.
1825–7	
	Elizabeth Stevenson attends Avonbank School, Stratford-upon-Avon.
1828	
	Elizabeth returns to London to live with her father and his second wife.
1829	
22 March	Elizabeth's father dies.
1831	
17 January	Charlotte starts boarding at Roe Head girls' school, Dewsbury run by Margaret Wooler (b.1792), meeting Ellen Nussey (b. 1817) and Mary Taylor (b.1817).
1832	
Mid-June	Charlotte leaves Roe Head and is appointed superintendent of Haworth's Sunday School.
30 August	Elizabeth marries Rev. William Gaskell (b.1805) in Knutsford.
1833	
July	Birth of Elizabeth's first daughter, stillborn.
1834	
12 September	Birth of Marianne Gaskell.
1835	
29 July	Charlotte rejoins Roe Head as a teacher, bringing Emily as a student, replaced in late October by Anne.
1837	
January	Elizabeth's first published first piece, a poem 'Sketches Among the Poor, No. 1' appears in *Blackwood's Edinburgh Magazine*. (5 February) Margaret 'Meta' Gaskell born.
1838	
September	Emily takes a teaching post at Law Hill school, Halifax until March 1839. December, Charlotte permanently leaves Margaret Wooler's school.

1840	
May	Anne Brontë becomes governess for the Robinson family at Thorp Green, near York.
1842	
8 February	Charlotte and Emily leave Haworth with Mary Taylor for the Hégers' boarding school in Brussels, arriving 15 February.
7 October	Birth of Florence Gaskell.
29 October	Death of Charlotte's aunt Elizabeth Branwell.
8 November	Charlotte and Emily return to Haworth from Brussels.
1843	
January	Branwell joins Anne at Thorp Green as a tutor.
29 January	Charlotte returns to the Hégers' school in Brussels.
1844	
1 January	Charlotte leaves Brussels for the last time.
23 October	Birth of Elizabeth's only son, William.
1845	
11 June	Branwell and Anne return to Haworth from Thorp Green; he is dismissed for gross misconduct.
17 July	Anne resigns.
10 October	Death of Elizabeth's year-old son William in Wales.
1846	
22 May	*Poems by Currer, Ellis and Acton Bell* published by Aylott and Jones.
3 September	Birth of Elizabeth's sixth child, Julia.
1847	
19 October	Charlotte's first published novel *Jane Eyre* released by Smith, Elder & Co.
15 December	Emily's *Wuthering Heights* and Anne's *Agnes Grey* published by T.C. Newby.
1848	
27 June	Anne's second novel *The Tenant of Wildfell Hall* published by T.C. Newby.
8 July	Charlotte and Anne reveal themselves to be Currer and Acton Bell to the staff of Smith, Elder in London.
24 September	Branwell dies at Haworth.

18 October	Elizabeth's first novel *Mary Barton* is published anonymously by Chapman & Hall.
19 December	Emily dies of tuberculosis at Haworth.
1849	
28 May	Anne dies of tuberculosis at Scarborough.
26 October	Charlotte's *Shirley* published.
1850	
April	The Gaskells move to Plymouth Grove, Manchester. Elizabeth begins writing for Dickens' *Household Words*.
20 August	Elizabeth Gaskell meets Charlotte Brontë for the first time in Windermere.
10 December	The new edition of *Wuthering Heights* and *Agnes Grey* edited by Charlotte is published.
1851	
27–30 June	Charlotte stays with Elizabeth in Manchester.
1853	
10 January	Elizabeth's novel *Ruth* is published.
28 January	Charlotte's final novel *Villette* is published.
Late June	Elizabeth's *Cranford* is published by Chapman and Hall.
19–23 September	Elizabeth stays with Charlotte in Haworth.
1854	
1–3 May	Final meeting between Elizabeth and Charlotte in Manchester.
29 June	Charlotte marries Arthur Nicholls (b. 1819).
1855	
31 March	Charlotte dies of morning sickness and is buried on 4 April at Haworth.
16 June	Elizabeth invited by Patrick Brontë to write her biography.
Mid-June	Elizabeth's *North and South* published by Chapman and Hall.
23 July	Elizabeth meets Patrick Brontë and Arthur Bell Nicholls at Haworth.
14 August	Elizabeth interviews Ellen Nussey.
8 October	Elizabeth interviews Margaret Wooler.

1856	
6 May	Elizabeth travels to Brussels to interview Constantin Héger.
20 May	Elizabeth returns to London.
17 June	Elizabeth meets George Smith.
1857	
25 March	*The Life of Charlotte Brontë* published by Smith, Elder & Co. to be redacted and reissued 9 May and 22 August.
7 June	Charlotte's first novel *The Professor* published posthumously.
1861	
7 June	Patrick Brontë dies at Haworth.
1865	
12 November	Elizabeth dies suddenly at her home in Hampshire and is buried on 16 November at Brook St Chapel, Knutsford.
1866	
12 February	Elizabeth's *Wives and Daughters* is published posthumously by Smith, Elder.

Notes

The following abbreviations have been used for the notes and index: CB – Charlotte Brontë; PB – Patrick Brontë; ECG – Elizabeth Cleghorn Gaskell; JKS – Sir James Kay-Shuttleworth; LJKS – Lady Janet Kay-Shuttleworth; *Life* – *The Life of Charlotte Brontë*; HM – Harriet Martineau; ABN – Arthur Bell Nicholls; EN – Ellen Nussey; GS – George Smith; WSW – William Smith Williams; MW – Margaret Wooler.

Chapter 1

1 Centre for Global Atmospheric Modelling, Department of Meteorology, University of Reading.
2 ECG to Anne Shaen, 20 December 1849.
3 ECG to Catherine Winkworth, 25 August 1850.
4 A. W. Fonblanque, *The Examiner*, 27 November 1847.
5 CB to Smith, Elder, 1 December 1847.
6 Martineau, *Autobiography*, vol. 2, p21.
7 ECG to Eliza Fox, 26 November 1849.
8 John Epps knew W.J. Fox, father of Eliza Fox, and WSW as friends and fellow members of medical and philosophical societies from the 1830s.
9 Epps, *Diary of the Late John Epps*, p470.
10 CB to WSW, 9 December 1948.
11 CB to ECG, 17 November 1849.
12 Ibid.
13 CB to WSW, 17 November 1849.
14 ECG to Catherine Winkworth, November 1849.
15 CB to PB, 20 August 1850.
16 CB to EN, 11 March 1850.
17 ECG, *Life,* p333.
18 CB to WSW, 3 January 1850.
19 Rev. William Heald to EN, 8 January 1850.
20 Ibid.
21 CB to WSW, 21 September 1849.

22 ECG to John Forster, 23 April 1854.

23 CB, *Shirley*, p589.

24 Ibid.

25 Turner, *A Springtime Saunter Around Brontë-Land*, p203.

26 The Haworth Mechanics' Institute was founded in the spring of 1849 at 2-4 West Lane, Haworth, the former butcher owned by William Garnett (Whitehead, p57) and eventually became the first Brontë museum.

27 CB to EN, 5 February 1850.

28 *London Morning Post*, 21 February 1850. The paper inaccurately cites its sources as the *Derby Telegraph*, which did not report it. They may have meant the *Blackburn Standard*, which mentioned it the day before without criticism.

29 *Blackburn Standard*, 3 April 1850.

30 Johnathan Berry (1821-1904) can be identified by the 1850 census of Spencer, Mass and the baptismal record for St Michael & All Angels, Haworth 18 March 1822. He was 7th in a family of 14 children and emigrated to the US in 1842, returning to England twice in 1844-46 and 1851-52, before settling with his wife and children in Michigan.

31 *Boston Weekly Museum*, 2 March 1850.

32 CB to EN, 30 March 1850.

33 CB to Lady KS, 5 March 1850.

34 CB to WSW, 16 March 1850.

35 CB to EN, 16 August 1850.

36 PB to EN, 12 July 1850.

37 CB to EN, 15 July 1850.

38 CB to EN, 26 August 1850.

39 CB to EN, 19 March 1850.

40 Frederick North's diaries, quoted by Selleck, 'James Kay-Shuttleworth' p294.

41 CB to EN, 2 September 1850.

42 ECG to Catherine Winkworth, 25 August 1850.

43 Hallam, *Tennyson*, p262.

44 ECG, *Life*, p83.

45 Ibid.

46 Ibid.

47 ECG to Eliza Fox, 27 August 1850.

48 CB to EN, 26 August 1850.

49 ECG, *Life*, p416.

50 Ibid.

51 ECG to Eliza Fox, 27 August 1850.

52 ECG to unknown, c25 August 1850.

53 Chadwick, *In the Footsteps of the Brontës*, p418.

54 CB to EN, 26 August 1850.

55 CB to James Taylor, 6 November 1850.

56 ECG to Charlotte Froude, 25 August 1850.

57 ECG to Catherine Winkworth, 25 August 1850.

58 CB to WSW, 22 May 1850.

59 ECG to Unknown, 25 August 1850.

60 ECG to Catherine Winkworth, 25 August 1850.

61 Ibid.

62 ECG to Lady KS, 14 May 1850.

63 Ibid.

64 ECG to Charlotte Froude, 25 August 1850.

65 ECG to Eliza Fox, 17 August 1850.

Chapter 2

1 CB to EN, 26 August 1850.

2 CB to ECG, 27 August 1850.

3 ECG to Eliza Fox, 27 August 1850.

4 ECG to unknown, 25 August 1850.

5 ECG to Catherine Froud, 25 August 1850.

6 ECG to Catherine Winkworth, 25 August 1850.

7 ECG to John Forster, *c* 29 September 1853.

8 ECG to Anne Shaen, 20 December 1849.

9 Emily Shaen to Catherine Winkworth, 30 August 1850.

10 CB to EN, 23 October 1850.

11 CB to ECG, 6 November 1851.

12 CB to Laetitia Wheelwright, 12 January 1851.

13 CB to James Taylor, 15 January 1851.

14 CB, 'Preparatory Note to Selections from Poems by Ellis Bell'.

15 The *Morning Post* of 8 January 1847 carries Newby's advert for *The Mcdermots* by Mrs Trollope. Newby posted the advert again the following week, with the author corrected to 'Mr Trollope'.

16 Anthony Trollope, Autobiography, p52.

17 CB, *Biographical Notice of Ellis and Acton Bell* in *Wuthering Heights and Agnes Grey* (1850).

18 CB to WSW, 5 September 1850.

19 CB to WSW, 27 September 1850.

20 CB to EN, 14 September 1850.

21 Ibid., 3 October 1850.

22 Ibid., 18 December 1850.

23 'The Three Guides' by Acton Bell, *Fraser's Magazine*, August 1848; 'The Narrow Way', *Fraser's Magazine*, December 1848.

24 CB, preface to *Poems by Acton Bell*.

25 CB to WSW, 4 September 1850.

26 CB, *Preface* to Poems by Acton Bell in *Wuthering Heights and Agnes Grey* (1850).

27 CB, *Editor's preface the new edition of Wuthering Heights*.

28 CB, *Biographical notice of Ellis and Acton Bell*.

29 Mary Taylor to CB, 5 April 1850.

Chapter 3

1 ECG to LJKS, 12 December 1850.

2 HM to LJKS, 13 December 1850.

3   HM to GH Lewes, 15 December 1850.

4   CB to HM, 8 December 1850.

5   Lucy Martineau to John 'Jack' Martineau, 10 December 1849.

6   Ibid.

7   HM, *Autobiography*, vol. 2, p23.

8   CB to WSW, 19 December 1849.

9   HM, *Autobiography*, vol. 2, p23.

10 HM, *A Personal Impression of Charlotte Brontë*, Cornhill Magazine, December 1900, pp778-95.

11 HM, *Biographical Sketches*, p48.

12 Ibid.

13 Ibid.

14 ECG, *Life*, footnote by Gaskell relating communication from HM, p415.

15 Lucy Martineau to John 'Jack' Martineau, 10 December 1849.

16 Ibid.

17 HM to Rev. William Ware, undated *c.*1849.

18 HM to Sarah Wetmore Story, 31 December 1845.

19 HM to William J Fox, 31 December 1845.

20 HM to Richard Cobden, 2 March 1846.

21 Meteorological data in Betty Burton, *Miss Brontë visits Ambleside*, BS, April 1999, p96.

22 HM to GH Lewes, 15 December 1850.

23 CB to EN, 18 December 1850.

24 ECG, *Life*, p368.

25 CB to EN, 28 December 1850.

26 CB to EN, 21 December 1850.

27 HM, *Autobiography*, vol. 2, p41.

28 Ibid.

29 Matthew Arnold to Frances Lucy Wightman, 21 December 1850, *The Letters of Matthew Arnold*.

30 Matthew Arnold, *Haworth Churchyard*, April 1855.

31 *Huddersfield Chronicle*, 4 January 1851.

32 *Blackburn Standard*, 5 February 1851.

Chapter 4

1   ECG to Marianne Gaskell, May 1851. She names the two servants as [Ann] Hearn and Maria [?].

2   CB to EN, 24 June 1851.

3   GS, 'Charlotte Brontë', *Cornhill Magazine*, vol. ix, p779.

4   ECG to Tottie Fox, April 1850.

5   CB to Elizabeth Smith, 1 July 1851.

6   Ann Hearn (1812-1892).

7   Snow Wedgwood to Effie Wedgwood, 3 November 1855.

8   Frances Wedgwood to Katherine Wedgwood, 6 November 1855.

9   CB to GS, 1 July 1851.

10 Ibid.

11 ECG to Marianne, May 1851.

12 The Gaskell daughters were Marianne b. 12/09/1834; Meta b. 05/02/1837; Florence b. 07/10/1842; Julia b. 03/09/1846.

13 CB to Elizabeth Smith, 1 July 1851.

14 CB to ECG, 6 August 1851.

15 ECG, *Life*, p384.

16 CB to ECG, 6 August 1851.

17 CB to GS, 1 July 1851.

18 Chadwick, Gaskell, *Houses, Haunts and Homes*, p260.

19 *Household Words*, vol. 7, no 158.

20 ECG, *Life*, p379.

21 ECG to Maria James, 29 October 1851.

22 CB to GS, 8 September 1851.

23 CB to GS, 15 September 1851.

24 CB to WSW, 14 August 1848.

25 WM Thackeray to WS Williams, 23 October 1847.

26 CB to WSW, 28 October 1847.

27 Ibid.

28 CB, *Jane Eyre*, Preface to the 2nd edition.

29 WM Thackeray to WS Williams, [no date], January 1848.

30 CB to WSW, 28 January 1848.

31 GS, 'Charlotte Brontë', *Cornhill Magazine*, vol. ix, 1900, p779.

32 CB to Mary Taylor, 4 September 1848.

33 Leonard Huxley, *The House of Smith and Elder*, p66-67.

34 CB quoted from memory by ECG to GS, 26 December 1856.

35 CB, *Villette*, p222.

36 Ibid.

37 Ibid.

38 GS, 'Charlotte Brontë', *Cornhill Magazine*, vol. ix, 1900, p779.

39 CB to WSW, 19 December 1849.

40 CB to PB, 5 December 1849.

41 CB to EN, 9 December 1849.

42 William Thackeray, 'The Last Sketch', *Cornhill Magazine*, vol. 1, 1860.

43 ECG, *Life*, p328.

44 Brontë, *Jane Eyre*, OUP, p260.

45 Leonard Huxley, *The House of Smith and Elder*, p68.

46 ECG, *Life*, p429.

47 CB to EN Nussey, 12 June 1850.

48 GS, *Recollections*, p168.

49 Anne Thackeray Ritchie, *Chapters from Some Memoirs*, p60.

50 Ibid., p61.

51 Ibid., p62.

52 Anne Thackeray Ritchie to Reginald Smith, 18 October 1906.

53 Charles M Brookfield, *Mrs Brookfield and Her Circle*, vol. 2, p 302.

54 Ibid., p 355.

55 Mrs Proctor to William Thackeray, 8 March 1853.

56 GS, 'Charlotte Brontë', *Cornhill Magazine*, December 1900.

57 *The Kickleburys of the Rhine* was published under the name M.A. Titmarsh by Smith, Elder for Christmas 1850.

58 *The Era*, Sunday 11 May 1851.

59 WM Thackeray to Richard Doyle, 21 May 1851.

60 *Morning Chronicle*, 30 May 1851.

61 CB to EN, 2 June 1851.

62 GS, 'Charlotte Brontë', *Cornhill Magazine*, vol. ix, p779.

63 ECG, *Life*, p376.

64 CB to EN, 2 June 1851.

65 There is a discrepancy between CB's and GS's versions. In his account written decades after the event GS says Thackeray introduced CB as Jane Eyre at the end of the lecture when he came down from the platform. In two letters written at the time CB says she was introduced to Thackeray's mother before it started, but that he came down at the end. I've accepted CB's version as it was written immediately and balanced it with the account she gave ECG who later incorporated Elizabeth Smith's memories. In all likelihood GS had to rely on his mother for an account, as he may have had to stand during the lecture rather than sit with them.

66 T.W. Reid, *Charlotte Brontë#; a Monograph*, p125. Reid is paraphrasing Milnes.

67 *Morning Chronicle*, 30 May 1851.

68 Gaskell, Gerin (ed.), *The Life of Charlotte Brontë*, p376.

69 ECG, *Life*, p376.

70 GS, 'Charlotte Brontë', *Cornhill Magazine*, vol. ix.

71 Ibid.

72 CB to EN, 2 June 1851.

73 WM Thackeray, 25 February 1852.

74 CB to ECG, 14 June 1851.

75 Chadwick, In the Footsteps of the Brontës, p428.

76 CB to Amelia Taylor, 11 June 1851.

77 CB to EN, 24 June 1851.

78 CB to Sydney Dobell, 28 June 1851.

79 CB, *Villette*, p323.

80 Ibid., p321.

81 Ibid., p323.

82 Ibid., p325.

83 *The Standard*, 29 July 1851.

84 CB to GS, 1 July 1851.

85 Calculated using the Bank of England's inflation calculator.

86 CB to GS, 1 July 1851.

87 Ibid., 26 February 1853.

Chapter 5

1 CB to ECG, 6 February 1852.

2 CB to EN, 14 January 1852.

3 Ibid., 16 January 1852.

4 CB, *Villette*, p198.

5 CB to GS, 30 October 1852.

6   CB to EN, 22 November 1852.

7   CB to WSW, 6 November 1852.

8   CB, *Villette*, p454.

9   GS, 'Charlotte Brontë', *Cornhill Magazine*, vol. ix.

10 GS, 'The Brontës', *Cornhill Magazine*, vol. 28, July–December, 1873, p70.

11 CB to GS, 3 November 1852.

12 CB to GS, 6 December 1852.

13 CB to EN, 15 December 1852.

14 ECG, *Life*, p410.

15 CB to EN, 15 December 1852.

16 CB to EN, 18 December 1852.

17 CB to EN, 2 January 1853.

18 Ibid.

19 Ibid., 19 January 1853.

20 PB to CB no date January 1853.

21 Ibid., *c.*17 January 1853.

22 CB to David Waldie, 19 January 1853 (unpublished).

23 CB to ECG, 12 January 1853.

24 *Manchester Times*, 2 February 1853.

25 CB to ECG, 12 January 1853.

26 *The Literary Gazette* and *The Globe*, 12 February 1853.

27 *Literary Examiner*, 5 February 1853.

28 CB to HM, 21 January 1853, quoted in HM, *Autobiography* (original lost).

29 HM, *Autobiography*, vol. 2, p24.

30 HM to CB, undated early February 1853.

31 CB to HM, *c.*3 February 1853.

32 *Daily News*, 3 February 1853.

33 CB to GS, 7 February 1853.

34 CB to MW, 11 February 1853.

35 ECG to John Stores Smith, 3 May 1853.

36 Catherine Winkworth to Emily Shaen, 23 March 1853.

37 Ibid., 25 March 1853.

38 Thackeray to Lucy Baxter, 11 March 1853.

39 GS to HM, 18 March 1853.

40 CB to EN, 18 April 1853.

41 CB to MW, 13 April 1853.

42 CB to EN, 6 April 1853.

43 Ibid.

44 Ibid.

45 CB to ECG, 14 April 1853.

46 ECG, *Life*, p420.

47 Ibid.

48 Ibid.

49 Charles W Bell (1811–1862); Barbara (b.1810); Margaret (b.1817); Caroline (b.1819). All four lived in Mosley Street, having moved there from Edinburgh where their details are captured on the 1841 census. ECG mentions to Maggie in her 22 April letter that Marianne will join her for music practice.

50 ECG to Maggie Bell, *c.*22 April 1853.

51 CB to ECG, 9 July 1853.

52 Chadwick, *Mrs Gaskell, haunts, homes, and stories*, p286.

53 Potter, Louisa, Eighty Years Ago: Memories of Old Manchester II, *Manchester Guardian*, Sep 2, 1896.

54 ECG, *Life*, p420.

55 'Carlisle Yetts', *Jacobite Relics of Scotland*, p198.

56 ECG, *Life*, p420.

57 Ibid.

58 Gaskell, Gerin (ed.), *The Life of Charlotte Brontë*, p421.

59 ECG, *Life*, p420.

60 ECG to LJKS, 7 April 1853.

61 Ibid.

62 Ibid.

63 Ibid.

64 ECG to John Forster, 3 May 1853.

65 CB to ECG, n.d April 1853.

66 CB to EN, 16 May 1853.

67 Ibid.

68 CB to EN, 19 May 1853.

69 CB to EN, 27 May 1853.

70 Ibid.

71 Ibid.

72 EN to TW Reid, 3 November 1876.

73 EN to Mary, 12 August 1853, not extant but quoted by Mary, 24 February 1854.

74 Mary to EN, 24 February 1854.

75 CB to GS, 3 July 1853.

76 CB to ECG, 18 June 1853.

77 CB to Laetitia Wheelwright, 8 March 1854.

78 CB to ECG, 18 June 1853.

79 Ibid., 9 July 1853.

80 Ibid.

Chapter 6

1 CB to the editor of *The Christian Remembrancer*, 18 July 1853.

2 *The Christian Remembrancer*, vol. 25: April 1853, p401.

3 CB to the editor of *The Christian Remembrancer*, 18 July 1853.

4 *The Christian Remembrancer*, vol. 26: October 1853, p501.

5 Ibid., vol. 15: June 1848.

6 Ibid., vol. 21: 1851, p395.

7 Ibid., vol. 21: 1851, p394.

8 ECG, *Life*, p426.

9 CB to MW, 30 August 1853.

10 CB to ECG, 1 June 1853.

11 CB to MW, 30 August 1853.

12 CB to ECG, 1 June 1853.

13 Ibid., 31 August 1853.
14 ECG, *Life*, p426.
15 Ibid.
16 ECG to unknown, 26 September 1853.
17 ECG to John Forster, *c.*29 September 1853.
18 Bennoch, *Poems, Lyrics, Songs and Sonnets*, 1877, pviii.
19 ECG, *Life*, MS p634.
20 ECG to John Forster, *c* 29 September 1853.
21 ECG, *Life*, p426.
22 Ibid.
23 Ibid.
24 ECG to John Forster, *c.*29 September 1853.
25 Ibid.
26 Ibid.
27 ECG, *Life*, p428.
28 ECG to John Forster, *c.*29 September 1853.
29 ECG, *Life*, p428.
30 Ibid.
31 John Stores Smith, *A Day with Charlotte Brontë*, Orel p 165.
32 ECG to John Forster, *c.*29 September 1853.
33 Ibid.
34 Ibid.
35 Ibid.
36 Ibid.
37 Ibid.
38 ECG, *Life*, p426.
39 ECG to John Forster, *c.*29 September 1853.
40 Ibid.
41 Ibid.
42 ECG, *Life,* p94.
43 Ibid.
44 ECG mentions Tabby's fairy anecdotes in *Life*, and the manor house in a letter to
    Caroline Anne Davenport of 27 December 1853.
45 ECG to John Forster, *c.*29 September 1853.
46 Ibid.
47 ECG, *Life*, p429.
48 Ibid.
49 Ibid.
50 ECG to John Forster, *c.*29 September 1853.
51 ECG, *Life*, p428.
52 ECG to John Forster, *c.*29 September 1853.
53 ECG, *Life*, p429.
54 Ibid., p427.
55 Ibid.
56 ECG to John Forster, *c.*29 September 1853.
57 CB to EN, 23 June 1849.

58 ECG to John Forster, *c*.29 September 1853.

59 ECG, *Life*, p428.

60 ECG to John Forster, *c*.29 September 1853.

61 ECG, *Life*, p133.

62 CB to WSW, 27 September 1850.

63 PB to GS, 2 August 1850.

64 ECG, *Life*, p463.

65 CB to ECG, 11 November 1853.

66 ECG, *Life*, p429.

67 CB to ECG, 25 September 1850.

Chapter 7

1 He was the Conservative member for Pontefract 1837–1863.

2 ECG to R. Monckton Milnes, 29 October 1853.

3 R. Monckton Milnes to Elizabeth, 30 January 1854.

4 ECG to John Forster, 17 May 1854.

5 CB to MW, 18 October 1853.

6 CB to ECG, 15 November 1853.

7 CB to Elizabeth Smith, 21 November 1853.

8 Elizabeth Smith to CB, 22 November 1853.

9 CB to Emily Shaen, 24 November 1853.

10 CB to WSW, 6 December 1853.

11 CB to GS, 10 December 1853.

12 Catherine Winkworth to Emma Shaen, 8 May 1854, describes hearing this from Gaskell.

13 CB to MW, 12 December 1853.

14 ECG to Marianne Gaskell, 13 December 1853.

15 CB to ECG, 27 December 1853.

16 *Bradford Observer*, 12 January 1854, p6.

Chapter 8

1 Mary Hewitt to EN, 21 February 1854.

2 Ibid.

3 Ibid.

4 CB to EN, 28 March 1854.

5 Ibid., 11 April 1854.

6 Ibid.

7 ECG to John Forster, 17 May 1854.

8 Ibid.

9 Ibid.

10 CB to EN, 11 April 1854.

11 Ibid.

12 CB to MW, 12 April 1854.

13 CB to EN, 11 April 1854.

14 CB to ECG, 18 April 1854.

15 CB to EN, 11 April 1854.
16 CB to ECG, 18 April 1854.
17 ECG to John Forster, 23 April 1854.
18 Ibid.
19 CB to GS, 25 April 1854.
20 Ibid.
21 Catherine Winkworth to Emma Shaen, 8 May 1854.
22 ECG, *Life*, p434.
23 Ibid.
24 CB to EN, 11 June 1854.
25 Ibid., 27 May 1854.
26 Ibid.
27 CB to EN, 27 May 1854.
28 Ibid., 11 June 1854.
29 Brontë, *Jane Eyre*, p288.
30 CB to EN, 16 June 1854.
31 ECG, *Life*, p436.
32 CB to EN, 29 June 1854.
33 Chadwick, *Footsteps*, p461.
34 EN to TW Reid, 3 November 1876.
35 PB to EN, 7 July 1854.

Chapter 9

1 'Announcements', *Leeds Mercury*, 1 July 1854.
2 Quotes from CB to EN, 29 June 1854.
3 CB to Catherine Wooler, 18 July 1854.
4 Alan Nichol (b.1816); Joseph Bell (1831-91); Mary Anna Bell, later Nicholls (1830–1915), Mrs Harriette Bell (1801–1902). ABN was the sixth of ten children to William Nichol and Margaret Bell. Her brother, Dr Alan Bell and his wife raised ABN with their own children.
5 Trollope, *An Autobiography*, p44.
6 CB to MW, 10 July 1854.
7 CB to EN, 28 July 1854.
8 Ibid., 9 August 1854.
9 CB to MW, 10 July 1854.
10 CB to EN, 29 June 1854; CB to MW, 10 July 1854.
11 ECG to John Forster, 14 May 1854.
12 CB to Catherine Winkworth, 27 July 1854.
13 ECG to Geraldine Jewsbury, 21 July 1854.
14 CB to MW, 10 July 1854.
15 Ibid.
16 CB to Catherine Wooler, 18 July 1854.
17 ABN to George Sowden, 10 August 1854.
18 CB to Catherine Winkworth, 27 July 1854.
19 CB to Katie Winkworth, 27 July 1854.
20 CB to EN, 28 July 1854.

21 CB to Martha Brown, 28 July 1854.
22 CB to MW, 19 September 1854.
23 Ibid., 22 August 1854.
24 Ibid.
25 CB to EN, 9 August 1854.
26 Ibid.
27 CB to MW, 19 September 1854.
28 CB to EN, 7 September 1854.
29 Ibid.
30 Wemyss Reid, *Memoir*, p240.
31 CB to MW, 19 September 1854.
32 CB, 'Emma' in *The Professor*, p252.
33 ABN to GS, 11 October 1859.
34 ABN to Clement Shorter, 8 December 1897.
35 CB to EN, 20 October 1854.
36 Ibid.
37 EN to ABN, 2? November 1854.
38 CB to EN, 7 November 1854.
39 Ibid.
40 Ibid., 7 December 1854.
41 Chadwick, *Footsteps*, p468. Recounts William Wood seeing ABN on his morning runs.
42 CB to EN, 29 November 1854.
43 Ibid., 7 December 1854.
44 ECG to Katie Winkworth, 1 January 1855.
45 CB to EN, 26 December 1854.
46 Ibid., 19 January 1855.

Chapter 10

1   Dr Amos Ingham (1827–1889) lived in Haworth all his life. His portrait, by an unknown artist, hangs in the parsonage.
2   ABN to EN, 29 January 1855.
3   PB to JKS, 3 February 1855.
4   ABN to EN, 14 February 1855.
5   Chadwick, *Footsteps*, p471 quoting Tabitha Ratcliffe.
6   Hannah Dawson (1819–1887) lived in Haworth all her life. She was the daughter of Ellis Dawson and Nancy Harrison and married George Smith (1804–1867) in 1857 and eventually worked as a drapery shopkeeper. Her sister Sally married George Feather, a notable local character.
7   Chadwick, *Footsteps*, p471 quoting Tabitha Ratcliffe.
8   CB to Laetitia Wheelwright, 15 February 1855.
9   Charlotte Brontë Last Will and Testament, signed 17 February 1855 and proof dated 18 April 1855 (seen in facsimile).
10 CB to Amelia Taylor, late February 1855.
11 CB to EN, March 1855.
12 PB to EN, 31 March 1855.
13 EBN to GS, 28 March 1860.

14 Ibid.

15 Lock & Dixon, *A Man of Sorrow*, p477.

16 T.W. Reid mentions the shutters were closed when EN arrived; *Charlotte Brontë: a monograph*, p182.

17 Babbage, *Report to the General Board of Health* (1850), p7. The report counted 509 households in Haworth in 1850.

18 HM to John Greenwood, ? April 1855.

19 Ibid.

20 HM to John Greenwood, 13 November 1857.

21 Ibid., ? April 1855.

22 ECG to John Greenwood, 4 April 1855.

23 PB to ECG, 5 April 1855.

24 Ibid.

25 *Bradford Observer*, 5 April 1855.

26 *Daily News*, 6 April 1855.

27 ECG to John Greenwood, 12 April 1855.

28 Ibid.

29 ECG to John Greenwood, 5 May 1855.

30 Ibid., 12 April 1855.

31 Ibid., 5 May 1855.

32 Ibid., 12 April 1855.

33 Matthew Arnold to John William Parker, 11 April 1855.

34 Matthew Arnold to Arthur Hugh Clough, 23 March 1853.

35 Matthew Arnold to ECG, 1 June 1855.

36 John Greenwood to ECG, circa April 1855, quoted to GS, 4 June 1855.

37 ECG to GS, 4 June 1855.

38 Ibid., 31 May 1855.

39 Ibid., 4 June 1855.

40 Ibid.

41 Ibid.

Chapter 11

1 EN to ABN, 6 June 1855.

2 Ibid.

3 ABN to EN, 11 June 1855.

4 Ibid.

5 PB to ECG, 16 June 1855.

6 ABN to EN, 24 July 1855.

7 ECG to GS, 18 June 1855.

8 Ibid.

9 PB to ECG, 20 June 1855.

10 Ibid.

11 HM to R. Monckton Milnes, 17 July 1855.

12 Elizabeth to unknown, 17 July 1855.

13 ECG to GS, *c.*22 July 1855.

14 Elizabeth to Hannah Kay, 11 July 1855.
15 Elizabeth to Marianne, 27 July 1855.
16 ECG to EN, 24 July 1855.
17 PB to ECG, 24 July 1855.
18 HM to ABN, 15 November 1857. ABN later denied telling Elizabeth and Greenwood he destroyed her papers.
19 ECG to EN, 24 July 1855.
20 Described by Elizabeth to John Greenwood, 25 July 1855.
21 'Dreadful Thunder Storm: Thornton', *Bradford Observer*, 26 July 1855.
22 ABN to EN, 24 July 1855.
23 Ibid.
24 ECG to EN, 24 July 1855.
25 EBN to ECG, 26 July 1855.
26 PB to ECG, 24 July 1855.
27 Ibid.
28 ECG to EN, 27 July 1855.
29 ECG to Jemima Quillinan, 4 August 1856.
30 ECG to GS, 1 August 1855.
31 ECG to unknown, 23 August 1855.
32 Ibid.
33 ECG to Maria Martineau, 19 August 1855.
34 Ibid.
35 Ibid.
36 Ughtred Shuttleworth, quoted in Frank Smith, *The Life and Work of Sir James Kay-Shuttleworth*, p332.
37 ECG to Maria James, 3 December 1855.
38 *The Life* ed. by Shorter, note by Gaskell quoted p78.
39 Susanna to Catherine Winkworth, 3? August 1855.
40 ECG to Maria Martineau, *c.*19 August 1855.
41 Ibid.
42 PB to ECG, 27 August 1855.
43 ECG to EN, 6 September 1855.
44 'British Association for the Advancement of Science': *Glasgow Herald*, 14 September 1855.
45 ECG to EN, 25 September 1855.
46 Ibid., 3 November 1855.
47 Ibid.
48 ECG to MW, 12 November 1855.
49 ECG to WSW, 15 December 1855.
50 ECG to EN, 20 December 1855.
51 Frances Wedgwood to Katherine Wedgwood, 6 November 1855.
52 Ibid.
53 *Cheshire Observer*, 8 December 1855.
54 ABN to EN, 24 December 1855.
55 ECG to EN, 20 December 1855.
56 ABN to EN, 24 December 1855.
57 PB to ECG, 23 January 1856.

58 ECG to GS, [?] July 1855. Ann Connor (1792–1857) taught at Cowan Bridge under her maiden name, Ann Evans.

59 ECG to EN, 20 December 1855.

Chapter 12

1 ECG to GS, 2 October 1856.

2 ECG, *Life*, p46.

3 ECG to Harriet Anderson, 15 March 1856.

4 Marianne to EN, 22 February 1856.

5 ECG to GS, 29 December 1856.

6 ECG to GS, 29 April 1856.

7 ECG to Frances Holland, 13 March 1856.

8 Ibid.

9 ECG mentions to Mrs Ludlow on 30 April she would be leaving London 'with my second girl' (Meta) for a fortnight, and to Marianne on 6 May that Eliza is with them and they leave 'tonight'.

10 ECG to Marianne, 29 April 1856.

11 ECG to Laetitia Wheelwright, 30 April 1856.

12 ECG to Laetitia Wheelwright, 22 August 1856.

13 Shorter, *Charlotte Brontë and her Circle*, p110.

14 ECG to Marianne, 6 May 1856.

15 Ostend–Ghent–Brussels railway timetable in *Bradshaw's monthly continental railway, steam navigation & conveyance guide* (1856).

16 Advert in *Bradshaw's Illustrated Handbook to Switzerland and the Tyrol* (1857), p13.

17 ECG, *Life*, p193.

18 Ibid., p196.

19 Ibid., p199.

20 CB to Heger, 8 January 1845.

21 CB to Heger, 18 November 1845.

22 ECG to EN, 9 July 1856.

23 Ibid.

24 ECG, *Life*, p292.

25 Ibid., p293.

26 Ibid., p266.

27 ECG to GS, 8 February 1857 mentions the return of all the material loaned to her by Smith Elder: letters, copies of reviews, and the manuscripts of her novels.

28 ECG to GS, 9 July 1856.

29 ECG to EN, 9 July 1856.

30 EBN to ECG, *c.*10 July 1856.

31 Ibid.

Chapter 13

1 Marianne to EN, 15 July 1856.

2 ECG to GS, 25 July 1856.

3 Ibid.

4 Ibid.

5 A lithograph of a page from 'The Secret' written in 1833 appears in *Life*.

6 ECG to GS, 1 August 1856.

7 Constantin Heger to ECG, 22 May 1856.

8 JKS to ECG, quoted by ECG to Emily Winkworth Shaen, 8 September 1856.

9 ECG to GS, 1 August 1856.

10 ABN to Clement Shorter, 30 April 1896: mentions JKS offered to edit it with Gaskell.

11 ECG to Emily Shaen, 7 September 1856.

12 ECG to GS, 13 August 1856.

13 ABN to GS, 26 September 1856.

14 ECG to Laetitia Wheelwright, 22 August 1856.

15 ECG to GS, 2 October 1856.

16 ECG to GS, 10 September 1856.

17 ECG to GS, [?18] December 1856.

18 ECG to Emily Shaen, 8 September 1856.

19 ECG to GS, 19 August 1856.

20 PB to ECG, 3 November 1856. He does not name the title of 'the pamphlet' he sends, or its male author, but his descriptions are that of *Jottings by Currer, Ellis and Acton Bell* by 'W.P.P' published in April 1856 by Longman.

21 ECG to GS, 19 August 1856.

22 Ibid., 2 October 1856.

23 Ibid.

24 Ibid.

25 Chorley to ECG, cited in ECG to GS, 15 November 1856.

26 ECG to GS, 15 November 1856.

27 Ibid., 22 November 1856.

28 ABN to GS, 28 November 1856.

29 Ibid.

30 ABN to GS, 3 December 1856.

31 Ibid., 1 December 1856.

32 ECG to GS, 11 December 1856.

33 ECG to Stewart, 11 November 1856.

34 ECG to GS, 11 December 1856.

35 Ibid., 15 November 1856.

Chapter 14

1 ECG, *Life*, p296.

2 ECG to GS, 26 December 1856.

3 Ibid.

4 CB to Mary Taylor, 4 September 1848.

5 ECG to GS, 26 December 1856.

6 Ibid.

7 Mary Taylor to EN, 19 April 1856.

8 Mary Taylor to ECG, 18 January 1856.

9 Mary Taylor to EN, 19 April 1856.

10 Ibid.
11 ECG to Charles Kingsley, 6 June 1857.
12 Gaskell, *North and South*, p109.
13 ECG to GS, 29 December 1856.
14 Ibid.
15 Catherine Winkworth to Emily Winkworth, 16 January 1857.
16 ECG to GS, 8 February 1857.
17 Ibid., 11 February 1857.
18 Ibid., 19 January 1857.
19 Ibid., 11 February 1857.
20 Ibid., 4 February 1857.
21 Ibid., 8 February 1857.
22 In the course of his long career James Charles Armytage (1820–1897) produced hundreds of reproductions of artworks for books and journals.
23 ECG to GS, 11 February 1857.
24 *Bradford Observer*, 12 March 1857.
25 *Morning Post*, 30 March 1857.
26 PB to GS, 30 March 1857.
27 PB to ECG, 2 April 1857.
28 PB to William Gaskell, 7 April 1857.
29 ECG, *Life*, p410.
30 Ibid.
31 ABN to GS, 2 April 1857.
32 EN to T.W. Reid, 15 May 1876.

Chapter 15

1 *Daily News*, 4 April 1857.
2 *Literary Examiner*, 11 April 1857.
3 *The Standard*: 'Jane Eyre' by WW Carus Wilson, 24 April 1857.
4 *Ibid*.
5 William to EN, quoting JKS 15 April 1857.
6 Charles Kingsley to ECG, 14 May 1857.
7 'To the editor of Littell's Living Age: Jane Eyre and the School at Cowan Bridge'; *The Living Age*, v.46, July-September 1855, p652.
8 Ibid.
9 ABN to *Leeds Mercury*, 20 May 1857.
10 William C. Wilson to the *Leeds Mercury*, 28 May 1857.
11 Quoted by ABN in letter to *Halifax Guardian*, 3 June 1857.
12 ECG to E.E. Norton, 3 June 1857.
13 Francis Leyland, notes on his visit to Haworth and the Brown family, 21 May 1874.
14 CB to EN, 17 June 1846.
15 ECG to GS, 29 December 1856.
16 James Stephen to Edward Backus Eastwick, 6 May 1857, *BST*: 21: 3, p72.
17 Ibid.
18 GS, *Recollections*.
19 Ibid.

20 William Shaen to Newton & Robinson, 26 May 1857.

21 Mary Taylor to ECG, 30 July 1857.

22 ECG to EN, 16 June 1857.

23 Ibid.

24 ECG to GS, 3 June 1857.

25 Sarah Baldwin to the editor of the *Halifax Guardian*, 8 July 1857.

26 Ibid., 9 June 1857.

27 Ibid., 8 July 1857.

28 Ibid.

29 PB to GS, 9 June 1857.

30 William Wilson to the editor of the *Halifax Guardian,* 18 July 1857 but published elsewhere by 16 July.

31 PB to GS, 16 July 1857.

32 Ibid.

33 ABN to the editor of the *Halifax Guardian*, 15 July 1857, published 18 July.

34 Ibid.

35 Sarah Baldwin, advertisement in *Halifax Guardian*, 1 August 1857.

36 Elizabeth G Smith, quoted by Sarah Baldwin, advertisement in *Halifax Guardian*, 1 August 1857.

37 Sarah Baldwin, advertisement in *Halifax Guardian*, 1 August 1857.

38 Sarah Baldwin to ABN, *c.*8 August 1857 (Barker, p972, note 97).

39 ABN to the *Halifax Guardian*, 5 August, printed 8 August 1857.

40 ECG to Charles Kingsley, 6 June 1857.

41 PB to GS, 9 June 1857.

42 Ibid.

43 Mr Woolven to Francis Leyland, 8 September 1875, recalls domestic violence in the Robinson household.

44 Francis Leyland to *The Athenaeum*, 21 July 1883.

45 PB quoted by William Dearden to Francis Leyland, *c.*28 August 1857.

46 Francis Leyland to William Dearden, 3 September 1857.

47 ECG to Maria Martineau, 23 August 1857.

48 CB to Hartley Coleridge, 10 December 1840.

49 William Dearden, *Bradford Observer*, 13 August 1857.

50 ECG*, The Life*, p72.

51 Francis Leyland, *The Brontë Family*, p48.

52 ECG to GS, 17 June 1857.

53 PB to ECG, 30 July 1857.

54 Ibid.

55 HM to ABN, 10 November 1857.

56 HM to Catherine Winkworth, 13 June 1857.

57 Francis Leyland, Notes on his visit to Haworth and the Brown family, 21 May 1874.

58 HM to R.P. Graves, 27 November 1857.

59 Ibid.

60 HM to John Chapman, 22 July 1857.

61 ECG to Maria Martineau, 23 August 1857.

62 HM to Katie Winkworth, 13 June 1857.

63 William Dearden to the *Bradford Observer*, 11 August 1857, published 13 August.
64 Martha Brown to William Dearden, 31 August 1857.
65 William Dearden to the *Bradford Observer*, 18 August 1857, published 20 August.
66 'Mrs Gaskell and the Rev Patrick Brontë', *Daily News*, 21 August 1857.
67 HM to *Daily News*, 24 August 1857, published 26 August.
68 Ibid.
69 William Dearden to Francis Leyland, *c*.28 August 1857.
70 ECG to William Dearden, 9 September 1857.
71 PB to ECG, 20 August 1857.
72 Ibid.
73 ECG to Maria Martineau, 23 August 1857.
74 PB to ECG, 24 August 1857.
75 Francis Leyland to ABN, 17 August 1883.
76 ABN to Francis Leyland, 15 August 1883.
77 PB to William Dearden, 31 August 1857.
78 William Dearden, letter to the *Bradford Observer*, 3 September 1857.
79 W. Brooksbank, letter to the *Bradford Observer*, 3 September 1857.
80 PB to William Dearden, 21 October 1857.
81 Francis Leyland's *The Brontë Family, with special reference to Patrick Branwell Brontë* was published in 1886.
82 ECG to GS, 23 August 1857.
83 Ibid., *c*.5 August 1857.
84 Ibid., 23 August 1857.
85 'Jane Eyre', *Manchester Times*, 29 August 1857.
86 Mary to EN, 28 January 1858.
87 HM to R.P. Graves, 27 November 1857.
88 PB to HM, 5 November 1857.
89 HM to PB, *c*.6 November 1857.
90 HM to R.P. Graves, 6 November 1857.
91 ABN to HM, 6 November 1857.
92 HM to ABN, *c*.7 November 1857.
93 Ibid., 10 November 1857.
94 Ibid., 17 November 1857.
95 ABN to HM, 9 November 1857.
96 PB to HM, 11 November 1857.
97 HM to PB, 13 November 1857.
98 HM to ABN, 13 November 1857.
99 Ibid.
100 James Stephen to Edward Backus Eastwick, 6 May 1857, *BST*: 21: 3, p72.
101 Ibid.
102 Ibid.

Chapter 16

1 'The Parsonage on the Moors', *The Ladies' Cabinet of Fashion, Music and Romance*, 1 December, 1857, p40–46
2 ECG to GS, mid-August, 1857.

3   Ibid., 26 November 1857.

4   *The Christian Remembrancer*, vol. 34 (October 1857), p48.

5   *Ibid.*

6   'A Day at Haworth', *Bradford Observer*, 19 November 1857.

7   Raymond, quoted by T.W. Reid, *Charlotte Brontë: a monograph*, p193.

8   Ibid.

9   'A Day at Haworth', *Bradford Observer*, 19 November 1857.

10 Ibid.

11 John Elliot Cairnes mentions buying one on his visit in 1858, as described in a letter, recounted in Lemon, p50. Walter White mentions declining them: Lemon, p42.

12 ECG to unknown, 23 June 1857. None of CB's letters to ECG survived.

13 ECG to GS, 17 March 1858.

14 MW to EN [?] September 1857.

15 EN to Mary Robinson, 24 July 1883.

16 EN to Francis Leyland, 17 October 1884.

17 EN, 'Reminiscences of Charlotte Brontë', *Scribner's Monthly*, May 1871, p18.

18 ECG to WSW, 20 December 1860.

19 PB to Rev. John Rand Bailey, 17 February 1860.

20 CB to PB, *c.*5 June 1849.

21 Ibid., 9 June 1849.

Chapter 17

1   Charles Lemon, *A Centenary History of the Brontë Society 1893–1993*, p9.

2   EN, *Reminiscences* in Smith vol. 1, p601.

3   Ibid.

Select Bibliography

Adamson, Alan H., *Mr Charlotte Brontë: The life of Arthur Bell Nicholls*. Montreal: McGill-Queen's University Press, 2008.

Allott, Miriam, *Charlotte Brontë: Jane Eyre and Villette, a selection of critical essays*. London: Macmillan, 1973.

Barker, Juliet, 'Saintliness, Treason and Plot', *Brontë Studies*, Vol. 21: 4, 1994: pp101–15.

—, The Brontës. London: Weidenfeld & Nicolson, 1994.

Bellamy, Joan, 'Mary Taylor, Ellen Nussey and Brontë biography', *Brontë Studies*, Vol. 21: 7, 1996: pp275–83.

Bennoch, Francis, *Poems, Lyrics, Songs and Sonnets*. Hardwick & Bogue: London, 1877.

Brontë, Anne, *Agnes Grey*. Oxford: Oxford University Press, 1847 (1991).

—, 'The Three Guides', *Fraser's Magazine*, August 1848.

—, *The Tenant of Wildfell Hall*. Oxford: OUP, [1848] 1993.

Brontë, Anne, and Clement and Hatfield, C.W. (eds.) Shorter, *The Complete Poems of Anne Brontë*. London: Hodder, 1920.

Brontë, Charlotte, 'Biographical Notice of Ellis and Acton Bell'. London: Smith, Elder & Co, 1850.

—, *Jane Eyre*. Oxford: OUP, [1847] 1993.

—, 'Preface to Poems by Acton Bell'. London: Smith, Elder & Co, 1850.

—, *Shirley*. London: Penguin, 1849 [1985].

—, *Villette*. Oxford: Oxford University Press, 1853 [1990].

Brontë, Emily, *Wuthering Heights*. London: Shakespeare Head , 1847 (1931).

Brontë, Emily, and C.W. (ed.) Hatfield, *The Complete Poems of Emily Jane Brontë*. New York: Columbia University Press, 1941.

Brontë, Patrick, and Horsfall (ed.) Turner, *Brontëana: The Rev. Patrick Brontë's Collected Works*. Bingley: Harrison & Sons, 1898.

Brugge, Roger, 'The weather of 1850',' *Weather*, Vol. 55, 2000: pp98–103.

Burton, Betty, 'Miss Brontë visits Ambleside', *Brontë Studies*, 1999: p96.

Chadwick, Ellis H., *In the Footsteps of the Brontës*. London: Pitman, 1914.

—, *Mrs Gaskell: Her Haunts, Homes and Stories*. London: Pitman, 1910.

Chapple, J.A.V. and Arthur Pollard, *The Letters of Mrs Gaskell*. Manchester: Manchester University Press, 1997 [1966].

Chapple, John and Alan Shelston, *Further Letters of Mrs Gaskell*. Manchester: Manchester University Press, 2003 [2000].

Cochrane, Margaret, *My Dear Boy: The Life of Arthur Bell Nicholls*. Beverley: Highgate, 1999.

Davies, Stevie, *Emily Brontë: The Artist as a Free Woman*. Manchester: Carcanet, 1983.

Dearden, William, 'Letter', *Bradford Observer*, August 13, 1857.

Dinsdale, Ann, *At Home with the Brontës*. Stroud: Amberley, 2013.

Dinsdale, Ann. 'Martha Brown: life after the Brontës, *Brontë Studies*, Vol. 24: 1, 1999: pp97–101.

Dinsdale, Ann, 'Mrs Brontë's Nurse', *Brontë Studies*, Vol. 30: 3, 2005: pp258–9.

Dinsdale, Ann, Sarah Laycock, and Julie Akhurst, *Brontë Relics: A Collection History*. Haworth: Brontë Society, 2012.

Duckett, Bob, 'The Letters of Francis Leyland', *Brontë Studies*, Vol. 42: 3, 2017: pp220–50.

Edgerley, Mabel, 'The Rev. Arthur Bell Nicholls', *Brontë Studies*, Vol. 10: 3, 1942: pp95–101.

Epps, Emily (ed.), *The Diary of the Late John Epps*. London: Kent & Co, 1874.

Field, W.T. 'Two Brussels Schoolfellows of the Brontës, *Brontë Studies*, Vol. 5: 23, 1913: pp25–9.

Gaskell, Elizabeth, and Angus (ed.) Easson, *Ruth*. London: Penguin, 1997.

Gaskell, Elizabeth, and C.K. (ed.) Shorter, *The Life of Charlotte Brontë*. London: John Murray, 1914.

Gaskell, Elizabeth, and Peter (ed.) Keating, *Cranford*. London: Penguin, 1976.

Gaskell, Elizabeth, and Winfred (ed.) Gerin, *The Life of Charlotte Brontë*. London: Folio Society, 1971.

Gerin, Winifred, *Anne Brontë*. Oxford: Oxford University Press, 1959.

—, *Branwell Brontë*. Oxford: Oxford University Press, 1961.

—, *Charlotte Brontë: Evolution of Genius*. Oxford: Oxford University Press, 1967.

—, *Elizabeth Gaskell: A Biography*. Oxford: Oxford University Press, 1980 [1976].

—, *Emily Brontë*. Oxford: Oxford University Press, 1971.

Green, Dudley, *Patrick Brontë: Father of Genius*. London: Nonsuch, 2008.

—. *The Letters of the Rev. Patrick Brontë*. Stroud: Nonsuch, 2005.

Haldane, Elizabeth, *Mrs Gaskell and Her Friends*. London: Hodder, 1930.

Huxley, Leonard, *The House of Smith, Elder*. London: William Clowes & Sons, 1923.

Jones, Marnie, 'George Smith's Influence on The Life of Charlotte Brontë', *Brontë Studies*, Vol. 18: 4, 1984: pp279–85.

Lang, Cecil Y., *The Letters of Matthew Arnold*, 2 Vols, Charlottesville and London: The University Press of Virginia, 1996.

Lemon, Charles, *A Centenary History of the Brontë Society 1893–1993*. Kendal: The Brontë Society, 1993.

—, *Early Visitors to Haworth from Ellen Nussey to Virginia Woolf*. Haworth: Brontë Society, 1996.

Leyland, Francis, *The Brontë Family, with Special Reference to Patrick Branwell Brontë*. London: Hurst & Blackett, 1886.

Logan, Deborah Ann (ed.), *The Collected Letters of Harriet Martineau Vol. 3: 1845–1855*. London: Routledge, 2007.

Logan, Deborah Ann (ed.), *The Collected Letters of Harriet Martineau, Vol. 4: 1856–62*. London: Routledge, 2007.

Lonoff, Sue, 'The Mystery Behind the History of the Brontë Heger Letters', *Brontë Studies*. Vol. 38: 1, 2013: pp1–7.

MacKay, Angus, *The Brontës: Fact and Fiction*. London: Service & Paton, 1897.

Martineau, Harriet, *Autobiography*. New York: Houghton Mifflin, 1877.

—, *Biographical Sketches*. New York: Leypold and Hunt, 1869.

—, *Letters of the Laws of Man's Nature*. Boston: H.G. Atkinson, 1851.

McDonald, Frederika, *The Secret of Charlotte Brontë*. London: T.C & E.C. Jack, 1914.

Miller, Lucasta, *The Brontë Myth*. London: Random House, 2001.

Nussey, Ellen, 'Reminiscences of Charlotte Brontë', *Scribner's Monthly*, Vol. 2: 1, 1871: pp18–31.

Orel, Harold, *The Brontës: Interviews and Recollections*. London: Palgrave, 1996.

Palmer, Geoffrey, *Dear Martha: The Letters of Arthur Bell Nicholls to Martha Brown*. Gainsborough: Brontë Society, 2004.

Pollard, Arthur, *Mrs Gaskell: Novelist and Biographer*. Manchester: Manchester University Press, 1965.

Potter, Louisa, 'Eighty Years Ago: Memories of Old Manchester II', *Manchester Guardian*, September 2, 1896: 8.

Preston, Albert H., 'John Greenwood and the Brontës', *Brontë Studies*, Vol. 12: 1, 1951: pp35–8.

Ray, Gordon (ed.), *The Letters of William Makepeace Thackeray, Vol. 1*. Cambridge, Mass.: Harvard University Press, 1946.

—, *The Letters of William Makepeace Thackeray, Vol. 2*. Cambridge, Mass.: Harvard University Press, 1946.

—, *The Letters of William Makepeace Thackeray, Vol. 3*. Cambridge, Mass.: Harvard University Press, 1946.

Reid, S.J., *Memoirs of T.W. Reid 1842–85*. London: Cassell, 1905.

Reid, T.W., *Charlotte Brontë: A Monograph*. London: Macmillan, 1877.

—, *The Life, Letters and Friendships of Richard Monckton Milnes*. London: Cassell, 1891.

Ritchie, Anne Thackeray, *Chapters from Some Memoirs*. London: Macmillan, 1894.

Scruton, William, *Thornton and the Brontës*. Bradford: John Dale, 1898.

Selleck, R.J.W., *Sir James Kay-Shuttleworth: Journey of an Outsider*. London: Routledge, 1994.

Shaen, Margaret, *Memorials of Two Sisters, Susanna and Catherine Winkworth*. London: Longman, 1908.

Shorter, C.K., *Charlotte Brontë and Her Circle*. London: Hodder, 1896.

Smith, George, 'Charlotte Brontë', *Cornhill Magazine*, 1900: p779.

Smith, George, 'The Brontës', *Cornhill Magazine*, 1873: pp54–71.

Smith, Margaret (ed.), *The Letters of Charlotte Brontë, Vol. 1, 1829–47*. Oxford: Oxford University Press, 1995.

—, *The Letters of Charlotte Brontë, Vol. 2, 1848–51*. Oxford: Oxford University Press, 2000.

—, *The Letters of Charlotte Brontë, Vol. 3, 1852–55*. Oxford : Oxford University Press, 2008.

Society, Brontë, '"Innocent and Un-Londony": Impressions of Charlotte Brontë', *Brontë Studies*, Vol. 19: 1, 1986: pp44–9.

Stanley, Arthur Penrhyn, *The Life and Correspondence of Dr Thomas Arnold*. London: B. Fellowes, 1844.

Stoneman, Patsy, *Brontë Transformations*. London: Prentice-Hall, 1996.

Stoneman, Patsy, '"Such a life..." Elizabeth Gaskell and Charlotte Brontë', *Brontë Studies*, Vol. 41: 3, 2016: pp193–204.

Tennyson, Hallam, *Alfred Tennyson: A Memoir* (in 2 vols). London: Macmillian, 1897.

Thormaheln, Marianne (ed.), *The Brontës in Context*. Cambridge: Cambridge University Press, 2012.

Trollope, Anthony, and David (ed) Skilton, *Autobiography*. London: Penguin, 1996.

Turner, Whiteley, *A Springtime Saunter Round and About Brontëland*. Halifax: The *Halifax Courier*, 1913.

Uglow, Jenny, *Elizabeth Gaskell: A Habit of Stories*. London: Faber and Faber, 1993.

Unknown, 'The Parsonage on the Moors', *The Ladies' Cabinet of Fashion, Music and Romance*, 1857: 40–6.

Unsigned, 'Charlotte Brontë', *Cosmopolitan Art Journal*, Vol. 1, No. 5, 1857: pp157–9.

Weir, Edith, 'Cowan Bridge: New Light from New Documents', *Brontë Studies*, Vol. 11: 1, 1946: pp16–28.

Whitehead, Barbara, *Charlotte Brontë and Her Dearest Nell*. Leeds: Smith Settle, 1993.

Whitehead, S.R., *The Brontës' Haworth*. London: The Brontë Society, 2017.

Wiltshire, Irene, *The Letters of Mrs Gaskell's Daughters*. London: Humanities-ebooks, 2000.

Wise, T.J., and J.A. Symington, *The Brontës: Their Lives, Friendships and Correspondence* (in 4 vols). Oxford: Oxford University Press, 1932.

Index

'Acton Bell' (pseudonym), *see* Brontë, Anne
Agnes Grey (1847), *see* Brontë, Anne
Ambleside, England 40–46, 73–74, 137,
    149–150, 154, 222, 227
Anglesey, Wales 119
Appleton & Co (publisher) 172, 200
Armytage, James 203
Arnold, Dr Thomas 25–26, 172
Arnold, Frances 25–26
Arnold, Mary (*née* Penrose) 25–26
Arnold, Matthew
    challenged on inaccuracy 142
    dislikes *Villette* 141
    family relationships 25
    meets CB and HM 45
    proposes elegy 'Haworth Churchyard'
        (1855) 141
    unfavourable impressions of CB 141
Aykroyd, Tabitha ('Tabby')
    Aylott & Jones (publisher) 33, 248
    ECG's impressions of 88
    employed by Brontë family 91, 94
    Haworth lore 94
    illness and death (1855) 132, 134
    relationships with CB 95, 108
    with Martha Brown 21

Baldwin, Sarah 214–218
Banagher, County Offaly, Ireland 120–122
Bangor, Wales 119
Belgium 155, 162, 173–176
Bell, Dr Charles W. 76, 258
Bell, Harriette Adamson 120, 123

Bell, Joseph 119
Bell, Maggie 76–77
Bell, Mary Anna (*later* Nicholls)
    family 119–120
    marries ABN 245
    meets CB 120
Bennoch, Francis 90–91, 93, 100–101
Berry, Johnathan 20, 253
Birstall, West Yorkshire, England 45, 64,
    81, 111, 145, 155–156, 160, 206
Black Bull, Haworth (pub) 185, 237–238
Blackwood's Magazine (journal) 89
Blake, William 186
Bradford Observer, The (newspaper) 139, 203,
    223, 225, 245
Bradford, West Yorkshire, England 14–19,
    45, 81, 105, 125, 132, 159, 162, 220
Branwell, Elizabeth (CB's aunt) 148, 220,
    246, 248
Briery Close, Windermere, England 13, 22,
    26, 31, 44–45, 144
Brontë Parsonage Museum 244–245
Brontë Society, The 242
Brontë, Anne (CB's youngest sister)
    birth in Thornton 148
    dealings with Newby 33–35
    described in CB's prefaces 38, 46, 87,
        99, 190
    illness and death 27, 37
    life and character 37–39
    painted by BB 98
    poems compiled and edited by CB 36
    relationship with EJB 17

uses Acton Bell pseudonym 34, 53, 77, 87, 181
visits London and meets GS 53, 181
WORKS:
Agnes Grey (1847, 1850) 33–35, 88, 98
Poems by Currer, Ellis and Acton Bell (1846, 1850) 33
The Tenant of Wildfell Hall (1848, 1853) 14, 33–35, 211
Brontë, Charlotte
LIFE:
accepts ABN
as governess 49
badly edits sisters' material 36–37
birth in Thornton 148
collaboration with BB 17
difficult courtship with ABN 104–105
domestic routine 94–95
education at Cowan Bridge 30
her engagement 108
her portrait by Richmond 90, 99, 195, 202–203, 238
illness and death 132–139
is bereaved 16, 130, 139
is exposed as Currer Bell 20
Jane Eyre published (1847) 14
juvenile writings 17, 33
literary ambitions 23
marriage 112–116
meets ECG (1850) 13
mystery over Currer Bell 13–20
negotiations with Newby for EJB and AB's rights 34
opinion of Haworth and its landscape 27, 89
painted by BB 98
Pensionnat Héger 45
proposes new edition of sisters' works 34
rejects ABN 68, 82, 100
rejects offer of serialisation 49
Roe Head school 160, 221
Shirley published (1849) 15
Villette published (1853) 71
writing process 42, 49
CHARACTER:
bitterness 25, 60
conversation 56
defiance 24, 82
dutifulness 80–84
faith 28, 75
her 'unique' nature as regarded by ECG 151, 171
kindness and generosity 104
reserve 78–79, 96
resilience 231
resourcefulness 109
shyness 24, 76–77, 120
sociability 56
social anxiety 21, 25–26
strength 80
HEALTH:
accidental poisoning by doctor 63
decline and death 132–135
insomnia 49
morning sickness 136
nightmares 63
potential consumption 63
pregnancy 131
recurrent seasonal ill health 63
RELATIONSHIPS:
admiration of EJB 97, 177
argues with HM about *Villette* 71–74
closeness lost with BB 33
conflicts with PB 67–68, 107–108
estrangement from EN 83–85, 88
her love and correspondence with Héger 178–179
hosts ECG in Haworth (1853) 90–100
learns of GS's marriage 103
professional relationships with GS and WSW 35, 103, 111
reconciliation with EN 104, 106–107
respect for AB 121
romantic idealisation of GS 57
severs relationship with GS 104
stays with HM (1850) 43–45
with MW 71–72, 102–107, 114–116, 126
WORKS:
Emma (published posthumously, 1860) 127, 151, 182, 186
Jane Eyre (1847) 13–15, 17–20, 23–24,

27, 34, 41–42, 45, 50, 55–60–61, 70, 86–87, 97–101, 103, 108–111, 114, 120, 139, 144–145, 151, 156–157, 161–162, 180, 182, 187, 203, 208–210, 216, 226, 236

Juvenilia 186

Poems by Currer, Ellis and Acton Bell (1846 and 1850) 23, 33, 39

The Professor (published posthumously, 1857) 151, 180–192, 213

Shirley (1849) 15–20, 40, 64, 92, 97, 110, 139, 156, 160, 190, 203, 243

Villette (1853) 45, 53, 58, 61, 63–74, 79–84, 98, 103, 112, 139, 141, 151, 154, 156, 162, 173, 176, 180–182, 187, 188, 197, 203, 227, 230

CULTURAL AFTERLIFE:

becomes representative of women's lives 238

memorials suggested by EN 145

pilgrimages to Haworth 17, 238

publicity after death 139, 238

readers' responses to *Life* 238

regarded as moorland ghost 235

Brontë, Elizabeth (CB's sister) 30, 148,

Brontë, Emily Jane (CB's sister)

attends Pensionnat Héger 176–179

birth in Thornton 148

illness and death 15–16, 27

life and character 177

relationship with CB and AB 37, 177

WORKS:

Poems by Currer, Ellis and Acton Bell (1846, 1850) 33

Wuthering Heights (1847) 33

revised by CB (1850) 35, 88, 98

Brontë, Maria (CB's eldest sister) 30, 97, 148, 209, 220–221

Brontë, Maria (née Branwell, CB's mother) 30, 94, 154, 148, 220

Brontë, Patrick Branwell (CB's brother) 95, 105, 110, 126, 154, 243

addiction 98

affair with Lydia Robinson 155, 192, 196, 211–213, 222

artistic career 148

birth in Thornton 148

characterised in *Life* 201, 225

collaboration with CB 17

decline and death 31, 33, 130, 192

estrangement from CB 211

friendships 211, 219, 226

life and character 33

Patrick refuses to sanction his biography 226

posthumous reputation 225, 227, 237

prolific childhood 33

relationship with PB 211

sculpted by Leyland 220

Brontë, Rev. Patrick (CB's father)

abusive towards CB 68, 108, 123, 223

approves of *Life* 203

makes objections 204–206

argues with HM 223–226, 230

as minister of Haworth 17, 148, 230

at CB's deathbed 135–136

autobiographical writing 147–149

controlling conflicts with CB 107–109

destroys household objects 219–221

disagreements with servants 30, 221

early life in Ireland 123, 148

emotionally distant from his children 91, 223

his charity 130

his fears 21–22

his grief 33, 241

his pride in CB 138

ignorance of daughters' novels 148–149

impressions of 92–93, 223

illness and death 242, 245

in Thornton 148, 220

is photographed 140–141

last visit from ECG 240

local gossip about 158

meets ECG 91, 150

objects to courtship with ABN 67–70

objects to marriage 67–68, 108, 138

possible stroke 85

proposes *Life* 146, 151

refuses to attend wedding 114–115

relationship with ABN 81–83, 108, 125, 153, 242, 245

relationship with CB 92
temper observed by servants 108, 220
Brookfield, Jane 56–57
Brooksbank, William 219, 224–225
Brown, John 19, 68, 81, 115, 225, 238
Brown, Martha 21, 68, 115, 124, 132, 222, 245
  early life 19
  employed by Brontë family 91, 94
  interviewed by ECG 223
  involved in controversy 223, 226
  relationship with CB 95
    identifies her as Currer Bell 19
    nurses her in terminal illness 133–135
    takes EN to view her body 135
Brown, Tabitha (*later* Ratcliffe)
  employed by Brontë family 133
  impressions of PB 136
  nurses CB in her terminal illness 133–13
Brown, William 238
Brussels, Belgium 45, 80, 97, 139, 148, 154–158, 162, 171–185, 187, 198, 209
Byron, Lord George Gordon 112, 121, 192

Carlisle, 7th Earl of (George Howard) 58
Carlisle, England 78, 89
Carlyle, Jane 56
Carlyle, Thomas 48, 56–57
Casterton, Cumbria 157, 215
Cator, Rev. Thomas 101
Chapter Coffee House, London 181
Chorley, Henry 192
Christian Remembrancer, The (journal) 86–88, 236
Coltman, Lady (Anna Duckworth) 173
Connor, Ann 162
Conwy, Wales 119
Cowan Bridge (School for the Daughters of the Clergy) 23, 30, 148, 162, 207–209, 213–217, 226
Cowan Bridge (village), Lancashire, England 157
Crowe, Catherine 56
Cuba Court, Banagher 122, 245

Currer Bell (CB's pseudonym)
  abandoned 70
  as distinct masculine identity from CB 15, 17, 64, 127–128
  attributes 50, 63
  comparisons to Thackeray 50
  confusion with sisters' pseudonyms 34
  creation of 17
  exposed in press 19–20
  in negotiations with Smith Elder 49, 66,149–150
  press speculation about 14–20
  progression from name to character 20
  used for protection 20, 65
  used in public 56

Daily News, The (newspaper) 72, 139–140, 142, 207
Darwin, Charles 160
Davenport, Caroline Anne 155
Dawson, Hannah 133–136
Dearden, William
  accusations to ECG 224
  arguments with HM 227–230
  connection to BB 219
  hears about BB's affair 219
  speaks to press about PB 223–225
  visits PB (1857 219)
Dewsbury, England 148
Dickens, Charles 48–50
Dixon, Mary 158
Dublin, Ireland 119, 122, 124
Dunoon, Scotland 159

Eastlake, Lady Elizabeth Rigby 192
Ellis Bell, (pseudonym), *see* Brontë, Emily
Elliot, Jane 56
Epps, Dr John 15–16, 252
Evesham, England 187–189
Examiner, The (magazine) 81, 207

Felix, Rachel 50, 60–62
Forbes, Dr John 58
Forster, John 81
Fraser's Magazine 37, 141

Garrs, Nancy 136, 162, 220–223, 226
Garrs, Sarah 221, 223
Gaskell, Elizabeth Cleghorn
  amassing CB's letters 156–161
  apology made by William 213
  begins discussions about *Life* with GS
    147
  career 49, 127
  concerns about CB's relationship with
    ABN 110
  concerns about content of *The Professor*
    180
  concerns about JKS editing *The Professor*
    187–190
  contacts the Wheelwrights 158, 189,
    202
  correcting proofs of *Life* 202, 226
  correspondence with Mary Taylor 214
  curiosity about CB 13
  encourages CB to talk about her life 60,
    80, 96–99, 220, 222
  dislike of ABN 110, 208
  family background and early life in
    Knutsford 48
  fascination with EJB 97
  'fear' of PB 92
  first edition of *Life* published 203
    second edition published 204, 212
    third edition published 226
  first meets CB in Windermere (1850)
    13–17
  GS coerces ABN to sign over CB's
    copyright 193–194
  her character 26
  hosts CB in Manchester in 1851 47–49;
    in 1853 76–81; and 1854 111
  hosts EN in Manchester (1857) 200–201
  in a 'hornet's nest' 201, 214
  interviews Héger in Belgium 175–180
  is nominated by EN as biographer
    145–146
  is proposed as a friend for CB 28
  is told of CB's death 138
  meets GS and WSW 181
  meets LJKS 28
  meets Margaret Wooler 160

  moves to Plymouth Grove (1850) 47
  plot to better ABN's prospects 101
  publishes article about CB 144
  puts *Life* behind her 236
  retracts material in *Life* 213, 226, 236
    defends claims 197, 221
    makes concessions 216
  social support for CB at the Arnolds
    26
  stays with CB in Haworth (1853)
    90–100
  visits ABN and PB in Haworth (1855)
    150–152
  visits ABN and PB with JKS to obtain
    manuscripts and permission to
    photograph the Richmond portrait
    185–188
  visits Cowan Bridge 157
  visits EN in Birstall (1855) 156
  visits family in Scotland (1855) 159
  visits France and Italy (1857) 203
  writes account of CB for friends 27
  writes *Life* in Silverdale 154–157
  RELATIONSHIPS:
  with William Gaskell 48, 89
  her children ,77,105, 144
  with the Arnold family 25
  with Dickens 48–49
  with PB 92
  with ABN 182–184
  with HM 149, 223
  with GS 159, 181
  with EN 152–156, 158–160, 162, 172,
    200–202
  WORKS:
  Cousin Phyllis (1864) 240, 245
  Cranford (1853) 49, 85
  The Life of Charlotte Brontë (1857) (*see*
    entry)
  Mary Barton (1848) 49, 203
  North and South (1855) 131, 191, 199,
    203
  Ruth (1853) 69–70, 203
  Sylvia's Lovers (1863) 240, 245
  Wives and Daughters (1866) 240, 245
Gaskell, Florence ('Flossy') 48, 173, 248

Gaskell, Julia ('Baby') 48, 77, 173, 248

Gaskell, Margaret ('Meta') 48, 160, 173–175, 180, 202–203, 210, 245

Gaskell, Marianne 48, 76, 105, 159, 160, 247, 172–175, 185, 203, 210, 219

Gaskell, Rev. William 29, 48, 89, 204, 208, 212, 218, 240, 247. 161

Gawthorpe Hall, Lancashire 20, 22, 31, 45, 131–132, 155–156

Glasgow, Scotland 159

Glengarriff, County Cork, Ireland 124

Grant, Rev. Joseph 115

Greenwood, John
  announces CB's death to associates 136–137
  capitalises on Brontë fame 238
  career in Haworth 136
  commissions photograph of PB 140
  disgruntled about CB 141
  exaggerates friendship with CB 137, 143
  interviewed by ECG 141–143
  supplies the Brontë family 136

Halifax Guardian, The (newspaper) 214–218

Hane, Melanie 162

Hartley, William 101

Hartshead–cum–Clifton, West Yorkshire, England 148

Haworth Parsonage 14, 16, 20, 26, 30–32, 43, 48, 67, 85, 88, 90–96, 99, 112, 115, 127, 130, 139–140, 146, 153, 237, 242–244

Haworth, West Yorkshire, England 17–22, 27–29, 31, 58, 65–69, 75, 81, 83, 89, 94, 99–104, 107, 114, 119, 121, 124–125, 132–135, 139, 142–150, 154–159, 171, 180, 184–190, 198, 202–203, 212, 214, 220, 229, 237, 239, 242–246

Heald, Rev. William 18

Hearn, Ann 48, 173, 255

Héger, Constantin
  as model for Paul Emanuel 112
  ECG's concerns about discretion 180
  ECG's impressions of 175, 180, 183
  first meets CB and EJB 176
  friendship with CB known to others 174, 183
  impressions of CB and EJB 177
  interview with ECG 175–180
  letters to CB 179
  Pensionnat Héger 174
  shows ECG letters from CB 178–180
  suggests tutorials 177

Héger, Zoe Claire (*née* Parent): 162, 175–176, 183

Hill, Anna Andrews 208

Hogg, James 77, 89

Holyhead, Wales 119

Household Words (magazine) 49, 105

Ingham, Dr Amos 32, 135–136

Ireland 120, 122, 131–132, 141, 148, 245

Jane Eyre (novel) *see* Bronte, Charlotte

Kay–Shuttleworth, Lady Janet
  background 20
  friendship with ECG and CB 20–28
  her chronic illness 27, 131, 157
  hosts CB in Gawthorpe 20
  and Briery Close (1850) 9–28
  introduces ECG and CB by letter 28
  relationship with husband 22
  relationship with Rosa Poplawska 22, 131, 157
  separation and removal to Europe 51, 131, 157

Kay–Shuttleworth, Sir James
  admiration for CB 20
  assists ECG 150
  background and character 22
  decides to edit *The Professor* 187
  hosts CB at Gawthorpe and Briery Close (1850) 9–28
  illness and infirmity 44, 150
  literary ambitions 24, 187
  obtains manuscripts and portrait of CB from ABN 185
  relationship with wife 22

separation from wife 51, 131
visits Haworth with ECG (1857) 185–186
Keighley, West Yorkshire 18, 89, 92, 99, 111, 119, 150, 171, 237, 242
Kilkee, County Clare, Ireland 123–124
Killarney, County Kerry, Ireland 124
Kingsley, Charles 208
Kingstown (*now* Dún Laoghaire), Dublin, Ireland 119
Kirkudbright, Scotland 89

Lawrence, Samuel 62
Leeds, England 102, 105, 155, 171
Leeds Mercury, The (newspaper) 119, 140, 209
Legouvé, Ernest 60
Leyland, Francis
  charges CB and PB for BB's medallion 220, 225
  connection to BB 219
  encourages controversy about *Life* 219–226
  offers BB's poetry for sale 225
  PB opposes his biography of BB 225
  publishes biography of BB 226
  visits PB (1857) 219
Leyland, Joseph
  friendship with BB 211
  sculpts BB 220
The Life of Charlotte Brontë (ECG)
  PRODUCTION:
  collaboration with EN 156–157, 172, 206, 239
  correspondence with Mary Taylor 214
  ECG suggested by EN 145–146
  first edition published 203
  first edition withdrawn 213
  identifying teachers at Cowan Bridge 162, 207
  interviews GS 181
  interviews Héger 175–180
  interviews HM 223
  interviews Laetitia Wheelwright 174–175
  interviews PB 147–148

interviews servants 94–95, 162
legal action threatened by Robinson 213–214
legal action threatened by Wilson 216
obtains CB's letters from interviewees 152, 154, 159, 201
opposed by Nicholls 146, 150–152, 205–206
redacted third edition published 226
second edition published and withdrawn 204, 212
seen as representative of women's domestic condition 239
sells UK rights 172
sells US rights 172
transcribes CB's letters 160–162, 173
visits Clergy Daughters School at Cowan Bridge and Casterton 157
writing of 171, 173, 189–192, 200–203
RECEPTION:
disliked by BB's friends 219
first reviews 207
popularity 213, 235
reaction from PB 204
reaction of EN 201–202
reaction of Mary Taylor 213
reaction of Nicholls 205
reviews and reception 236–237
responses from readers 238–239
threats of legal action 208
Limerick, County Limerick, Ireland 124
London, England 14, 19–21, 35–36, 40–41, 45, 47–49, 52–58, 66, 69, 73, 76, 99, 101–105, 111, 120, 138–144, 150, 155, 162, 173–175, 180–181, 203, 245
Lowood school (in *Jane Eyre*) 209, 217

MacTurk, Dr William 132
Manchester, England 24, 29, 47, 60, 62, 76–79, 89, 99, 111, 120, 138, 150–155, 160–162, 172–176, 185–186, 200–201, 210, 226
Manchester Guardian, The (newspaper) 77
Manchester Times, The (newspaper) 70
Marseilles, France 203

Martineau, Harriet
  anger about third edition of *Life* 221,
    227
  CB's impressions of 44
  changes perspective on CB 231
  conflicts with ABN and PB 223–229
  conflicts with Dearden 227
  demands return of her letters to CB 222
  doubts CB's truthfulness 222
  estrangement from CB 72–74
  her independence 44
  hosts CB in Ambleside (1850) 40, 43
    and relationship with CB 31, 42, 71
  interviewed by ECG 223
  life and career 15
  life in Ambleside 25, 45
  meets CB in London (1849) 15, 41
  opinion of ABN and PB 230
Martineau, Lucy 40–43
Martineau, Richard 40–43
Maxwell, Sir John 159
Milan, Italy 210
Milnes, Richard Monckton 58, 101–108, 159
Moseley, Rev. Henry 23

New York Times, The (newspaper) 237
New Zealand 39, 156, 213
Newby, Thomas Cautley (publisher)
  disagreements with CB 35
  ECG's intention to villainise 196, 200
  negotiations with Smith Elder 35
  publishes Antony Trollope 35
  publishes EJB and AB 34
Newman, Cardinal John Henry 23
Nichol, Alan 119, 262
Nicholls, Rev. Arthur Bell
  CB's death 135
  character 18, 110
  claims to have destroyed CB's papers
    151, 180, 186, 228; proven to not
    have destroyed CB's papers 229
  clerical career 112
  confronts CB about authorship 19
  depicted in *Shirley* 18–19, 110
  disagreements with EN 84, 107, 206
  disputes with PB 67–70, 74, 81

  early life and background 119–123
  embroiled in Cowan Bridge controversy
    208–221
  engagement and marriage 107–109, 115
    honeymoon 119–125
  family 120
  impressions of 67, 76, 112
  in conflict with HM 228–231
  is refused incumbency at Haworth 242
  is rejected by CB 68
  leaves Haworth 82
  married life in Haworth 125–127
  meets ECG 150
  opposes *Life* 205
  PB's death 242
  PB's dislike of 96, 105
  protectiveness of CB 120, 123
  resumes relationship with CB 75, 81, 83
  returns to Ireland 245
  tells EN to burn CB's letters 128
  vigour and good health 113, 130
Nussey, Ellen
  anger at PB's obstruction of CB's
    wedding 116
  at wedding of CB and ABN 115
  CB's death and funeral 135–136
  character 17–18, 201
  collaborates with ECG 172
  conflicts with PB 116
  denies collaboration with ECG 239
  discontent with lack of recognition 239
  dislike and distrust of ABN 67, 127–128
  disliked by ABN 128–129, 205
  falls out with CB 83–85, 88, 96,
    104–106
  family 17
  growing anger at PB and ABN 146, 206
  hopes for condemnation of PB and
    ABN 206
  hosts CB in Birstall 45, 64, 81
  mythologising of CB 240
  possessiveness of CB 84
  preserves CB's letters 129, 245
  recalls EJB and AB 172
  receives CB's letter to ABN by accident
    107

reconciled with CB 107
refuses to be named in *Life* 201
Rev. Heald threatens to expose CB 18
stays with CB at Haworth 18, 83
suggests ECG write memoir 145–146
upset by press speculation about CB 145
visits Haworth and Brontë Museum in
    old age 242–244
with Mary Taylor 83–84

Ostend, Belgium 175, 180
Oxenhope, West Yorkshire, England 104,
    115

Paris, France 105, 175, 203
Pensionnat Héger, Brussels 156, 158, 160
    ECG's visit 171–180
    location 175
    the Brontës' attendance 174–176
Penzance, Cornwall, England 190
Perry, Kate 56
Plymouth Grove, Manchester 48, 76, 90,
    105, 111, 122, 149, 161, 182–183, 219,
    245
Poplawska, Rosa
    intimate relationship with Janet Kay–
        Shuttleworth 131, 157
    meets CB 22
Potter, Louisa 77
Proctor, Adelaide 56–57
Proctor, Anne Benson 56–57

Quillinan, Edward 154

Raymond, Henry Jarvis 237
Redman, Joseph 81
Richmond, George
    portrait of CB commissioned by GS 99
    reproduced 195, 202–203
Robinson, Lydia (Lady Scott)
    employs AB and BB 211
    identified by ECG 155, 196
    letters from 222
    marriage 155, 211
    PB's impressions 212
    relationship with BB 211–213

threatens to sue 212–213
    conflict settled 226
Robinson, Rev. Edmund 219
Roe Head (school), Mirfield, West
    Yorkshire 160, 221, 247
Rome, Italy 202–203
Ruskin, John 48, 202

St Michael and All Angels, church of,
    Haworth 20, 70, 82, 90–94, 114, 125,
    136, 139, 142, 195, 202, 237, 238,
    243–245
Scarborough, North Yorkshire, England
    37, 95, 241
Scoresby, Dr William 159
Scotland 89, 102, 150, 159
Scott, Lady Lydia *see* Robinson, Lydia
Scribe, Eugene 60
Shakespeare, William 77
Shirley (1849) *see* Brontë, Charlotte
Silverdale, England 154–157
Skipton, England 125, 152, 171
Smith, Elder & Co (publisher) 15, 23,
    34–35, 53–57, 71. 102–103, 180–185,
    200, 203, 206, 212, 214
Smith, Elizabeth (*née* Gauntlett) 217
Smith, Elizabeth (*née* Murray) 53, 58–59,
    69, 103, 161, 174, 181, 196–197
Smith, George
    adopts EJB's and AB's novels 34–35
    attempts to dupe ABN of CB's
        copyright 194–195
    CB's idealisation of 65
    commercial acumen 182
    commissions CB's portrait 99
    congratulates CB on her engagement
        110
    corresponds with ECG 143, 150, 159
    courtship 84–85
    death 245
    determination to sign Thackeray 51–53,
        60, 62
    friendship terminated by CB 111
    handles scandal 212–214, 226
    his discomfort about his representation
        in *Villette* 61, 64–66, 181

hosts CB in London in 1848 181; in
 1849 40, 52–53; in 1850 55–56; in
 1851 47, 57; and in 1853 53
inherits Smith Elder 52
interest in *Emma* 186
legal issues with *Life* 211–213
life and family background 34
lowers CB's advance 66
marriage 102–103
meets AB (1848) 181
meets CB 53
meets ECG 174
negotiations with ECG 172
publishes *Jane Eyre* 14
publishes *The Professor* 192
raises objections to *Life* 196–199
reduces advance to ABN for *The
 Professor* 188
relationship with mother 174, 181, 197
uses controversy to commercial
 advantage 188
work and stress 47
Sowden, Rev. Sutcliffe 115, 119, 129, 136
Spectator, The (newspaper) 24, 207
Stephen, Sir James 212
Stewart, John 194–195, 202

Taylor, Amelia Ringrose 89, 111
Taylor, Joe 89, 111
Taylor, Martha 156
Taylor, Mary
 admiration of *Life* 213, 227
 at Roe Head School 160, 221
 background and family 89
 co–operates with ECG 198
 emigrates to New Zealand 198
 destroys CB's letters 198
 disagreements with EN 83–84
 dislike of PB 198
 friendship with CB 39, 198
 in Brussels 156
 scepticism about *Life* 198
 tries to persuade CB to leave Haworth
 198
Tenant of Wildfell Hall, The (1848) *see*
 Brontë, Anne

Tennyson, Alfred 23, 26, 60, 101
Thackeray, Mrs Anne (*née* Becher) 58–59
Thackeray, Anne (*later* Ritchie) 54–57, 59
Thackeray, Minny 56–57
Thackeray, William
 argument with CB 59
 career 50
 courted by GS 52–62
 curiosity about CB 53
 daughters 55–56
 dislike of 'clever women' 56
 first marriage 51
 first meeting with CB (1849) 52; third
 and final meeting (1851) 59
 his portrait delivered to CB 62
 hosts CB and GS for dinner (1850) 53
 identifies CB as Jane Eyre at London
 lecture 58
 irritated by *Jane Eyre*'s dedication 51
 open derision and sarcasm about CB 54,
 59–60
 paid extravagantly by Smith Elder 57
 use of pseudonyms 59–60
 WORKS:
 Henry Esmond (1852) 62, 80
 Paris Sketchbook (1840) 52
 Vanity Fair (1848) 50–51, 56, 60
Thornborrow, Eliza 173
Thornton, West Yorkshire, England 148,
 152, 220
Thorp Green Hall, York 211
Times, The (newspaper) 236
Trollope, Anthony 35, 120
Trollope, Mrs Frances (*née* Milton) 35
Trulock, Alice Jane 57

Verona, Italy 210
Villette (1853), *see* Brontë, Charlotte

Waldie, David 70, 258
Wedgwood, Frances 'Snow' 161
Wellington, Duke of (Arthur Wellesley)
 91, 153
Wellington, New Zealand 39, 213
Wheelwright, Laetitia 174, 189, 202
Williams, William Smith

editorial relationship with CB 15
    impressions of 182
meets with ECG 182
with GS 15
Wilson, Rev. William (Jnr) 207–218, 236
Wilson, Rev. William Carus 207–214, 218
Winkworth, Katie
    friendship with ECG 16, 131, 150, 185,
        200–204, 210, 223
    interest in CB 16, 73, 112, 122
    meets CB 111
Winkworth, Susanna 73, 112, 157
Wooler, Margaret
    celebrated as 'Miss Wooler' from *Life*
        239
    co–operates with ECG 160
    friendship with CB 72, 89, 102, 104,
        106

headmistress at Roe Head School 247
    intervenes at CB's wedding 114–116
    recollections of CB 221
    reluctance to participate with *Life* 176
Woolf, Virginia 212
Wordsworth, Dora 44
Wordsworth, William 25, 44, 190
Wright, Martha (*née* Heaton) 30, 162, 220,
    223
Wuthering Heights (1847), *see* Brontë, Emily

York 155, 211
Yorkshire 13, 17–18, 30, 59, 71, 73, 94, 96,
    101, 120, 237, 241

You may also enjoy …

978 0 7509 6525 5

Anne Brontë, the youngest and most enigmatic of the Brontë sisters, remains a best-selling author nearly two centuries after her death. This revealing biography opens Anne's most private life to a new audience and shows the true nature of her relationships with her siblings, in particular with her sister Charlotte.

'Touching and extraordinary … a hidden story longing to be told.'
DAME JOANNA LUMLEY

WRITING
BLACK BEAUTY

ANNA SEWELL
AND THE STORY OF
ANIMAL RIGHTS

CELIA BRAYFIELD

978 1 8039 9164 1

Black Beauty is a novel that changed our world. Intended to 'induce kindness' in a Victorian audience who relied on horses for transport, travel and power, it remains a children's classic. *Writing Black Beauty* is the story of the remarkable woman who wrote it and shows how Anna Sewell developed extraordinary resilience to rouse the conscience of Victorian Britain.

The destination for history
www.thehistorypress.co.uk